Fashion and the Unconscious

Books By Edmund Bergler, M.D.

FRIGIDITY IN WOMEN
(In collaboration with E. Hitschmann)

TALLEYRAND-NAPOLEON-STENDHAL-GRABBE

PSYCHIC IMPOTENCE IN MEN

UNHAPPY MARRIAGE AND DIVORCE

DIVORCE WON'T HELP

THE BATTLE OF THE CONSCIENCE

CONFLICT IN MARRIAGE

THE BASIC NEUROSIS

THE WRITER AND PSYCHOANALYSIS

MONEY AND EMOTIONAL CONFLICTS

COUNTERFEIT-SEX

THE SUPEREGO

FASHION AND THE UNCONSCIOUS

KINSEY'S MYTH OF FEMALE SEXUALITY
(In collaboration with W.S. Kroger)

THE REVOLT OF THE MIDDLE-AGED MAN

HOMOSEXUALITY: DISEASE OR WAY OF LIFE?

LAUGHTER AND THE SENSE OF HUMOR

PSYCHOLOGY OF GAMBLING

ONE THOUSAND HOMOSEXUALS

PRINCIPLES OF SELF-DAMAGE

TENSIONS CAN BE REDUCED TO NUISANCES

CURABLE AND INCURABLE NEUROTICS

JUSTICE AND INJUSTICE
(In collaboration with J.A.M. Meerloo)

PARENTS NOT GUILTY!

SELECTED PAPERS OF EDMUND BERGLER, M.D.: 1933-1961

Fashion and the Unconscious

By EDMUND BERGLER, M.D.

International Universities Press, Inc.
Madison Connecticut

Foreword by Dr. Melvyn L. Iscove

First printed by Robert Brunner.

First Paperback Printing, 1992

Library of Congress Cataloging-in-Publication Data

Bergler, Edmund, 1899-1962.
Fashion and the unconscious.
Reprint. Originally published: New York:
Robert Brunner, 1953. With new foreword.
Includes index.
1. Fashion—Psychological aspects. 2. Psychoanalysis. I. Title.
GT524.B47 1987 391′.01′9 87-3935
ISBN 0-8236-8046-0

PRINTED IN THE UNITED STATES OF AMERICA

Contents

Foreword to the 1987 Printing

THE AVERAGE PERSON GLANCING through the pages of a fashion magazine reacts with a combination of admiration for the styles depicted, fascination with their esthetic or sensual qualities, and—disbelief. Sometimes there is blanket rejection of the styles from the start: "They've gotta be kidding!" This often proceeds to the rhetorical question: "Who on earth is going to *wear* this stuff?" The critique then turns from the creations to the creators: "What kind of person dreamed up these outfits?" There the matter rests, with a resigned shrug of the shoulders and perhaps the cynical afterthought that it's all just a big racket to make money for the fashion industry.

The essence of this typical reaction is that haute couture is paradoxical, extreme, fantastic—anything but realistic and practical. A comment by a female colleague recently confirmed this: "Men don't realize how uncomfortable it is to be dressed up in style." This raises a number of questions: Why do men expect this of women in the first place? What kind of women go along with these styles? Do women ever say no to the dictates of fashion, and if so, why don't they say it more often?

All the facts would indicate that irrational elements play a large role in both the production and the acceptance of fashion creations. Psychoanalytic psychiatry has been demonstrating for the last century that the irrational in human behavior cannot be fully understood except in terms of the unconscious part of the personality, with its repressed infantile wishes, defenses, and guilt. This accounts for the present volume, which explains the irrational in fashion by considering the unconscious tributaries.

By 1952 Edmund Bergler had been in full-time psychoanalytic practice for twenty-five years, on two continents, and had extensive clinical experience with patients working directly or indirectly in the fashion industry. These included a range of occupations, from designers and manufacturers to models, fashion writers, and photographers (Personal communication from Mrs. Bergler). In addition, numerous patients presented inexplicable predilections or "peculiarities" in their manner of dressing which proved under analytic scrutiny to have a specific and important meaning within the overall framework of their neurosis.

This rich and thought-provoking panorama of clinical experience provided the basis for *Fashion and the Unconscious*. Although this was not the first major psychoanalytic work on clothing (having been preceded by J.C. Flugel's 1930 work, *The Psychology of Clothes*)*, it was the first time that newer psychoanalytic ideas about the deepest layers of the unconscious were specifically applied to this subject. These concepts were developed and worked out largely by Bergler in independent clinical investigation.

Those reading Bergler for the first time here may require some additional information about his contributions to psychoanalytic psychiatry and his place in the history of the psychoanalytic movement. Following Freud's lead in the early 1930's and a significant minority of Freud's pupils, Bergler concentrated his attention on the earliest phase of unconscious psychic development, the oral phase. (Even today the majority of analysts focus on the Oedipus complex, a later psychological stage.) Bergler emphasized the emotional importance of the infantile fantasy of magic omnipotence, which is unavoidably frustrated constantly during the child's first interactions with external reality. The child reacts to each "refusal" with helpless fury and aggression; this boomerangs, flooding the ego. The beleaguered ego is left with a tremendous quantity of "displeasure" which somehow must be handled, and the outcome of the hopeless battle is a "brilliant" solution: psychic masochism—"sugar-coating" the pain. This childhood aggression is not to be confused with the later defensive

*Flugel reviewed *Fashion and the Unconscious* favorably (1954). In acknowledging Bergler's criticism of the earlier book, he conceded: "No doubt much of this criticism is justified."

*pseudo*aggression which permeates the adult neurotic (see text). It was Bergler who identified the "pleasure-in-displeasure" pattern as the basis of neurotic suffering: neurotics unconsciously repeat the infantile feeling of being *refused*, and *enjoy* that feeling *unconsciously*. He worked out the clinical picture which he called the "Mechanism of Orality," and showed how applying this understanding could lead to success in treating a wide array of neurotic symptoms and personality problems.

For the sake of brevity, and to avoid word-for-word duplication of what has already been said at length elsewhere, the interested reader is referred to the present writer's introductions to reprints of three other Bergler works (1949, 1954, 1958). In these introductions considerable background material is presented on the man, the ideas, and the scientific career spanning three-and-a-half decades (1927–1962). This career began at Freud's psychoanalytic clinic in Vienna in the stimulating environment generated by Freud himself and the brilliant first and second generation of Freud's pupils, at a critical time in the development of psychoanalytic theory. It was toward the last decade of Freud's long life, and the issues of that decade and the next centered around Freud's late theoretical revisions and the attempt to expand psychoanalysis in order to incorporate them. It was Freud who first pointed out, in 1931, that the Oedipus complex was not the crux of neurosis, suggesting instead that the pre-Oedipal issues were decisive.

The best way to familiarize oneself with Bergler's work is to read as much Bergler as possible. I would encourage the reader to refer to the growing number of available reprints and to consult libraries for out-of-print works in order to acquire a more complete picture.

For instance, the clinical technique demonstrated here via lengthy excerpts from actual cases, beginning in chapter 1, may arouse curiosity as to the underlying rationale for this approach. The reasons will be more apparent from a thorough study of the other Bergler literature.

The same applies to aspects of the theory, notably the role in neurosis of unconscious irony directed at the parents, as noted in the case illustrations in chapter 9. The mechanism whereby irony is incorporated in the neurotic symptom was first described by

Bergler and labeled "the pseudo-moral connotation of neurotic symptoms" in a paper published a year before the present book's appearance (see also Bergler, 1952, 1959, 1961 where this topic is discussed at greater length). This particular issue is so central to the understanding and treatment of neurosis that Bergler, in his last months, drafted an outline for an entire book on the subject. He called it *Ironizands: People who are too Ironic for their own Good* (Archives of Edmund and Marianne Bergler Psychiatric Foundation). The neologism "ironizand" was created by Bergler from the word *analysand*; in the course of analyzing a patient's ironic resistance, Bergler said, "Make up your mind—are you an analysand or an ironizand?"

Any attempt to summarize here the main thesis of *Fashion and the Unconscious* would be quite redundant. Once again, I must direct the reader's attention elsewhere, this time to Bergler's own foreword. Here, he outlines in a remarkably concise condensation the psychological problems in fashion and the comprehensive thesis he constructed to solve them.

The central point in Bergler's thesis—man's unconscious fear of the female body—merits further comment. Given the concept that fear led man to invent clothing in the first place, and determined the form that clothing would take (i.e., uncomfortable—spell "punitive!"), several questions arise. Have fashion developments in the last thirty-odd years borne out Bergler's conclusions? Have new trends or events shown that this book is no longer relevant in our "more liberated" era? What has changed in fashion as a result of the feminist movement?

Bergler's own further observations appeared in print twice after the publication of *Fashion and the Unconscious*. The first time was in an interview published in *Cosmopolitan* (February 1960), entitled "A Psychoanalyst Looks at Women's Clothes." There he reiterates the importance of male fear of women as a propelling motive: "Unconsciously, and I stress 'unconsciously,' the man—and I am speaking of the heterosexual male—is to some degree afraid of the woman's body. Hence, he finds it necessary to cover it up. Women's interest in clothes stems from this psychological necessity." He goes on to state that "most men, to an extent more than they realize, have some *inner* doubts about their masculinity. . . . Feminine clothes serve as man's unconscious reassurance that he is the he-man by providing a sort of inner alibi for his masculinity. . . . If he chooses to undress the woman mentally and to glory in fantasies, he can freely do so and yet avoid the danger of being put to the actual test." By implication we may conclude that since the unconscious makeup of the male does not change over the course of time, the *basis* of fashion is static, despite changes in social attitudes.

A recent scholarly book by Alison Lurie, *The Language of Clothes*, offers some welcome if unintentional corroboration. The author provides a historical survey of fashions up to 1981, as well as an analysis of their symbolic meaning. We may note with interest how her descriptions of absurd female styles are in basic agreement with Bergler's observations. Her conclusions, on the other hand, miss the underlying unconscious fear element, leaving obvious contradictions unexplained.

For instance, she notes that:

> By the 1830's, female fashions . . . continued to suggest—and to promote—physical frailty. Early Victorian costume not only made women *look* weak and helpless, it made them weak and helpless. The main agent of this debility . . . was the corset, which at the time was thought of not as a mere fashion but as a medical necessity. Ladies "frames," it was believed, were extremely delicate; their muscles could not hold them up without assistance. . . . By the time they reached late adolescence they were wearing cages of heavy canvas reinforced with whalebone or steel and their back muscles had atrophied to the point where they could not sit or stand for long unsupported. The corset also deformed the internal organs and made it impossible to draw a deep breath [p. 217]*.

She goes on to describe the "ten to thirty pounds of clothing" worn over this garment, adding that the lady was "still not protected from the climate since fashion . . . often demanded that her neck, shoulders and chest be exposed" (p. 218).

*Reprinted from Alison Lurie, *The Language of Clothes*, 1981, by permission of Random House, Inc.

Lurie's sarcasm in describing Victorian man's idea of woman's "helplessness" overlooks a salient point: that the "helpless" image of the female represents an *unconscious defense* against a more deeply repressed image of the woman as a powerful and frightening being. The irony of the situation is that Victorian women were not placed in "*cages* (sic!) of *heavy* canvas *reinforced* with whalebone or *steel* (italics added)" for their *own* protection; they were rendered helpless to this degree in order to protect the *male*, unconsciously afraid of *his own fantasy* of their power to hurt him! Similarly, the obvious *cruelty* toward the woman, as in exposing her upper body to the cold after constricting it in the corset, is inconsistent with the superficial image of her alleged helplessness and need for protection. It is on the contrary a mistreatment entirely in accord with the infantile fantasy of a dangerous, threatening creature who must be first *subdued*, then punished for her very existence.

Lurie is also quite correct in comparing the Victorian lady with the modern expense-account blonde and in observing "the principle still in force, that clothes which make a woman's life difficult and handicap her in competition with men are always felt to be sexually attractive" (p. 220). Recognizing the unconscious fear factor clarifies why immobilizing the woman is deemed the necessary prerequisite for attractiveness. Clinical experience confirms this unconscious link: in my own practice I have encountered a series of male patients who literally immobilized the woman in sex. Any sign of active participation from the woman led to impotence.

The impact of man's unconscious fear on a more recent fashion trend is also written between the lines of Lurie's book. The Annie Hall Look, based on Woody Allen's movie character, and introduced in the late 1970's:

> involved the wearing of actual men's clothing; elegant three-piece suits, vests, shirts, ties and hats . . . worn very large and loose . . . sleeves and trouser legs rolled up . . . accompanied by huge handbags and kooky childish costume jewelry . . . these clothes convey an ironic antifeminist message . . . they suggest a child dressed up in her daddy's or older brother's things for fun, and imply "I'm only

> playing; I'm not really big enough to wear a man's pants or do a man's job." This is a look of helpless cuteness, not one of authority [p. 229].

Here we are back to the "helpless" theme again 150 years later, but now the *reassuring* aspect of the childish tomboy image is recognized. But reassurance against what, if not man's fear of the reality of the grownup woman?

One major advance toward rationality has been women's greater rejection of the "punitive" in fashion. In the *Cosmopolitan* interview, Bergler already noted that "Women are becoming more discriminating in their choice of clothes and do not necessarily follow blindly the dictates of the fashion designers." He predicted that "fashion designing will probably become more and more the domain of women—and women are much more realistic about the clothes they wear than are men. Accordingly one would also guess that the beauty and utilitarian element in their clothes will become more and more prevalent." Today the names of prominent female fashion designers are household words: Gloria Vanderbilt, Coco Chanel, and Anne Klein spring to mind. In a 1960 paper on the demise of the hat industry, Bergler put it more strongly: "It is more likely that the rebellion against the hat is part and parcel of the general feminine trend towards greater ease (meaning less constriction) in dress generally. Fashion is now paying the penalty for its cruelty toward women" (1960a). The current widespread introduction of modified jogging suits and sweat suits as trendy casual wear bears this out, with the emphasis on practicality and comfort.

Designers are coming to realize that there is a limit now to how much "fashion nonsense" women will tolerate. However, the punitive elements still stubbornly refuse to bow out graciously and stay out. Lurie notes with some dismay that "during the last few years . . . women have begun wearing tight high-heeled shoes again, even with pants; and the most fashionable styles are those that, like clogs and ankle-strap sandals, give least support to the feet and make walking most difficult. . . . Another ominous sign is the narrowing of the skirt to the point where ordinary gestures like sitting on a low sofa or stepping over a puddle become difficult" (p. 228). And recent advertisements in *The New*

York Times offer a garment called the "shaper" which sounds suspiciously like the old "girdle." This parallels a 1926 instance of the same disguising technique cited by Bergler on page 121. The unconscious (hence irrational) definition of what makes for attractiveness continues to play havoc with all attempts at reforming the fashion industry, and the indications are that this problem allows for no simple solution.

We come now to a consideration of the clinically oriented last two-thirds of the book. Here Bergler examines the issue of how clothes are secondarily adapted for the expression of unconscious neurotic conflicts. These center around the universal neurotic problem of psychic masochism and its elaboration in the areas of voyeurism and exhibitionism. The complexities of the problem are outlined in chapter 5.

Once again, a supposedly clear-cut psychological attitude such as female narcissism and vanity, expressed through an obsession with clothes, turns out to be more complicated: it is in part a defense against the deeper masochistic fantasy, "nobody loves me!" Similarly, the problem of conspicuous tastelessness in dress is explained as the result of a neurotic inhibition. This signifies a psychological problem which can and should be analytically resolved (p. 205). Especially significant is Bergler's prediction that "female analytic patients and analysands will in the future draw the analyst's attention to this point, and request that this specific symptom be included in the scientific scrutiny of their 'total personalities'" (p. 206). Today's female analytic patients would do well to heed this prediction in light of the important "clues" hidden in the sartorial message. The clinical application is thoroughly documented in the case histories of chapter 9.

An up-to-the-minute clinical example from a patient currently in treatment illustrates the therapeutic potential of Bergler's conclusions. The patient, a young dental technician in her mid-twenties, came for treatment of "boyfriend troubles." She had become involved twice with immature men who were emotionally unready to make a commitment to marriage. Although she half-heartedly maintained that she really wanted to marry her boyfriend, she was partially aware herself that something was wrong with her choices: in this instance his emotional "marriage block" made it very unlikely that the relationship would work. She spoke wistfully of "wanting to settle down," but her words had a hollow ring. Resignation to her sad fate was written all over her.

It did not take long to establish "under the analytic microscope" (Bergler) that this woman was unconsciously a psychic masochist, and that she had unconsciously chosen her two boyfriends not despite but because of their unavailability. Their unconscious value to her was as providers of disappointment and rejection.

Her appearance and manner of dressing contributed to the defeatist message she conveyed. In fact they turned out on examination to be an important link in the meaning of her neurosis. To begin with she was thirty pounds overweight. This would not have been so bad in itself, but in combination with her clothes it became part of the rejection game she played out. Her wardrobe did nothing to minimize her size; in fact her choice of clothes absolutely accentuated her weight, drawing attention to bulges and emphasizing disproportion. Her typical workday outfit was a bright-colored sweater or sweatshirt, with "loud" tight-fitting sweatpants. The ensemble was completed by a pair of shabby tennis shoes. The colors and fit of the clothes drew attention to her waist and thighs; these appeared all the larger in contrast to slender calves outlined by the skin-tight pants. In addition she wore no lipstick or other make-up, had large glasses, and her hair hung limp and lifelessly straight.

Interestingly, she was fully aware of her artificially exaggerated unattractiveness. She smiled when I questioned her reasons:

"I know I could look better, but I do this on purpose," she explained. " I always thought if people would love me fat they would love me for me, not what I look like. When I'm thin people who wouldn't otherwise look at me stop and whistle."

"What's wrong with that?"

"I dislike that form of attention intensely, because it means they only like me for my body. It's *not sincere.*"

"But you have set it up so that you lose either way," I pointed out. "If you're overweight and unattractive and men reject you, you can feel sorry for yourself because they are judging by externals only, and nobody appreciates the wonderful person beneath the surface. If you're thin and attractive, and men show an interest in you, it's also no good because they only like your looks, not you. So once more you feel unloved and unappreciated. This time, though, instead of being rejected, *you* reject the man and again end up with nothing."

"But that makes it sound like I planned this all out!"

"Well, who was it, if not you?"

"True, no one else did it but me. Still, I had no idea I was doing it. I certainly never thought of it in those terms."

"That's right. You created the pattern, but *not consciously*, therefore consciously you know nothing about it. You just act in accordance with the *unconscious* pattern that you yourself constructed. The main point is that you spoil it for yourself. Although you tell yourself you're fighting hypocrisy and seeking sincere affection, the result is only that you create the situation where you lose out. How are you helping yourself with this? You merely reinforce your pre-existing feeling of being unloved. Furthermore, you haven't said anything about how being overweight makes you feel about yourself. How do you feel about sex when you are in your unattractive phase?"

"That's a good point. I don't enjoy sex when I'm fat. I don't feel right. I'm uncomfortable about my size and the way I must look to him. But I must say that's independent of my knowing that *he* doesn't care for my weight."

"You see how you have constructed an approach that perpetuates your own unconscious fantasy that you are the innocent victim deprived of satisfaction. We will have to find out what specific psychic leftovers from childhood you are unconsciously using to form the content for your repetitive pattern."

Her history provided the necessary information to reconstruct the inner basis of her illogical and self-defeating behavior. As a child she had been admired as a beauty, but she had devalued and negated this attention, inwardly choosing to concentrate instead on the feeling that her older sister got "*all* the attention." The fact behind this was the sister's chronic illness, which demanded much of the parents' time and energy. As the "good" child she had felt neglected—actually her mother told her much later what a relief it had been to have a second child who was so pleasant and undemanding (she "never cried"); this had freed the exhausted mother to devote herself to the more needy sister (who "cried all the time"). The patient had taken the extra time given to her sister as proof that mother didn't love *her*. "Whether I was bad or good I never got any attention from my parents," was her summation.

At her next visit she was again wearing an outfit that accentuated her weight: a patterned sweater and tight yellow sweatpants. I pointed out to her:

"Aren't you dramatizing the inner complaint 'Nobody pays any attention to me, therefore there's no point in trying to look good?'"

Her confirmation came quickly in the form of tears. "If you don't have anything it can't be taken away from you."

"But the only one taking things from you now is you, and even that is based on a *fantasy* of neglect from earliest childhood. Why ruin your happiness over old *fantasized* grievances? And why cling to suffering when the suffering could be corrected?"

At least this time it was possible to discuss her statement with her analytically in relation to the masochistic pattern of self-defeat which was emerging.

Several additional connections became apparent, linking current contradictions with their past origins. As a defense against the wish to feel unloved and lose out to her sister the patient had secondarily identified unconsciously with her sister. The defense read: "You love her, not me. I am like her, therefore you must love me." Thus she became a crier; by her teens she "cried all the time," as the sister had done earlier. She made herself fat, whereas she had always been a skinny child; her sister had always been fat. (It was of interest that in complaining that there were no pictures of her as a baby, she said there were "tons" of her sister—the weight reference was not lost on her when brought to her attention.) Finally, she developed a "big mouth" and became difficult, again like her sister; she hounded her mother with complaints until the woman cried.

In the long run this defense merely reinforced her masochistic pattern—the parents who previously "ignored" her now actively disliked her and resented her. To complete the picture she tormented herself with guilt over upsetting her mother.

There was even a "pseudo-moral connotation" to her overeating defense. The parents had a bad marriage and frequently quarreled. When the patient became upset about this, they both apparently appeased their guilt by offering her treats in the form of food. Now, in using food as a "comfort" when depressed, she was using irony, unconsciously reducing their solution to absurdity: "*their* brand of consolation" made her fat and miserable!

After analyzing this material with the patient, a "transformation" occurred. She arrived at her next appointment smiling, her hair done up, wearing cosmetics, contact lenses, and—a different outfit. She wore a loose sweater in a subdued shade, black slacks, and matching shoes. "I just want you to see that I *can* look better!" The twinkle in her eye indicated that therapy was making an impact unconsciously, and even though the sudden change may turn out to be a positive transference mirage requiring analysis and resolution, the over-all impression is that the prognosis is favorable.

The foregoing excerpt offers a glimpse of the clinical side of the fashion phenomenon. Although styles have changed since Bergler treated his "fashion neurotics" thirty years ago, we see in this contemporary case how the unconscious masochistic misuse of clothes continues as ever. Neurosis, unfortunately, does not go out of fashion; it just changes its outward trappings to suit the new occasion.

The syndicated columnist, Dorothy Kilgallen, wrote in 1953: "Seventh Avenue will flip when Dr. Edmund Bergler's book *Fashion and the Unconscious* is published." By focusing on the "fashion" half of the title she implied that this book was primarily of interest to the fashion industry. The impact of this volume, however, is not limited to Seventh Avenue. Only a small minority of the populace is actively involved in making clothes; everyone wears them, for better or for worse. In neurosis it is often for worse, and this brings fashion into the province of psychotherapy. Beyond that, this book strikes a chord on *every* Avenue and in *every* culture—in fact, wherever the inquisitive male eye stops to scrutinize, secretly, the veiled beauty of a woman.

MELVYN L. ISCOVE, M.D., F.R.C.P.(C)

Toronto, November 1986

REFERENCES

Bergler, E. (1949), *The Basic Neurosis*. New York: Grune & Stratton, 1977 (with a new Preface).
——— (1952), *The Superego*. New York: Grune & Stratton
——— (1954), *The Revolt of the Middle-Aged Man*. New York: International Universities Press 1985 (with a new Foreword).
——— (1958), Counterfeit-Sex, 2nd ed. New York: Grune & Stratton, 1982 (with a new Introduction).
——— (1959), *Principles of Self-Damage*. New York: Intercontinental Medical Book Corp., 1974.
——— (1960a), Psychological factors in the decline of an industry. *Dis. Nerv. Syst.*, 11/8.
——— (1960b), A psychoanalyst looks at women's clothes. Interview. *Cosmopolitan*, February.
——— (1961), *Curable and Incurable Neurotics*. New York: Liveright.
Flugel, J. C. (1930), *The Psychology of Clothes*. London: Hogarth Press.
——— (1954), Review of *Fashion and the Unconscious* by Edmund Bergler. *Psychoanal. Quart.*, 23/4:587.
Freud, S. (1931), *Female Sexuality*, Standard Edition, 21:215–220. London: Hogarth Press, 1961.
Lurie, A. (1981), *The Language of Clothes*. New York: Random House.

ACKNOWLEDGMENT

My thanks to Rose J. Orente my co-trustee in the Edmund and Marianne Bergler Psychiatric Foundation, for many hours of editorial review that provided invaluable assistance in the preparation of this manuscript.

Foreword

IS THERE REALLY LESS than meets the eye in a well-dressed woman? Is it correct, as the cynic claims, to declare that fashion is no more than a common meeting ground for the vanity of women and the greed of manufacturers, and that each season's style changes are merely a trick of exploitation, artificially limiting the life of a garment? Is fashion really "a racket to sell clothes," as *The New Yorker* declared recently? Are men the innocent victims, caught in the middle, grudgingly paying for their wives' "extravagance?" In short, is the paradox of fashion a purely conscious problem of vanity and commercial enterprise, or has the unconscious any part in it?

Anatole France once ventured this opinion: If he were allowed to look into all the books published a century after his death, he would choose a fashion journal as the best source of information about the world as it would be, and more revealing than books of philosophy, belles lettres, or science.

To date, psychological and anthropological investigations of the problem of clothing have established a triad of motivations: decoration, modesty, protection. Beyond these generalized findings, progress has been achieved in only two points: modesty and repressed exhibitionism have been correlated, and the so obvious aim of decoration has been connected with the long forgotten custom of wearing magical amulets. Here, with few exceptions, the matter rests.

The popular theory about clothing, that women dress as they do for two alleged reasons: to "attract" men and to "anger other women," is partially correct, but it is at the same time so general that it loses all value. The general formula does not even begin to explain the specific basis of either attitude.

This book admits to a few ambitious aims. Using the clinical psychiatric-psychoanalytic method, it sets out to prove several highly "unlikely" theories. This element of "improbability" is one which is common to all theories concerning the unconscious. Only naive people try to apply to the unconscious, where irrational wishes, defenses and guilt dominate, the working methods of consciousness—namely, good, sound, horse-sense. Their method has the advantage of "probability"; it leads, however, to invariably erroneous conclusions. I shall not, therefore, be surprised to see repeated the statement of a not-too-smart critic who some time ago thundered against me: "It's getting to the point where a fair question would be: Can you think straight, or were you educated in Vienna?" I have to admit to the crime: I was "educated in Vienna."

Having unburdened my conscience, here is the thesis I wish to prove:

Clothes are a masculine invention, secondarily thrust upon women. Investigating the peculiar *unconscious* reasons which prompted men to take this sartorial step, one comes upon another, and even more peculiar, reversal of the generally accepted dictum that fashion is a feminine prerogative and a feminine interest. If the typical man is, indeed, above "fashion-nonsense," how are we to explain his concupiscent peeping at women's clothes, and his alleged He-Man attitude of joyfully undressing her, in thought? The theory is suggested that feminine attire is man's *unconscious* reassurance against his own repressed fears of woman's body, and the equally repressed fantasies connected with it: the magic of the intervening thin layer of material—the improved skin—seems to do the trick. Nevertheless, man—for whom the neckline plunges, for whom the skirts are shortened and swirled, who whistles, either in actuality or in thought, after every good-looking "babe"—is not, as he believes, running after Lady Godiva, and is—as he does not believe—whistling in the dark. What he is looking for, frantically, is inner reassurance that he is THE HE-MAN—which he is not.

The interconnection between man's inner and deeply repressed masochistic fears (it will be proven that fear, and fear exclusively, lies behind the masculine invention of woman's clothes) and, used as inner defense, his two pseudo-aggressive "transgressions into the forbidden" (peeping and mental undressing), lie at the crux of the matter.

Finally, an answer is proposed for the entirely unclarified, although repeatedly and scientifically stated, riddle: why is the innuendo attached to a half-exposed, half-dressed feminine body sexually more alluring to man than full exposure?

To complicate matters, feminine clothes—children of man's unconscious fears—have become independent, and seem to have a life of their own. What do women live out in their obsession with fashion, and are there sartorial "anti-talents" among them? Can "lack of taste" be defined? The thesis is promoted that there are—sartorially speaking—no "tasteless" women, only neurotically inhibited ones.

In addition, a scrutiny of different fashions is attempted, and some of the motives of their promoters probed. Since it is common knowledge that male homosexuals in extraordinary numbers are involved in fashion-creation, there is a tentative discussion of whether or not the *unconscious* hatred of women* typical for every homosexual (and conse-

* This hatred is a covering cloak for fear.

quently, also for the czars of fashion-creation), has been responsible for some of the dress absurdities of the last half-century. The paradoxical fact that women are dressed by their bitterest enemies allows one to draw some ironic conclusions from the existence of specific constrictive and "uncomfortable" fashions, provided that misconceptions centering around the psychic make-up of male homosexuals are clarified. There is an old objection to fashion, formulated by Christian Nestell Bovee, "There would not be so much harm in the giddy following the fashions, if somehow the wise could always set them." This objection can be answered from a new angle: "Perhaps it is the unconscious, and not the unwise, who set the fashions."

One has to admit that this sketchy outline describes a large program—large in its scope, aside from any consideration of subject matter, and large in proportion to what some readers may consider the minor importance of its theme. But the problem of fashion is no longer confined to the very few who can afford to buy the expensive and exclusive new styles created by Paris or Fifth Avenue. Each new fashion is immediately popularized by manufacturers in the medium of low price ranges, and nearly half the population is shortly wearing a simplified version of the new creation, or a reasonable (or unreasonable) facsimile thereof. "Fashion is that by which the fantastic becomes for a moment the universal," said Oscar Wilde. Fashion, in these days, therefore concerns every woman in progressive and not impoverished countries. It is exactly the universality of the problem which justifies a prolonged investigation.

To sum up the practical vistas: Assuming for the sake of argument that feminine clothes are a masculine invention, designed to alleviate man's repressed fears and to bolster up, unconsciously, his tottering He-Man attitude, where does this leave the stereotype of the enraged husband, railing at his wife's extravagant purchases of new clothing? Is he justified in "hitting the ceiling" and "blowing his top"?

EDMUND BERGLER

New York 1952

Acknowledgments

MOST OF THE PHOTOGRAPHS reproduced are through the courtesy of the Metropolitan Museum of Art. The photograph of the Minoan Snake Goddess is reproduced through the courtesy of Mr. N. Platon, Director of the Museum in Candia, Crete. The photograph of two Burmese hill-women in metal collars is from Ewing Galloway, New York.

Thanks are expressed to the publishers and copyright owners for permission to quote from *John Ruskin and Effie Gray,* by Admiral Sir William James, published by Charles Scribner's Sons, New York, 1947; from *Nobody's Fool,* by Charles Yale Harrison, published by Henry Holt & Co., New York, 1948; and from the Encyclopædia Britannica.

Fashion and the Unconscious

1 The Suspicion of a Fantastic Fashion-Hoax, Perpetrated on Women by the Unconscious of Some Designers

TEN YEARS AGO, on a sunny spring morning, I sat in my office trying to concentrate on the work at hand—analysis of the resistance of a homosexual who happened to be a fashion designer. That resistance was directed against my explanation of his self-damaging tendencies. At the same time, I was applying myself with equal diligence to the attempt to suppress a certain irritation at the fact that my profession forced me to spend most of my life indoors. My patient cooperated by putting me on the alert with a sudden outburst. He shouted: "I HATE WOMEN, I HATE WOMEN, I HATE THEM!" His emotionalism was by no means unusual; for him, such scenes were the order of the day. What struck me was my own association: "If he hates women, his fashion creations must reflect this pseudo-hatred, too. Women who trust this type of 'guidance' are delivering themselves into the hands of their worst enemies."

The irony of this vista, which had opened up so unexpectedly, intrigued me. I had by then analyzed some forty homosexuals, many of them directly or indirectly connected with the fashion field (in the next ten years this figure more than doubled, reaching over one hundred), but the association had never occurred to me before. I began to explore the new vein; my first move called for reconstruction of the preceding "discussion." The patient had been talking about the "stupidity" and garrulity of women, delivering a self-eulogy that was typically homosexual in its superciliousness. In the course of that expectoration, he had remarked in an irritated tone:

"Can you explain why I don't design men's suits, instead of wasting my time on idiotic women's dresses?"

"Is there a market?"

"Of course not. Men don't count in fashion. They don't go in for novelties. But what puzzles me is that I always wanted to design women's dresses."

"I've told you, repeatedly, that a homosexual is only a fugitive from women. As the French say, 'On revient toujours à son premier amour,' one always returns to one's first love."

It was then, after a second's pause, that the man had shouted: "I HATE WOMEN! I HATE WOMEN! I HATE THEM!"

Following up my clue, I said: "Well, if you hate women as passionately as you claim, isn't it possible that you are using your profession to revenge yourself on them—that you're not dressing women, but caricaturing them?"

The patient's violence vanished at once. He became pleasantly animated, and exclaimed: "That does it! I don't have to mourn over my wasted time. Thank you for the wonderful story!" [1]

[1] The next day the "story" had a different aspect. The patient came gloomily to his appointment, and asked immediately: "If you change my homosexuality will my designing talent collapse, too?"—"The answer is —no. Your talent represents a sublimation, hence the result of an inner conflict *productively* solved. A sublimation is resistant to any change in the personality structure. It represents the normal part of you."—"Are you sure? I was thinking about giving up analysis. I can't afford to lose my gift—it's my only source of income." I replied: "There's no danger on that score. The identical objection you brought forward is presented by *every* artistically creative person, inside and outside of analysis. Writers, especially, have this unwarranted fear. Experience proves that after losing

"Your triumph is slightly premature," I told him. "The fact that you rescued part of your *superficial* defenses and alibis in your sublimation—designing women's clothes—does not change the fact that your psychic structure is still masochistic. If I attest to you your defensive aggression, you are triumphant. But if I so much as hint at the real underlying masochistic reason for your behavior, you are furious."

"Don't evade the issue! Just a minute ago you yourself said I was right when I claimed that I hate women. Does hatred make one masochistic?"

"I appreciate the high-class irony. You are overlooking a salient fact. There are different types of hatred: real *and* defensive. Defensive hatred covers fear, and that is the type of hatred you feel for women. May I remind you of something very frequently discussed here? You ended your infantile conflict with an overdose of unsolved *masochistic attachment* to your mother, or more precisely, to the distorted image of your mother. To avoid the danger zone, you unconsciously built up your *defensive hatred* for her. This went so far that you rejected, not just your mother, but the whole species, woman. You became attached to boys, thus rescuing yourself to another continent. To bolster this defense, you began to identify with girls, secretly parading up and down in front of the mirror in your sister's—and later your mother's—dresses. You used perfumes, lipstick; you imitated their gestures, and so on.

"There is no contradiction here," I added. "Your terror of women is *basic;* your identification with them is only

---

their neuroses, they still have their talent." The patient was persistent. "Are you sure?" he asked. "I am positive about it," I replied.

As was to be expected, the patient's fears were unfounded. Today, many years after the change to heterosexuality (he is married and has children), he is still in the same field of endeavor, and is one of the important men in it.

superficial. The basic terror pertains to your earliest distorted fantasy of the 'cruel' pre-Oedipal mother. The superficial identification, developed later, pertains to the 'harmless' and demoted Oedipal image of your mother."

"Well," the patient retorted, "since I'm making my living by designing women's dresses, this identification seems to be more stable than you assume."

"In *one* sector, yes. But see how shaky the identification must be if you yourself have to invoke the deeper layer of pseudo-hatred so often. Didn't today's discussion start with your declaration of your alleged hatred of women? Weren't you shouting at the top of your lungs, 'I hate women'? And weren't you flattered when I brought up the possibility that your fashion creations are meant to make women into caricatures?"

"So I've used up two layers so far. I wouldn't be at all surprised if you proved to me that the deepest layer, the masochistic one, was 'mobilized,' too."

"You meant that as irony, but it happens to be good crystal-gazing. Yes, I will remind you of the masochistic layer. Remember the incessant conflicts with your long list of quick-change boy friends? Aren't these quarrels fashioned after the principle of *injustice-collecting?*"

"Now you are blaming me for their neuroses!"

"Far from it. I am holding you accountable for choosing, and not avoiding, these neurotics."

"There aren't any others around."

"And this doesn't make you skeptical of your repeated statements that homosexuality is just a way of life, an exact parallel to heterosexuality, as you put it? Isn't the worst heterosexual relationhip peaceful compared with the best homosexual one?"

"I'm not the sedate suburban type who's in search of quiet!"

"Is that so? Then why do you complain so bitterly about the injustices inflicted upon you by your boy friends?"

"Oh, stop it. What interests me more is this suspicion of yours that I'm making caricatures of women by designing peculiar and uncomfortable dresses. That's a new one; let me think about it."

Was the fashion field the scene of an unconscious hoax perpetrated upon women? And—a necessary check—was it possible to determine whether there really are a substantial number of male homosexuals employed in the creation of women's fashions? Queries directed at people "in the know" produced astonishing replies; according to my informants, the majority of the really creative persons in the field are male (and to a much lesser extent, female) homosexuals.

Of course, the only part of this statement that is "news" is the fact that it is a summing-up of precise information from people actually in a position to know. It has never been publicly acknowledged that the majority of the great male fashion creators and hair stylists, both foreign and domestic, are homosexual. But it has been whispered for decades. This has been "forgiven" them even by otherwise prudish women because "they are so gifted." The popular error which defines a homosexual as an effeminate man, and therefore psychologically a woman, here worked to the homosexual's advantage. This otherwise rejected trait was assumed to be an asset in fashion creation. Women took it for granted that these "feminine" men, because they were effeminate, could "understand" and "express" their customers' personalities. And it is of course true that many of these homosexuals excel in fantasy and in sartorial ingenuity.

The homosexual's commanding position in the fashion

field is a fact, but is that proof of a "hoax?" One could object that the results of a talent are more important than the unconscious reasons for it, and this is a point. But "by their fruits ye shall know them," and many fashion features, each season, are so silly and even preposterous, so nearly a caricature of clothing, so awkward or uncomfortable to wear, that they invite speculation. It seems to me that inventions of this sort should be credited to the homosexual's hidden enmity against the female customer, a defensive enmity which originated in the unsolved homosexual conflict with the infantile image of the Giantess of his individual nursery.

This statement, based on clinical material, is to be taken with all possible mental reservations;[2] it is intended to explain, not everything, but only one curious facet of the situation.

The battle-cry, "Fashion is foolish," is timeless; the regretful aphorism, "There would not be so much harm in the giddy following the fashions if *somehow the wise could always set them*," has already been quoted. Perhaps the "foolish" who set them are not so foolish after all, but rather are propelled by the inner wish to reduce women to absurdity. If, to use a comparison, a Jew were to retain an anti-Semite as financial advisor, one could suspect that the advice received, although persuasive and perhaps even given in good faith, might contain the seed of future damage.

What might be called "*punitive* fashions," are a recur-

[2] Not all fashion czars, of course, are homosexual. The extent of women's participation in this field is still increasing; perhaps things will change when women "take over"—that is, assuming that the proportion of Lesbians in this field does not exceed their proportion in the total population. The assumption is rather doubtful. Paradoxical as it may sound, Lesbians have as many unconscious grievances against women as do male homosexuals. The genetic basis is identical: masochistic fixation, pseudo-aggressive defense, secondarily warded off with *pseudo*-love. For elaboration, see chapter on Lesbianism in *Neurotic Counterfeit-Sex* (Grune & Stratton, N.Y. 1951).

rent theme in dress. It is difficult to explain, except in terms of unconscious ill-will, the opposition so frequently offered by the big-wigs of la haute couture to the substitution of styles which are easy and comfortable to wear.

The hobble skirt popular in the early part of the century,[3] which was almost as successful in making walking difficult as the Chinese bound foot, the figure-forming (as opposed to the figure-controlling) corset, the whalebone-stiffened high collar of the Gibson Girl—all these and many other "I don't care if it hurts, I want to be beautiful" fashions, arouse skepticism as to the motives of the designers, not to mention the peculiar mental processes of the wearers. So do the comparatively minor aberrations, such as the vogue starting in the twenties for coats without buttons, requiring the wearer to get along with the use of only one arm, the other serving as a buckle to hold the two sides of the coat together.

Unconscious motives, again, must have been responsible for the flapper fashion introduced after the first World War. The styling of women as garçonnes, even to their haircuts, is undoubtedly an imitation of the familiar boy type so highly valued by homosexuals.[4]

The comedy of quid pro quo is still incomplete: the women who accepted and adopted the flapper style did so for reasons of their own, quite apart from those of the homosexual designers. In every war, there is a preponderance of soldiers who are in the army "for the duration, and six months after." Because of their "masculinity complex," girls identified with these men.

The way in which fashion shuttles back and forth between "masculine" and "feminine" ways of dressing some-

[3] Not so extinct as one might believe, at least among the designers; the Paris showings of 1950 featured the "return" of the hobble skirt, but it never to my knowledge ventured beyond the show rooms.

[4] This type sees in his partner a narcissistic reduplication of himself as a boy (the type described by Sadger-Freud).

times gives the impression that women must, from time to time, recapture their right to be—feminine. Recapture from whom? Obviously not from heterosexual men, but perhaps from a type one columnist called "a man among men but not among women."

In every case I have encountered, analysis of homosexuals proved that a truly fantastic fear of women lay behind the universal façade of "distaste" or "indifference," a fear which was warded off with pseudo-aggression. Discussions of this specific element regularly produced strong resistance on the part of these patients. To reproduce some details of these "differences of opinion":

Mr. A: "How can you talk such nonsense! I don't hate *or* fear women—I'm just indifferent to them."

"If that is so, how can you explain your repeated dreams about threatening, or even cannibalistic women? You told me you had these dreams before we even met, so you can't blame them on analysis."

Mr. A: "Dreams are nonsense. I am not responsible for them."

"You are mistaken. Dreams represent the nightly newspaper—written in code, it's true—which tells us specifically what is going on in the decisive part of your personality, your unconscious."

Mr. A: "I can only account for my life outside of sleep."

"What makes you assume that your 'life outside of sleep' is not permeated by identical attitudes? Time and again we've discussed your quarrels with your boy friends. Weren't they all reducible to one common denominator, 'someone is unjust to you'? And isn't it true, as we established in many of your conflicts, that these 'injustices' were unconsciously self-created?"

Mr. A: "That's what you claim!"

"That's what the record shows. Take your present friend as an example. You told me that you met him at a party where he flirted with you; another friend warned you that he was extremely promiscuous. You yourself observed this, too. Still, you chose to have exactly this unreliable person for your friend. You go into tantrums every time the boy runs around with someone else. What reason did you have to assume that this psychopath was good material for a steady affair?"

Mr. A: "Everybody can make an error in judgment."

"Make an error in judgment again and again? When this happens, the error is obviously part of a pattern, repeated ad nauseam."

Mr. A: "What has all this got to do with my alleged fear and hatred of women?"

"Only this: the pattern of masochistic injustice-collecting originally pertained to mother, and was later shifted to men."

Mr. A: "You're wrong. But assuming your theory is right, this would only account for fear, not hatred."

"Now you are confusing wish and defense. Fear of one's own masochism comes first. Later, as a defense, comes pseudo-hatred."

Mr. A: "But I don't hate women. I'm just indifferent to them."

"That's the last stage of defense, secondarily denying even the peudo-hatred."

Mr. A: "But look at my profession—I'm a designer, I have a friendly-indifferent attitude towards women. Why, I even beautify the bitches!"

"Is the derogatory word 'bitches' in your opinion a proof of a friendly-indifferent attitude?"

Mr. A: "Stop catching me on phrases. 'Bitches' is a colloquialism, that's all."

"Why not give up and admit that contradictions have to be solved? First you told me the common homosexual tale about how you loved to wear girls' dresses when you were a child. The theory behind this, you claimed, was that you were 'biologically a half-girl.' Is that a proof of indifference towards women?"

Mr. A: "But you demolished this idea. You told me that homosexuality has no connection with inherent femininity. I accepted that."

"Fine. But it was because of your mistaken assumption, you claimed, that you went into the field of feminine fashion, developed great skill, and moved ahead very fast. How does your interest in designing feminine clothing prove your indifference towards women?"

He laughed heartily. After exhausting himself, he said triumphantly:

"Well, it doesn't prove my hatred!"

"Let's see. I told you that the basis for your skill, and your predilection, was an attempt to defend yourself, inwardly, against accusations that you have masochistic fears of women. The defense runs: 'How can I be afraid of them? They are putty in my hands, they wear what I tell them to wear.' "

Mr. A: "I admit to only one contradiction. Why, indeed, did I choose to work in a field where I am in constant contact with women?"

"As you correctly stated, 'Why, indeed?' Perhaps because you aren't as indifferent to women as you claim?"

Mr. A: "Now wait a minute. First you want to prove that I'm afraid of women. Then you want prove that I hate them, then that I love them. Make up your mind!"

"I have already. I claim that you are masochistically afraid of women. This feeling is warded off in two ways. First alibi: 'I'm superior; I dress them as I wish; they follow *my* dictates, therefore I cannot be afraid of them.' Second alibi: 'I hate women, and force them into uncomfortable clothes.' Didn't you report that you are incessantly quarreling with the other top designer in your firm, because she constantly complains that no reasonable women will buy your creations—they're *too* uncomfortable? And didn't you tell me that these pitched battles about fashion almost always end with your saying 'I'm disgusted,' and then letting this woman designer modify the touches that she says come from 'the sadist in you'?"

Mr. A: "She is wrong. Fashion-crazy women would accept any extravagant style, even if they had to be pressed between two steamrollers before they could fit into it."

"Quite possible. The point you didn't explain is this: Why do you want to make it so tough for your clients to breathe and eat in over-tight dresses?"

Mr. A: "Let them wear corsets so tight that they can't eat at all. Who cares?"

"But why do you have this 'sadistic' streak in your designs? Why do you make your creations to fit so tightly that they are uncomfortable even over an empty stomach?"

Mr. A: "Fashion is fashion."

"Tautologous, redundant, *and* evasive. If you are indifferent to women, why torture them?"

Mr. A: "Well, so I *am* a sadist. Anyway, I like it better than being called a masochist—a blank-blank masochist."

"If you observe your pride when you are called a sadist, and your anger and deflation when you're called a psychic masochist, you can study the whole difference between inner defense and inner wish."

Mr. A: "So I'm not even a sadist?"

"Sorry, no. Just a masochistic—"

Mr. A: "Stop it! I don't want to hear it!"

Not all homosexual fashion designers are so difficult; nor are *all* difficult fashion designers homosexuals. A very reasonable heterosexual woman in the field of fashion came into analysis with me because of a short-lived marital conflict, and her explanation was illuminating.

"These homos," she said, "are impossible in every respect. They are arrogant, conceited, supercilious, unreliable, and what not. But it must be admitted—they are extremely gifted. And don't forget that a new collection and line is needed every season. That means sixty to eighty new ideas, brand new, every season. A good deal of the time the new ideas don't sell, but they aren't really meant to. Women marvel at the new creations, try them on, and then buy a *modified* outfit, a more reasonable one. Or, if they actually buy these bizarre creations, the clothes have to be discarded after a short time and new ones bought—to the great satisfaction of the manufacturers.

"But to produce these new ideas, without running to the library and modifying the old ones, the industry needs the male homos. However, it also needs protection from them, and so they are constantly watched. Left to themselves they can do real damage. Many firms work it this way: they have a down-to-earth person who takes these crazy ideas and changes them into something possible. Of course, you can't do this when the homo-artist has a name and a position. Then, you can't even protest. God have mercy on the women *they* dress!"

I continued to test the fashion-hoax theory by submitting the idea to other homosexuals working in the fashion field who, for one reason or another, were in analysis with me. The reactions were so uniform that they could be schematized. In all the cases I tested, the *unconscious* aggression—which manifested itself in specific fashion creations—was (as the term implies) not in the conscious mind. When it was brought to the surface by the interpretation, there was an immediate and universal reaction in the form of a smile of half-recognition. The smile was as good as a confession; the interpretation had hit the mark.

The immediate reaction was jovial because I had assumed responsibility with my suggestion of the aggressive possibility, and consequently had freed, for a second, the repressed tendency. As a later reaction, the interpretation was for the most part promptly accepted, because the male homosexual's aggression towards women in his *second* line of inner defense, and serves to keep in deeper repression the real problem, which is masochistic fear of women. Real resistance began only when masochistic fear of women was shown to be at the core of the situation.

I asked such a homosexual designer:

"How do you explain the fact that fashions are so often *uncomfortable, unbecoming,* in short, *unfair,* to women?"

Mr. B: "Well, they run after everything new. What's a designer to do?"

"Couldn't he invent something comfortable, becoming, and fair to his customers?"

Mr. B: "Women wouldn't cherish it. The more uncomfortable, the better."

"But isn't the whole approach unfair? You are talking about these women as if they were guinea pigs, who have to pay, and dearly, for that matter, for being made uncomfortable."

Mr. B: "Why don't you analyze the masochism of the female consumer, instead of bothering me with your so-called proof that I'm masochistic towards women, using my so-called fake aggression as defense?"

"Aren't you shifting the problem? We are not talking about the customer. We're talking about the unconscious motives of homosexual designers."

Mr. B: "Don't you agree that you should never give a sucker an even break?"

"Do you or don't you agree that unconscious aggression comes into the picture?"

Mr. B: "I never thought of that. Off the record, I can tell you: I wouldn't be surprised." [5]

Another homosexual, Mr. C, was at first skeptical. Later he accepted the fact that unconscious motives could creep into his "rational life." He asked:

"Why are some male homosexuals so good at everything connected with fashion and interior decoration?"

"The answer is simple. Homosexuals' typical, superficial, defense is feminine identification, plus the narcissistic wish to outdo women. On *that* basis, something like a talent can be constituted."

Mr. C: "But you told me that feminine identification is only a half-conscious blind!"

"Correct. And exactly because it is a blind, the next—slightly deeper—defense enters. This one is pseudo-aggression towards women. Both defenses cover the real thing, the end-result of the infantile conflict. In homosexuals, this means psychic masochistic attachment to the mother."

Mr. C: "If this is so, a homosexual designer whose creations are really caricatures is unconsciously doing something 'moral' with his aggression—he's proving to his conscience that he isn't masochistic. Is that what you call 'admission of the lesser crime'?"

"Quite correct."

Mr. C: "Very strange. Why hasn't anybody pointed this out before?"

"Simply because homosexuals have been constantly misunderstood—even psychiatrically." [6]

Mr. D, also a homosexual fashion designer, had reached a phase in analysis in which he was toying with the idea

[5] In a very few cases, homosexual fashion designers had this pompous attitude: "My business activity and my pyschic situation (homosexuality) are not interconnected." This hypocrisy could easily be reduced to absurdity.

[6] See "The Myth of a New National Disease—Homosexuality and the Kinsey Report." *The Psychiatric Quarterly*, 1948.

of "switching to heterosexuality." He constantly bewailed the fact that he had been born just a little too late; his lot, he claimed, would have been easier in the twenties:

"The flapper type was at least half-way possible. Nowadays women are impossibly dressed."

"Meaning?"

"The flapper type approached the boy. All the distasteful female characteristics were more or less hidden."

"You seem to forget that women are dressed for heterosexuals."

"That's regrettable. Don't you know that, according to Kinsey, every third man has had *some* homosexual experiences in his adult life? Who takes care of that one-third of the male population?"

"In my opinion, Kinsey's statistics on homosexuals are quite inaccurate. His anti-psychiatric bias and his ignorance of psychology led him to overlook the fact that many of his volunteers were homosexuals. I also believe that his figures will be revised downwards when he gets a cross-section more representative than the 12,000 originally questioned."

"So what? There are enough homosexuals around."

"That's true, especially in fashion and other artistic fields. But you're forgetting that in analysis you are not being asked to compromise with your homosexuality. You're asked to change it. Your regret at the extinction of the flapper type proves that you haven't gone as far as you gratuitously assume."

"Come, come."

"All your homosexual friends were boys in their late teens, and we traced your 'type' back to a narcissistic duplication of yourself in puberty. That's a well-known homosexual predilection.[7] But heterosexuality presupposes a different

[7] It is not exclusive, of course; there are many types. Homosexuality is not a unit, but a set of different pictures. See *Neurotic Counterfeit-Sex*, Grune & Stratton, New York, 1951.

approach. I'm curious about this: How do you function in designing feminine clothes?"

"I try to revive the flapper type."

"Which leads to conflicts?"

"Sometimes. To prove how silly the other approach is, I sometimes design a burlesque of femininity in clothes. Amusingly enough, some of these designs go over big!"

"Did it ever occur to you how fantastic it is that the enemies of women decide what women should wear?"

"Never thought of it."

The patient, after a few seconds of silence, burst into hilarious laughter.

"Say, that's a good one! So we homosexuals have more power over women than we knew!"

My suspicion of a fashion-hoax, unconsciously perpetrated by homosexuals, was now on firm ground, but the surrounding terrain was an unbroken vista of implications and related possibilities. The homosexual is not alone in his use of fashion for neurotic purposes; in virtually all analyses of women clothing is a theme of some importance. One of the most familiar of popular clichés is that women dress to "express their personalities"; very often a woman's dress reveals that she is not consciously aware of the personality she is expressing. It is a commonplace to find that the way a woman dresses is a key to her specific unconscious elaboration. One example will suffice here; additional examples will be found in the chapter on "Dresses and Three Types of Reputation."

Mrs. X., a woman in her thirties, was an inhibited and deeply depressed writer in analysis with me. She dressed well and inconspicuously. Her behavior pattern was composed of apology for being in this world at all, exorbitant verbal malice, and masochistic (though subdued) complaints. She was conspicuous in only one way: her favorite (only?) hat was in the shape of a helmet, a long pointed affair that unduly and unfavorably emphasized her skinniness and towering height. The purpose of this procedure—unconscious, to be sure—was *an unspoken reproach directed at her mother:* "See what an enormous misfit you produced!" Obviously, this reproach, which attempted defense and achieved merely pseudo-aggression, was only a cover for more deeply repressed psychic masochism. In the woman's appearance she deprecated not her mother, but herself.

But every "case" is different. I analyzed a poetess with conflicts similar to those of Mrs. X. Here the seemingly identical symptom of the "helmet hat" had exactly the opposite meaning; her height was one of the few features this lady approved in herself, and was proud of. In her specific case the hat, accentuating her height, had symbolic innuendoes as well as the pseudo-aggressive defensive meaning: "My height is the only thing bad mother could not prevent!"

As for the normally heterosexual male, his interest in woman's clothing, at least at first glance, seems obscure. Not that "what my wife wears" is a theme infrequently encountered in analyses of husbands; nor that references to women's clothing, either bitter or admiring, are rare in analyses of unmarried men; nor that men are unlike women and do not dress to reveal their unconscious personalities. But the theme here is submerged: men are not "interested" in women's clothes. Their contention is that they are "interested" in how much their wives spend on their clothes, they are "interested" in their wives' "stupid obsession" with fashion, they are "interested" in—and impressed by—the effect created by their girl-friend's outfits, and they are "interested" in making a good appearance in their own clothes—presumably for the sake of "business contacts."

Even if this false front of disinterest were genuine, it

would be difficult for men to prove that they are not involved with and concerned with women's clothes in a larger sense. If there were no other proof, the very existence (not to mention the popularity) of the institution known as the strip-tease would suffice. For here is a spectacle which depends entirely upon clothing for its effectiveness. The ostensible object is the split second of nudity or apparent nudity at the end of the routine; the real attraction is the gradual removal of clothing, layer by layer, with each discarded layer revealing the girl still clothed. Clothing, far from being an impediment to the sexual object, advances to the position of a sexual object itself.

These are of course the most superficial of the connections suggested by the homosexual fashion-hoax. They are enough, however, to indicate that fashion in general supplies an unusually rich lode for the exploration of human motives and reactions. Less superficial is this related question: Is the use of fashion for neurotic purposes merely fortuitous; is clothing, like every other human institution, seized on by neurotics merely because it is there, or is clothing a preferred vehicle of neurotic expression? Since psychology recognizes no accidents, but only more or less successfully hidden origins, this point is basic.

One further preliminary step remained to be taken, since the entire question of homosexuality is still a delicate—not to say explosive—one in our society. I called in a man who had been analyzed for homosexuality and cured by me nine years before. I had always had a great respect for this man; his personality was quite different from the morbid narcissism and psychopathic trends of the average homosexual. After his homosexuality was analytically changed, we remained on friendly terms. He is a top-notch fashion designer, grateful to analysis both for his marriage and for having rescued him from a truly "impossible" situation, the

THE HINDU GODDESS KALI

MINOAN SNAKE GODDESS,
2000 B.C.

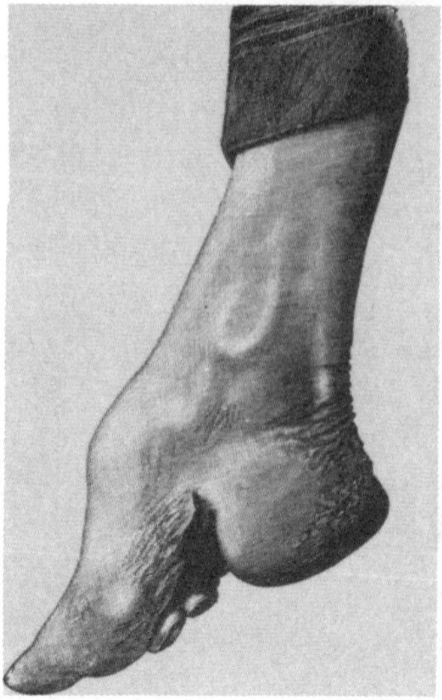

CONTRASTS IN CONSTRICTION: THE BOUND FOOT OF THE CHINESE WOMAN AND THE WASP WAIST OF THE WEST, CIRCA 1900

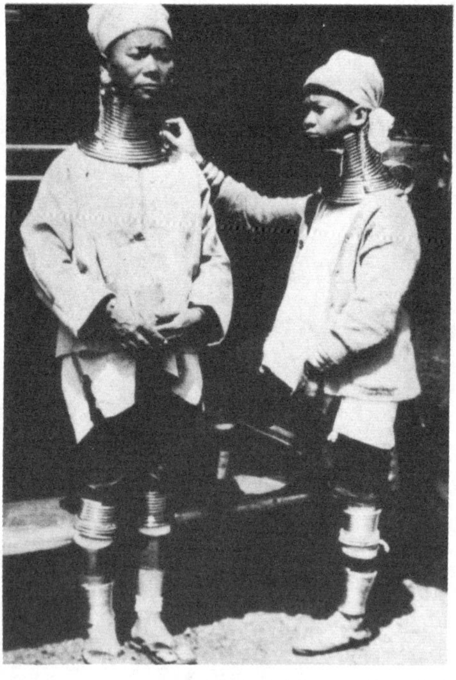

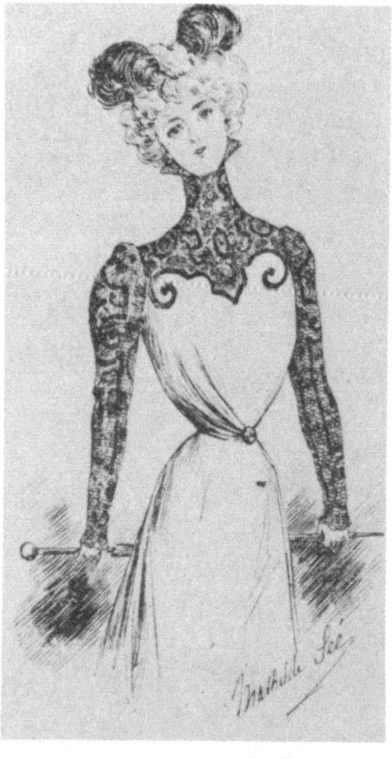

by Ewing Galloway, New York

THE NECK AS OBJECT OF CONSTRICTION: THE BURMESE HILL WOMAN, WITH METAL COLLAR AND THE GIBSON GIRL, WITH COLLAR OF WHALEBONE, SILK AND LACE

HOLBEIN'S "LADY OF BASLE"

THE EMPIRE STYLE

THE CRINOLINE

THE BUSTLE

THE HOBBLE SKIRT AS WORN IN 1910

details of which cannot be discussed. I am reproducing parts of a conversation we had in June, 1950.

I explained the conclusion I had reached about the part played by homosexuals in fashion creation, emphasizing the fact that I was talking about excesses and extremes and not the daily work done. I then outlined the general ideas of this book, and told him:

"I am quite sure of my results; still, the idea of the unconscious homosexual hoax in fashion is such an unfamiliar one that I want your criticism. Be as harsh as you wish."

My friend was silent for a long time, obviously thinking with concentration. Finally he said:

"You know, of course, what you are letting yourself in for—I mean external criticism from both parties, the victimized women and the unconscious avengers, the homosexual designers."

"Of course. I am not interested in that. I am asking for objections to the deduction itself."

"It is a strange idea."

"That's true. But is it—in your opinion—a correct idea? Please be more outspoken. You are not on the witness stand."

After a still longer silence, the answer came.

"I have been going over in my mind some of the fashions you would call 'foolish,' and remembering their inventors. Your formula fits. And it's difficult to disprove. But—and I mean this seriously—I don't think you should make it public."

"Why?"

"Because it would confuse both the customers and the designers. Both will be furious."

"When did you become so timid? And when did public criticism become more important than scientific truth?

Come to the point. This is what I want to know: is this idea possible or probable?"

"You don't seem to understand the effect this idea is likely to produce, and not only on the people who work directly in the fashion field. It would be worse than a middle-sized earthquake. You can see from my answers that I myself am rather stunned. I don't seem to want to come to grips with the idea; I talk around it. And as you know, I'm generally very precise in my answers."

"I understand, though I believe you exaggerate the expected 'earthquake' reaction. Anger, and rejection, are of course unavoidable. I'll repeat the question: On the basis of your personal knowledge of the genesis of homosexuality, and your personal knowledge of fashion designers, would you say that my idea of the unconscious homosexual hoax in fashion is possible, or probable?"

Fortunately for my friend, I was called to the telephone at that point, which gave him a breathing spell of a few minutes. When I returned, I found him in a different mood. He was smiling, and had evidently recovered, to an extent, from his first reaction.

"Well?"

"Well, let's put it this way. The idea seems correct. At least, I can't find a flaw in it. I admit that I tried. But in the meantime, I began to see the irony of the situation. I believe my evasiveness came from resentment—you were so matter-of-fact when you presented the idea. Of course that's reasonable—you are not personally involved. But if someone came to you and proved that everything in psychopathology that you believe in is a hoax—how would you react, *at first?*"

"I believe I would try to argue, to find objections."

"And if you couldn't find any?"

"I would still try to find objections which would convince myself."

"And after exhausting those?"

"I would give up—if at all—only after a very long fight."

"Still, it's interesting that I should have made the silly suggestion that you suppress the material. Your deduction must have hit a sore spot to bring out the ostrich in me."

"Your rationalization was just as interesting—telling me that I ought to protect myself from unavoidable criticism."

"That was a beauty. Are we all so infantile when something hits us, let's say, below the fashion-belt?"

"We all are."

"Without malice: I would like to see how you would react if the bottom were knocked out of something you value. And with unimpeachable arguments, too."

"I can assure you I would be—at first, anyhow—no less silly. I believe I would even feel 'it's unfair!' "

"Me, too!"

My friend has finally forgiven me: in a letter received a few days later he admitted that he had gone on trying to find arguments with which to confound my assumption, and had been unsuccessful. "You convinced at least *one* person in the fashion field. But don't quote me recognizably. I would be a dead duck in the industry."

2 *In the Beginning Was Fear*

SOME ANTHROPOLOGISTS[1] have already exploded the contention that the idea of clothing originated from the human being's innate sense of modesty. As far back as 1901, Westermarck observed, in *The History of Human Marriage*, that the facts pointed to the existence of shame as a *result* of the custom of clothing the body, not as a *cause*. The origin of clothing, in Westermarck's opinion, in some cases can be traced to the need for protection from the elements, and in many other cases can be traced to the individual's desire to make himself or herself attractive to the opposite sex.

Westermarck's theory of "clothes as sexual lure" is certainly not a satisfactory clarification. On the contrary, it prompts a further question: why should covering exactly the body constitute a sexual lure, and how does covering the body make it sexually attractive? If modesty and its concomitant, a feeling of shame, are not primary human attitudes, who should be credited with the invention of these feelings?

Comparative anthropological observations confuse the issue even further. Contradictions are rampant; even the conservative Encyclopædia Britannica can but regretfully register the following cross-statements:

[1] Anthropology is a science, hence its disciples behave exactly like those of every other science: not even adherents to the same school of thought agree among themselves.

"*Modesty is not innate in man,* and its controversial nature is easily seen from the consideration of the different ideas held by different races on the same subject. With Mohammedan peoples it is sufficient for a woman to cover her face; the Chinese women would think it extremely indecent to show their artificially compressed feet, and it is even improper to mention them to a woman; in Sumatra and Celebes the wild tribes consider the exposure of the knee immodest; in Central Asia the fingertips, and in Samoa the navel are similarly regarded. In Tahiti and Tonga clothes might be discarded without offense, provided the individual were tattooed, and among the Caribs a woman might leave the hut without her girdle but not unpainted. Similarly in Alaska women felt great shame when seen without plugs they carried in their lips. Europeans are considered indelicate in many ways by other races, and a remark made by Peschel is to the point: "Were a pious Musselman of Ferghana to be present at our balls and see the bare shoulders of our wives and daughters, and see the semi-embraces of our round dances, he would silently wonder at the long-suffering of Allah who had not long ago poured fire and brimstone on this sinful and shameless generation." Another point of interest lies in the difference of outlook with which nudity is regarded by the English and the Japanese. Among the latter it has been common for the sexes to take baths together without clothing, while in England mixed bathing, even in full costume, is even now by no means universal. Yet in England the representation of the nude in art meets with no reproach, though considered improper by the Japanese. Even more striking is the fact that in civilized countries what is permitted at certain times is forbidden at others; a woman will expose far more of her person at night in the ballroom or theatre, than would be considered seemly by day in the street; and a bathing costume which would be thought modest on the beach would meet with reprobation in a town.

"*Modesty therefore is highly conventional,* and to discover its origin the most primitive tribes must be observed. Among these, in Africa, South America, Australia and so forth, where clothing is at a minimum, the men are always more elaborately ornamented than the women. At the same time it is noticeable that no cases of spinsterhood are found; celibacy, rare as it is, is confined to the male sex. It is reasonable, therefore, to conclude that ornament is a stimulus to sexual selection, and this conclusion is enforced by the fact that among many comparatively nude people clothing is assumed at certain dances which have as their confessed object the excitation of the passions of the opposite sex. Many forms of underclothing, moreover, seem to call attention to those parts of the body of which, under the conditions of Western civilization at the present day, it aims at concealment. Certain articles of dress worn by the New Hebrideans, the Zulu-Xosa tribes, certain tribes of Brazil and others, are cases in point. Clothing, moreover—and this is true also of the present day—almost always tends to accentuate rather than to conceal the difference between the sexes. Looking at the problem, then, from the point of view of sexual selection, it would seem that a stage in the progress of human society is marked by the discovery that *concealment affords a greater stimulus than revelation;* that the fact is true is obvious—even to modern eyes a figure partially clad appears far more indecent than a nude. That the stimulus is real is seen in the fact that among nude races flagrant immorality is far less common than among the more clothed; the contrast between the Polynesians and Melanesians, living as neighbours under similar conditions, is striking evidence on this point. Later, when the novelty of clothing has spent its force, the stimulus is supplied by nudity complete or partial.

"One more point must be considered: there is evidence of competent observers to show that members of a tribe accustomed to nudity, when made to assume clothing for the first time, exhibit as much confusion as would a European compelled to strip in public. This fact, considered together with what has been said above, compels the conclusion that *modesty* is a feeling merely of acute self-consciousness due to appearing unusual, and is the *result of clothing rather than the cause.*"

Thus the game of asking what came first, modesty or clothing, just like the other time-honored question about the chicken and the egg, can be shelved as unusable for research. The sense of shame, as moderns understand it ("are you decent?") *presupposes* the knowledge of the differentation between the nude and the dressed. This being the case, the problem still remains: what preceded the introduction of clothing, and its maintenance as an institution? What strong emotional impetus lies behind it? I suggest for this powerful emotional agent the term "*presartorial terror.*" [2]

To clarify the term, we have first to outline what psychoanalysis has already discovered about the unconscious motivations in the circumscript zone under discussion.

One of Freud's first steps in elucidation of the unconscious consisted of the postulation of a male castration complex.

The castration complex has had a strange fate in psychoanalytical science. First, it was confirmed on the basis of clinical material obtained by analysts all over the world in the past fifty years. On the other hand, more and more "precursors" of the complex were discovered. This was only natural, because of what might be called the "geology" of psychoanalysis. Freud's first discoveries were made during the treatment of hysterical neurotics, people regressed to the most superficial levels of the unconscious. Hence, he was confronted with *phallic* castration fear. As neurotics in deeper stages of regression came under analytic scrutiny, deeper fears were encountered. But the sequence of analytic discoveries was in exactly the opposite order from the sequence of stages through which the child passes in the course of its psychic development. Freud's earliest discov-

[2] For an explanation of nudity in some primitive tribes, see Chapter Eleven.

eries were at the apex of the psychic pyramid, and proceeded downward; the child's psychic development begins at the bottom of the pyramid and proceeds to the apex. Consequently, the difficulty of correlating actual development with actual discovery resulted in some confusion. Today the term castration complex is still used, although mostly for sentimental reasons; however, every author is forced to add an explanation in order to indicate the psychic level to which he is referring (phallic, anal, oral). This is not to say that the original discovery of "phallic castration fear" has lost its validity. Quite the contrary. Phallic castration fear is the culmination point of all other types of fear encountered on deeper levels of regression.

Personally, I believe that the "*septet of baby fears,*"[3] fantastic as they may sound, offers the best approach to an understanding of later castration fears.

Scrutiny of this septet of fears shows clinically that Wordsworth's opinion, "The child is father of the man," is an understatement: the *baby* is father of the man. Adults, with massive layers of repression, may ironically scoff at these precursors of their own "opinions." The clinically observable phenomena exist none the less; irony is cheap, and only facts carry weight.

In the order of their appearance, baby fears (as later reconstructed from neurotic manifestations) are:

Fear of being starved, devoured, poisoned, choked, chopped to pieces, drained, castrated.

This Grand Guignol of unbelievable fears becomes less fantastic when four facts are considered.

First, the newborn has been "spoiled" by the paradisiacal effortlessness of his prenatal existence, when not even eating, swallowing or breathing were necessary; oxygen and

[3] For elaboration, see the author's books, *The Superego*, Grune & Stratton, 1952; *Neurotic Counterfeit-Sex*, l.c.; *The Basic Neurosis*, Grune & Stratton, New York, 1949.

foodstuff were automatically pumped into his blood-vessels via his mother's blood-vessels. Birth changed all this, and not even an infant gives up a preferential position without some struggle.

Second, since the child has had these specific experiences in utero, he tries to duplicate them after birth, disregarding the radical change in conditions which has taken place. At the same time, he builds up the fantasy of megalomania and autarchy, in which everything "good" is provided by himself, and everything "bad" stems from the outside world. Thus, acknowledgment of the mother's loving kindness is impeded.

Third, a tragic biological inadequacy comes into play. The child is born with the potential aggression of an adult, and a muscular apparatus entirely incapable of expressing it. As a result, a mechanism of projection is used: a great deal of the child's own aggression is attributed to an outside source, as the English school of analysis has suggested. Unfortunately, the only person available to play the role of deus ex machina is—mother. In this early stage of the child's development, his mother's love and benevolence are not recognized. On the contrary, she is mistrusted as a designer of all varieties of evil.

And fourth, the child's ignorance of reality factors helps both to create and to maintain all these "silly" misconceptions.

These baby fears are either misconceptions of reality, projections of the child's own unusable aggression, or "reformulations" of already discarded fantasies. For example:

Fear of starvation. Mothers do not let babies starve: if proof of this statement is needed, it can be found in the fact that the candidate for future neurosis is alive, even though he harbors that fear in his unconscious. "Starvation" here is a reflection of megalomania; dependence upon the breast or bottle, plus a waiting period of even a few seconds, are unconsciously magnified out of all proportion.

In later years, the reproach is modified from "starvation" to "refusal," and the complaint becomes denial of love, kindness, gifts, attention, etc., instead of food.

Fear of being devoured. This grotesque fear has been clarified by the English school of psychoanalysis as a projection of the child's *own* aggressive designs upon the nipple or bottle. The formula reads: "I don't want to bite; mother wants to devour me." Fairy tales, dreams, animal phobias and unconscious fantasies, enshrine these early infantile concepts.

Fear of being poisoned. Sooner or later, even the child who cherishes his "starvation grievance" must admit that he is being fed. At this point, a reformulation takes place: "It is true that mother feeds me, but the food is harmful because it is poisoned." Pathologic fear of impregnation, neurotic intestinal disturbances, and hypochondriacal complaints centering around food are remnants of this fear.

Fear of being choked. Analysis of neurotics who are afraid of "confined places"—those suffering from true claustrophobia, and those with neurotic fear of elevators, subways, buses—proves that repressed fantasies of being choked by the mother's breast or body lie under the hysterical palimpsest. (Contributaries of this fear are also visible in the psychological aspects of asthma.) The fear has little to do with the disproportion between the mother's breast and the child's miniature mouth, or with the clumsiness with which the breast or bottle is sometimes forced between the baby's lips.

Fear of being chopped to pieces. Here the adult's harmless actions in the course of washing or cleaning procedures are misunderstood, and used as a point of departure for projection of the child's aggressive designs.

Later, the cutting of meat, fish, fowl, is adduced as a positive proof of a woman's "capabilities."

Fear of operations and phallic castration fears can be traced back to the irrational "chopping" fears of infancy.

Fear of being drained. This fear arises from the child's feeling of helplessness when it is confronted with "propelling forces" which it can neither understand nor control, in the elimination of urine and feces. The child feels "drained" against his own wishes, and retaliates secondarily with megalomaniacal and aggressive ideas connected with both products.

In later life, one encounters that neurotic fear behind the façade of miserliness in money, sex, and even words.

Fear of castration. This fear is the rationally disguised culmination of all the "ancestors" described above. It may be seen in its clearest form during the Oedipal phase. The subsequent elaboration of phallic castration fear is endless in its variations. It ranges from impotence to any inhibition of function of any organ or any inhibition of activity. Often what seems to be a superficial castration fear proves to be only a cover for more deeply repressed precursors and constituents of "baby fears."

It is important to note that in all these fears the child is on the passive-receiving end. Strong passivity and weak counter-actions are the common denominator which links together all these unconscious terrors.

The pattern which emerges, paradoxical as it may seem, indicates that *unconsciously every man is afraid of woman.*[4] Of course, the septet of baby fears disappears from consciousness. No man claims that women want to "starve, devour, poison, choke, drain, or castrate" him, or "chop him to pieces." What he says is, "women are cruel; they

[4] Interestingly enough, the first analyst to stress this fact misjudged the reasons. Karen Horney, in a paper published in the *Internationale Zeitschrift für Psychoanalyse*, 18:5-18, 1932 entitled "Die Angst Vor Der Frau," reduces that fear to an offense to self-esteem, alluding to the boy's narcissistic lesion resulting from rejection and ridicule by the mother in the Oedipal wish-period.

want to exploit me, hook me, drain me of money and sex, make me a cuckold, make me a sucker, make me a doormat," etc. Whether they admit it or not, men attribute "cruelty" to women. In making the accusation, the terms used are adult, but the fears they describe are still infantile.

There is abundant evidence that baby fears, culminating in phallic castration fear, are not an analytic fairy tale but are clinical reality. Instead of adducing clinical material once more (see *Basic Neurosis*), I am quoting a short story by the famous French novelist, Guy de Maupassant, and the testimony of a victim of her famous husband's castration fear, Mrs. John Ruskin.

The Maupassant story is *L'Inconnue*, obviously a tale uninfluenced by analysis, since the author died in 1893, a date at which there was no analysis in its present sense. Freud was then only beginning his as yet unpublished observations.

The story describes the gallant adventures of Roger des Annettes. The hero invites to his house a voluptuously beautiful woman whom he had long known by sight without ever having had the courage to approach her. To his surprise the lady accepts the invitation:

". . . I slept badly and awaited her. She arrived at about ten o'clock, very calm, very quiet, and held out her hand as if we were old friends. I offered her a chair, removed her hat and veil, her coat, and muff. After that I began with some confusion to be more gallant, for I had no time to lose. As a matter of fact, I had not long to wait and we had hardly exchanged a dozen words before I began to undress her. She thought to the rest herself. I have never succeeded in doing it myself. I prick my fingers on the pins, tie the laces up into knots instead of undoing them. I get everything disordered, lose my time and *lose my head*.

"O dear friend, do you know more precious moments in life than those in which we watch the woman as she allows each garment in turn to fall with a slight rustle to her feet . . . We watch it at a slight distance discreetly so as not to outrage their modesty, which they all have when they undress themselves for us. And what can be more charming than their movements in removing these soft garments which drop limply as if they had been touched by death. How wonderful and exciting is the appearance of their naked body, bare arms and bosom, after the corset has been removed, and how confusing the line of the body that we sense beneath the final wrap!

"But suddenly I noticed something astonishing, a black spot between the shoulders, for she had her back to me, a large, raised, deep black spot. What was that? I could not doubt it; the memory of the suspicion of a beard, or the eyebrows that met above the eyes, and the plentiful hair that covered her head like a helmet, should have prepared me for this surprise. As a matter of fact I had promised her not to look.

"In spite of this I was astonished and suddenly strange pictures and memories came into my mind. *I seemed to see one of those witches from the Arabian Nights, one of those sly, dangerous beings, who are created to draw human beings into unknown abysses.* I thought of Solomon, who made the Queen of Sheba walk over a mirror to make sure that she had not goats' feet.

"And . . . *and when I was to sing my love-song I noticed that I had no more voice, not even the slightest trace.* Forgive me, *I had a voice like one of the Pope's singers* . . . She was at first astonished, then highly indignant at this, for she dressed again hurriedly and said: "It was very pointless to ask me here" . . . That is the whole of my adventure. But the worst of it is, I am now in love with her, hopelessly in love, I cannot look at another woman without thinking of her . . ." [5]

[5] At first glance one could erroneously assume that Maupassant's hero was afraid of homosexuality. Nothing of the kind; I treated a series of men because of impotence whose conscious complaint was fear of female pubic hair. Under that rationalization was something else: lack of the female penis, not discernible beneath the pubic hair. A typical psychic shift was revealed: the identical, by the way, as in the Samson and Delilah myth. Why should a man's "power" be concentrated in his—hair?

And here are excerpts from a letter written by Effie Gray Ruskin to her father, shortly before her successful application for an annulment of her marriage to John Ruskin:

"I have received my Mother's and George's kind letters this morning and feel very thankful that I have your and their approval in the course of conduct I have been endeavouring to pursue for some time—and in fact unless matters had become so sad for me as to threaten my life I should not have on any account, but feeling that the necessity of acting in concert with you might, by being longer delayed, cause you and the others connected with my life greater sorrow in the end. I, therefore, as I fell now so ill and in perpetual nervous distress, feel that perhaps I may be adding to yours by a silence which I have kept on John Ruskin's conduct to me ever since I left your care, although I have lately and on my last visit home shown you how very unhappy I was. You are aware that since 1848 to this last year (1854) I have never made any formal complaint to you—there were many reasons for my silence the principal being of course my great love for you and my dear Mother—fearing to trouble you when you were in great difficulties yourselves, when I tried to look on my unfortunate position as one where whatever I internally suffered—at least removed me from being a burthen on you—and I resolved that no annoyance which I suffered should give you any . . . I have duly considered the step I am about to take in telling you all . . . I have therefore simply to tell you that I do not think I am John Ruskin's Wife at all—and I entreat you to assist me to get released from the unnatural position in which I stand to him— To go back to the day of my marriage the 10th of April 1848. I went as you know away to the Highlands—I had never been told the duties of married persons to each other and knew little or nothing about their relations in the closest union on earth. For days John talked about this relation to me but avowed no intention of making me his Wife— He alleged various reasons, hatred toward children, religious motives, a desire to preserve my beauty, and finally this last year told me his true reason (and this to me is as villainous as all the rest) that *he had imagined women* were quite different to what he saw I was, and the reason he did not make me his Wife was because he was *disgusted*[6] with my person the first evening 10th April. After I began to see things better, I argued with him and took the Bible but he soon silenced me and I was not sufficiently awake to what position I was in—then he said after six years, he would marry me when I was 25. This last year we spoke about it. I did say what I thought in May— He then said as I professed quite a dislike to him that it would be SINFUL to enter into such a connexion as if I was not very *wicked* I was at least insane and the responsibility that I might have children was too great, as I was quite unfit to bring them up."

The following document was the end of the Effie Gray Ruskin story:

"Therefore we John Hazzard Doctor of Laws the Commissary aforesaid having heard counsel learned in the Law in this behalf on the part of Euphemia Chalmers Gray falsely called Ruskin DO PRONOUNCE DEGREE AND DECLARE that he the said John Ruskin being then a Bachelor did at the time lebellate contract a pretended Marriage with the said Euphemia Gray then and still a Spinster but since falsely called Ruskin and we do also pronounce decree and declare according to the lawful proofs made in the said cause as aforesaid that the said Marriage howsoever in fact had between the said Ruskin and the said Euphemia Gray falsely called Ruskin was had and celebrated while the said *John Ruskin was incapable of consummating the same by reason of incurable impotency* WHEREFORE and by reason of the premises WE DO pronounce decree and declare that such Marriage or rather show or effigy of Marriage so had and solemnized or rather profaned between the said John Ruskin and Euphemia Chalmers Gray falsely called Ruskin was and is null and void from the beginning to all intents and purposes in the Law whatsoever and by reason

[6] The "disgust" was based on the "discovery" that women are "quite different" as far as the anatomy of the genitals is concerned, and it was this which so violently activated the castration fear in Ruskin, camouflaged by "disgust."

thereof that the said Euphemia Chalmers Gray falsely called Ruskin was and is free from all bond of Marriage with him the said John Ruskin by this our definitive sentence of final decree which we give and promulge by these presents."

Man entered the arena of action burdened with inwardly undigested fears. We could reasonably expect that his actions, especially those concerned with women, would reflect his inner fears. This is all the more marked because the patriarchal family gave to man the power of decision over woman's conduct as well as his own. Among the attitudes attributed to women were decency and modesty. Were these attitudes invented by women, or men?

A short recapitulation of prevailing psychological opinions is to be found in Havelock Ellis, who in his *Psychology of Sex*[7] concludes that modesty is composed of the following factors:

1. Sexual refusal: it is a method whereby the female conveys the fact that she is not receptive to male advances;

2. Fear of arousing disgust: clothing is a means of negating the proximity of the sexual organs to the anal and urethral openings;

3. Fear of the magic power of sexual manifestations: the elaborate ceremonies which originally grew out of this fear tend ultimately to be reduced to simple rules of behavior which both represent and ensure modesty;

4. The adoption and development of clothing and personal decoration: the dual result is the creation of an attitude of modesty, repressing male sexual advances, and of coquettishness, which is an attempt to arouse them.

5. The status of woman as property: this gave an external authorization to an emotion already existing, but based on what Ellis calls "more natural and primitive facts."

The next question reads: Is this all?

[7] Vol. 1, "Evolution of Modesty," pp. 1-84.

"Books," said Joseph Conrad in his *Personal Record,* alluding to the fact that he finished writing the tenth chapter of *Almayer's Folly* on the deck of a steamer frozen in at Rouen, "may be written in all sorts of places." Scientific progress, also, may be achieved in all sorts of places, by all sorts of people—with and without diplomas—and for all sorts of reasons. Tracing back the very few people who have aphoristically contributed to the elucidation of the *real* reasons for modesty, we start at dinner tables in Paris and Milan around the year 1820: the bored bon vivant Henri Beyle (better known as Stendhal, one of the greatest of psychological novelists) scribbles on the backs of menu cards his ideas of love, later elaborated and published in *L'Amour.* The book had no success; the publisher ironically reported to the author that he had written a holy book, one which nobody dared to touch . . . (In the eleven years after its publication in 1822, the book sold exactly seventeen copies.) Still, the book contains a fascinating theory of love, and one which was scientifically corroborated a century after it was written.[8] For Stendhal, the phenomenon of romantic love consists of fantasies projected upon the object of admiration: "In love only one's own illusion is enjoyed." Stendhal created the theory of "crystallization" in love, equating the growth of romantic love with the process taking place when,

"At the salt mines in Salzburg, a branch stripped of its leaves by winter is thrown into the abandoned depth of the mine. Taken out two or three months later, it is covered with brilliant crystals . . ."

Since fantasy is the basis of romantic love, Stendhal concludes:

"These souls burning too vehemently or too suddenly *fall in love on credit,* we might say, and act too rashly instead of wait-

[8] See Chapter Ten, also Jekels-Bergler *Transference and Love,* Imago (Vienna), 1934, and *The Psychoanalytic Quarterly* (New York) 1949.

ing for things to happen. Before there is a possibility of becoming impressed with the true nature of things, they envelop them—from afar and before they are even visible—in that imaginary charm which springs inexhaustibly from them. Then they approach and see things, *not as they are but as they themselves have made them*; and while under cover of the respective subjects, they take pleasure in themselves, believing they are enjoying the subject. But one day they tire of bearing all costs alone; they find out that the imaginary subject does not return the ball; their prejudice diminishes, and the blow suffered by their egotism makes them unjust toward the overrated subject."

In this strange book, we also read:

"It is clear that three-quarters of modesty is *taught*. This is, perhaps, the only law born of civilization which produces nothing but happiness . . . I can see no other natural foundation for modesty. Love is the miracle of civilization. Among savage and very barbarous races we find nothing but physical love of gross character. It is modesty that *gives to love the aid of imagination*, and in so doing imparts life to it. Modesty is very early *taught*, to little girls by their mothers, and with extreme jealousy, one might say, by esprit de corps. They are watching in advance over the happiness of the future lover . . . The advantage of modesty consists in the fact that the latter is the mother of love . . . The soul is occupied with being ashamed, instead of desiring; one does not allow oneself to desire, and desire leads to deeds."

Thus, according to Stendhal, modesty is subsumed into the technique of *leaving undisturbed* the fantasies which are to be projected onto the beloved, and its purpose is to prevent "deeds." [9]

In 1898, seventy-odd years after the publication of *L'Amour*, a Frenchwoman, Mme. Celine Renooz, published a book entitled *Psychologie Comparée de l'Homme*

[9] The second part of this theory is more easily understood when one knows that Stendhal was—impotent. See the author's book *Talleyrand-Napoleon-Stendhal-Grabbe*, Internationaler Psychoanalytischer Verlag, Vienna, 1935.

et de la Femme, and in this book attempted to prove that modesty is not really a feminine characteristic:

"Modesty is *masculine shame attributed to women* for two reasons: first, because man believes that woman is subject to the same laws as himself; second, because the course of human evolution has reversed the psychology of sexes, attributing to women the psychological results of masculine sexuality. This is the origin of the conventional lies which by a sort of social suggestion have intimidated women. They have, in appearance at least, accepted the rule of shame imposed on them by men, but only custom inspires modesty for which they are praised; it is really an outrage to their sex. This reversal of psychological laws has, however, been accepted by women with a struggle. Primitive woman, proud of her womanhood, for a long time defended her nakedness, which ancient art has always presented. And in the actual life of the young girl today there is a moment when, by a secret atavism, she feels the pride of her sex the intuition of her moral superiority, and cannot understand why she must hide her cause." [10]

The scene now switches to the India-Baluchistan border: an English colonel stationed at that forsaken place has read Ellis and Freud, has combined his own lay observations on Indian taboos with his own unconscious notions, and—though unanalyzed—has created a new scientific concept, "the menstruation complex." The name of this colonel was C. D. Daly; the essentials of his theory are contained in two papers published by *Imago* in 1927 and 1928.[11] Daly's interest in the menstruation taboos amounted to an obsession; he centered *everything* around these taboos. Hence he subsumed the question of modesty and the question of clothing under his "menstruation complex"; he suspected that "clothes were originally worn to hide the fact of men-

[10] Mme. Renooz' book is inaccessible to me; it seems to be forgotten and extinct. Havelock Ellis knew of it: he disagreed with the lady.

[11] The studies are entitled "Hindu-Mythologie und der Kastrations-Komplex," and "Der Menstruations Komplex."

struation, and that certain perfumes[12] had the identical purpose; *women* having observed that clothes constituted an attraction, used clothes and perfumes also at times when they themselves were not taboo, this time, however, to attract men.

Daly credits men with fear of menstruation, and disgust for it. Seemingly, however, he puts it up to women to find an ingenious remedy for this reaction. Daly has no explanation for the fact that the "attraction" goes beyond fear—in short, he does not touch upon the real problem. Moreover, he bases all these fears on the phallic-anal castration problem, omitting the masochistic substructure. Finally, Daly's deduction fails to clarify why the game of half-exposure and half-concealment, as symbolized in clothes at the times when the taboo is not in force, should be attractive to men. The possibility that man is playing with fear is not elaborated. Nor is this other question touched upon: since man's reaction to the bleeding genitalia is one of disgust, why is not the clothing which covers women regarded merely as protection? Why is man, somehow, attracted to feminine clothes—beyond the biological urge?

Stendhal in Milan, scribbling his theory of love and modesty on the backs of menus; Mme. Renooz in Paris some seventy years later, carrying on her suffragette-like fight against male prerogatives; after thirty more years, Colonel Daly in Baluchistan developing his cherished menstruation complex from his studies of old Indian goddesses—the way of scientific inklings, protracted over a century, is strange and picturesque. True enough, none of these three pioneers (a partial exception may be granted to Daly) had

[12] A similar theory concerning perfumes has been suggested by our distinguished Indian colleague, Dr. Girindrashekhar Bose, in his book *Concept de Repression*, Kegan Paul, Trench, Trubner, London, 1921.

precise ideas of the complexity of the problem. Still, theirs is the priority of half-vision.

Independently, anthropologists and sociologists confirmed Westermarck's contention: "the scanty covering was found to act as the most powerful obtainable sexual stimulus." This, by the way, had already been suspected by Robert Burton, who, in his *Anatomy of Melancholy* (published in 1621!) claimed that "the greatest provocations of lust are from our apparel."

The frequently adduced arguments that clothes can be used as a means of female coquetry, that clothes allow for the play of imagination, are true enough, but they sidestep the *real* question: what causes the moth-to-the-flame attraction which women's clothes have for men? The argument of fear put forward by Daly merely complicates the problem: if man is afraid of woman, he covers her up; if his biological urge proves stronger than his fear, he uncovers her and enjoys her in sex act proper. *But why—even at times when there is no question of sexual activity—man's attraction to the half-clothed woman, symbolized in dresses? Why is the half-clad more "alluring" than the nude?* And if "imagination" is of so much importance, what does it signify? What is imagined?

In short, the observations recorded on this subject, although initially correct, bogged down at exactly this point. Utilizing my previous investigations, therefore, I attacked the over-all problem from a new starting point: the clinical observation that man's at best half-digested, passive, baby fears unconsciously lead him into building up an unconscious portrait of himself, which I have called *The Hoax of the He-Man.*[13]

In our culture, man's activity is conveniently taken for

[13] First stated in *Divorce Won't Help;* chapter "The Myth of the Superior Male," Harper & Bros., New York, 1948.

granted. The "sissy" and "weakling" are disparaged; the "hero" who conquers all obstacles is the theoretical norm.

Elsewhere,[14] I have sketched the popular concept of the He-Man, thus: A real man is virile, active, determined. He is sound but daring, faithful but conquering—in short, a hero. In life, love, and work he is classed as superior. Where other mortals would despair, he remains undaunted, merely inquiring (pleasantly), "What do we do next?" If the remote possibility were to eventuate, and someone dared to ask, "Are you a man or a mouse?", He-Man would have no hesitation in answering. He is a Man. His vocabulary does not include the word "fear"; he cannot even begin to understand the meaning of that shameful word, "impossible." He-Man at work is fast, efficient, willing to take chances even against overwhelming odds (and when He-Man takes chances, he always wins). He-Man's approach to women? Chivalrous, protective, superior. He pays homage to the "weaker sex." After all, he can afford to be magnanimous; he is the kind, if supercilious, giant and woman is the dwarf . . . Physically, He-Man is composed of a miraculous material, firm but resilient, hard as steel and at the same time elastic. If the worst comes to the worst, he rolls with the punch . . . He-Man never takes "no" for an answer. He never has to, for all doors fly open at his approach, through the sheer force of his enviable reputation . . . He-Man, and the heroes of fairy-tales, are made of the same stuff; so is Superman, of the comics.

Unfortunately, this redoubtable hero casts a curious shadow—that of a baby. For can anyone deny the banal fact that once-upon-a-baby-time He-Man was completely helpless, and completely dependent upon a woman? To put it succinctly: Was he not a parasitic, passive infant, born of a woman, fed, reared, and taught by a woman? It is true enough that the infant outgrew his dependence and be-

[14] *Conflict in Marriage,* Harper & Bros., 1949.

came an active boy and man. But *how* was this mysterious transition accomplished?

The instrument of this transition was the "unconscious repetition compulsion," a general unconscious tendency in the human being to repeat *actively* what has been *passively* borne. The purpose of this peculiar reversal is to eradicate a lesion to one's self-esteem. In this strange system of psychic bookkeeping, reversing the tables makes one active once more, and the wound inflicted upon one's delicate narcissism heals—of itself.

Freud's original deduction grew out of a series of observations of a young girl. The child had been to a dentist; in the chair she had refused to open her mouth, but had finally been forced to do so. When she returned to her home, she played a game of "dentist" with a younger sibling. This could easily have been dismissed as a simple repetition, except that the child who had lately been the "victim" of the dentist now cast herself in his "active" role, and placed the younger child in the "chair" as the passive patient. The reversal of roles disclosed that the unconscious repetition compulsion was at work.

It is this instrument which accounts for the fact that the *passive parasitic baby* changes, as a man, into the *active family provider*. Now he actively *gives*, where previously he *was* passively *given*.

What happens when a man fails to make the unconscious identification with the pre-Oedipal *giving* mother? He will act, neurotically, the *refusing* mother. His wife will justifiably complain that he refuses love, tenderness, sex, money, interest. Especially in money matters,[15] he will jealously hold on to his purse strings to disguise the fact that he is really clinging to his mother's apron strings.

Or, if a different neurotic elaboration takes place, the husband will constantly work his wife into a position in

[15] See *Money and Emotional Conflicts*, Doubleday, 1951.

which her actions are "unjust" to him, "cruel," "malicious." Parasitically, he will want to be cared for. He will become a masochistic "dependee" and injustice collector. No matter how much he gets, he will consider it too little; he will always feel that he is being refused. This identification need not be based on a reality situation. The identification is with an unconscious image, not with a real person; to the neurotic child even a good mother appears as refusing.

The psychological consequences of these early misconceptions are far-reaching in later life. They color man's whole attitude towards women. Half-consciously, nearly every man must sometimes or even frequently suppress the thought that his wife is a sponging parasite, for whom he is working himself to death.

The typical man considers women "inferior"; and although he no longer dares to admit it in public, feels that man is somehow "superior" to her.

The equality of women has no sponsor in man's unconscious. Basically, he is afraid of women, and consequently deprecates them in a silly-supercilious way.

The typical man does not consider housework, cooking, child rearing or supervision of all three to be "real work" in any way comparable to his own chores. The old nutritional and educational dependence on mother is unconsciously devaluated.

The height of absurdity is reached by the He-Man when he calls his wife "baby"; here the reversal of roles (his own babyhood and his strong mother) is nearly on the surface. Nobody seems to wonder at this rather widespread pattern. Nor does anyone marvel at man's assumption that women are in need of constant protection, The masculine dictum, "She is so weak and childish," so often applied to adult women, is rather a joke when one knows of the "baby in the man."

The entire concept of the He-Man is a compensatory fantasy of activity, concealing the undecided battle of passivity which rages in the unconscious of every man from the cradle to the grave. This compensatory activity, needed to counteract his ever-threatening inner passivity, accounts for the fact that every man lives to some degree above his emotional means.

The ironic contradictions of the myth of the superior male become apparent in the last years of his life, when the typical organic diseases of the late forties and fifties develop. Whatever is ordered: a strict diet, abstention from sweets, alcohol, sports, or overexcitement; whatever the disease: diabetes, high blood pressure, heart—it is the wife who is in charge of executing the doctor's orders. The man's reaction to this situation is seldom one of mature resignation and adaptation to reality factors. On the contrary, he reverts to an attitude of infantile cheating. He seems to believe that his enemy is not the disease, but his wife. Therefore he smuggles a box of forbidden cigars into the house, and snatches an illegal shot of whiskey when her back is turned. In short, He-Man once more forces his wife into the role of the refusing mother.

He-Man's superiority is built on a conspiracy of inner negation of passivity, a fact which I consider to be of paramount importance for the understanding of man, whom Pascal calls "the glory and the shame of the universe."

Psychologically, man's attitude towards women amounts to this: he can never inwardly forgive the fact that in the past he was completely dependent on them. The offense to his narcissism is never overcome.

On the other hand, there is no point in underestimating his difficulties. He-Man labors under an initial disadvantage in his fight with the world: he is an inner fake. Once He-Man recognized, unconsciously, his early passivity and attempted to counteract it by magical means, it was inevitable that his picture of the ideal towards which he would strive would be enlarged out of all proportions. It is thus that a myth is born.

Unfortunately, a parthenogenetic myth needs constant replenishment. The upkeep of the myth consumes more energy than He-Man can reasonably afford. If you buy a house that is above your means, you will certainly not be able to take the taxes in your stride. When the load is too heavy to begin with, the inevitable additional burden of upkeep becomes intolerable. Without knowing it, He-Man is constantly on the watch for the tilted eyebrow, the amused or mocking smile, the derogatory or deprecating gesture, which would hint that woman has seen through him and is merely tolerating his pose of sexual conqueror.

The odds are decidedly against He-Man; he plays the "big shot"—with whom? The person who changed his diapers, knew he was a bed-wetter, washed his miniature naked body, carried him easily in the crook of one arm, watched from an unbelievable height as he crawled on his hands and knees, listened condescendingly to his first stammered words! We must admit that it is an uneasy business for He-Man— trying to ward off his constant suspicion that women are not taking him seriously.

Literally, the adult is of course not trying to impress the same individual who witnessed his humble and rather passive beginnings. But psychologically, he is, for the species woman is psychologically an entity, especially for the antihedonistic inner conscience. This exclusively punitive branch of the unconscious personality is repeatedly reminding He-Man of the baby he once was. He-Man goes through life feeling that he is known, not by his real name, but by an alias, and constantly fearing that his real identity will become known. The result is that the unproductive task of guarding against exposure claims a good part of his psychic energy.

Of course, even the future He-Man reaches later developmental stages in which he demotes the all-powerful mother of his infancy. Between the ages of two to five he enters the Oedipal phase and in this phase once more reverses the roles. By identifying with the father and borrowing strength from that source, he is enabled to see in the mother a passive,[16] weak, "castrated," dependent person; in my opinion, the *image of his own baby-passivity.* Now he becomes the all-powerful, and mother—the baby!

This wholesale borrowing of strength, first from the mother and then from the father, with which the child tries to save himself from being submerged into passivity, is a two-part technique. First, the child uses identification with the mother as a *crutch.* Later, he uses exactly this crutch as a *stick,* to beat up the "weak woman" to whom he feels superior. That the latter attitude is but defensive is eradicated from memory.[17]

One's reactions to He-Man's real story are necessarily mixed. There is pity for this poor human being whose emotional books are never balanced, and who must desperately go on trying to keep up an "active" front, despite inner passive demands. There is irony, when one realizes how illogical is the cultural yardstick which forces man, the weaker sex,[18] to act the stronger sex. Finally, there is rejection of He-Man's supercilious attitude towards women. Of these, pity is the strongest reaction. He-Man is reminis-

[16] The idea of mother's "passivity" is fostered by the "discovery" that women have no penis. See Ruskin's fears, p. 34.

[17] That Oedipal pseudo-superiority has its drawbacks: the Oedipal wishes are "shattered by the castration complex" (Freud). This time it is the father who is feared. Thus, the grandiose rescue attempt, via strength borrowed from the father, is also doomed, with the result that the whole problem is shelved during the latency period, to be taken up again during puberty, when the destiny of the boy is finally decided. The chances are that if the boy lost out in childhood, the "higher court" will not reverse the decision.

[18] Woman's longevity proves that. There are more widows than widowers around.

cent of the little eighteenth-century potentate who always wore extremely tight collars on festive occasions. Circulation was thus partially impeded, making his face the applauded martial red.

Decisions on morals, mores, *and feminine attire* were originally in the province of man—man, with his burden of undigested fears and costly inner defenses in the form of pseudo-superiority. His decisions could be foreseen. In one way or another, they must be designed to counteract his passive fears, and to substantiate his inner alibi of "aggression"—or at least activity.

This is precisely what happened. Man's unconscious fears were cloaked in his moralistic standards of decency. Having first exorcised his devil, fear, he was committed to the task of sustaining an alibi which would be convincing, and need not be put too seriously to the test. That alibi of anti-fear was twofold; the results are still present. In his thoughts, he undresses the dressed woman, and in that fantasy acts as if he could hardly restrain himself from tearing her clothes from her body. Isn't he "active?" And he peeps at every suggestion of nakedness in dress. Isn't he "active"?

These pseudo-active (though really infantile) attitudes towards woman's dress explain what anthropologists have observed without being able to explain: "concealment affords a greater stimulus than revelation." Indeed it does. *Infantile* peeping and *infantile* undressing in thoughts give He-Man the essential illusion of masculinity. And that, basically, is what he is always after.[19]

[19] Compensatory *pseudo-activity* in pseudo-sexual matters does not exclude the possibility that the typical man may have at his disposal a good share of real activity, in business, for instance. It is only in his relation to women that one can spot his Achilles' heel.

3 Not Fear but Terror: The Case of the Homosexual

The normally heterosexual male protects himself against women with the hoax of the He-Man. The homosexual has no equivalent armor. He protects himself with self-delusion, claiming that he is "indifferent" to women; he protects himself with malicious pseudo-aggression, expressed in a variety of ways, all covering his masochistic regression. If he happens to be a fashion designer, he encircles his sphere of legitimate conduct with a shady borderland that is suffused with *unconsciously* illegitimate and malicious intentions. This is the homosexual's fashion-hoax, and like all his other deceptions it can be punctured by the needle of scientific assessment and observation. The motivations of the homosexual's attitude towards women can be uncovered; the difficulty is that there is a fantastic maze of confusion surrounding the whole psychiatric-psychoanalytic approach to homosexuality.

Male homosexuality is a *specific* elaboration of oral regression—*plus*. The path of discovery which revealed the oral regression in male homosexuals was rather tortuous. The oral base was first observed and described by myself in collaboration with L. Eidelberg, in our joint paper, "The Breast Complex in the Male," published in *Internationale Zeitschrift für Psychoanalyse* in 1933. The paradigmatic case was psychoanalyzed by both of us; when Eidelberg had to interrupt treatment over a long period because of illness, I took over the patient during the interim. Upon Eidelberg's recovery, the patient continued treatment with the first analyst. This rather unusual opportunity of checking and counterchecking observations and conclusions convinced us that we were on the right track.

At that time, we used three examples to prove our contention that Freud's "unconscious repetition compulsion" was both universal and *clinically important*. These examples were male homosexuality, pseudo-mental debility, and writing cramp. We came to the conclusion that the trauma of weaning is a profound offense to the narcissism of every child, and that the child overcomes the trauma by application of the unconscious repetition compulsion. This fully unconscious technique, as discussed in Chapter Two, is a reenactment in reverse of any event which has forced the individual into the passive position. The event is recast, with the passive victim in the active role, and then dramatized. The aim is to cancel out the narcissistic wound by supplying evidence of activity to balance the evidence of passivity already recorded.

At bottom, of course, the offense is against the individual's infantile megalomania, and the active repetition of the passive experience is the only restitution which is acceptable. Moreover, this need for restitution is so indispensable that it goes beyond the pleasure principle; the unconscious repetition compulsion is operative as a retort to both pleasurable and painful passive experiences.

The most far-reaching application of the unconscious repetition compulsion is that of the male infant, who overcomes the trauma of weaning and maintains his fiction of omnipotence by identifying breast with penis, milk with urine (and later with sperm). Instead of being the *passive* recipient of milk, he becomes the *active* bestower of a "similar" fluid.

There was a significant flaw in this deduction, as it was presented in 1933. Although the application of the unconscious repetition compulsion to the problem proved correct and valuable, the definition of orality proved to be wrong. We assumed, in accordance with prevailing opinions, that oral regression meant *the wish to get. Historically*, that is exactly what orality denotes. But *clinically*, in the adult, this original wish appears in altered form, clothed in masochistic elaboration, and denotes *the wish to be refused.* I have devoted a book, *The Basic Neurosis* (1949), to proof of this contention.

Moreover, the clinical statement that *beneath* the homosexual's search for the penis of the partner is hidden the original search for the mother's breast was so important that is overshadowed, for a time, the need to incorporate this point into the over-all problem, and clarify the entire story. The same temporary overemphasis applied to the Oedipal surface: what homosexuals are repeating is the baby—pre-Oedipal mother relationship. All this is proved and true, but it is insufficient.

In short, without clarifying the unconscious aim—the psychic masochistic wish to be refused—the personality structure and actual behavior of the adult male homosexual remains incomprehensible. (I have stressed this fact repeatedly.)[1] Thus, colleagues who accept the oral structure in male homosexuality, but remain aloof from the "plus"

[1] See, in addition to "The Breast Complex in Men"—"The Present Situation in the Genetic Investigation of Homosexuality," *Marriage Hygiene* (old series), 4:16-29, 1937; "Eight Prerequisites for the Psychoanalytic Treatment of Homosexuality," *Psychoanalytic Review*, 31:253-286, 1944; "Psychology of Frendship," *Medical Record*, 159:101-104, 1946; "Differential Diagnosis between Spurious Homosexuality and Perversion Homosexuality," *Psychiatric Quarterly*, 21:399-409, 1947; "The Myth of a New National Disease; Homosexuality and the Kinsey Report," *Psychiatric Quarterly*, 22:66-88, 1948; specific sections in my books *The Basic Neurosis, Neurotic Counterfeit-Sex* and *The Superego*, Grune & Stratton, New York, 1949, 1951 and 1952 respectively.

specified above, which is the wish to be refused, may be very "modern"—judged by 1933 standards; nevertheless, they are misjudging the real problem of male inversion. *The wish to get, in male homosexuals, is but an inner defense against the wish to be refused.* This masochistic regression was observed some twenty years ago, in the case originally reported; it was noted that "some of the tortures the patient complained of from the governess were self-provoked" (p. 561); still, the reason then given was the need of placing his *aggression.* This point was later clarified by my contribution on the masochistic foundation of orally based male homosexuality.

In my opinion, these are the reasons for male homosexuality:

Perversion homosexuality is characterized by conscious acceptance of sexual gratification derived from a relation with an object of the same sex. Feelings of guilt may or may not be present; this point is important for the therapeutic prognosis, but it does not affect the diagnosis. On the conscious level, the homosexual's story is that he is merely imitating a heterosexual relationship. As "convincing" evidence, therefore, the passive partner is "feminine" in his dress, in his mannerisms, in his use of perfumes and cosmetics. This surface identification, deliberately assumed to strengthen the impression of "husband and wife" relationship, is at the bottom of the typical notion that every man whose appearance or mannerisms are "effeminate" must be a homosexual. The clinical facts decidedly contradict this assumption. Anyone who is naive enough to accept the appearance of "effeminacy" as proof of homosexuality is the dupe of the homosexual's unconscious alibi.

On the unconscious level, the perversion homosexual is regressed to the earliest level of psychic development, the oral stage. The universally experienced trauma of weaning has already been mentioned, earlier in this chapter; so has the normal solution for the boy: consolation via the conviction that his "similar" organ, the penis, is a supplier of "similar" fluid and therefore a fully satisfactory, and active, substitute for the withdrawn giver of milk, the breast. Since the boy's major purpose is to safeguard the remaining fragments of infantile megalomania, his "breast substitute" is absurdly over-valued; the disproportionate "penis-pride" of the boy is the result.

The homosexual's solution to this infantile conflict is only one of the many abnormal solutions encountered. The homosexual's resentment is not satisfied by simple substitutive rejection of the breast or bottle; his rejection overflows until it encompasses the whole disappointing sex. Instead of pursuing women in later life, so that assumption of the active role can directly restore his self-esteem, he seeks out men as sexual partners, thereby *duplicating and re-enforcing his own defense mechanism*—the misuse of the penis. But behind this pursuit is the persistent image of the disappointing breast—a fact confirmed in every analysis of a male homosexual.

Clinical proof of this connection may be found in any unbiased analysis of a male homosexual. All male homosexuals are controlled by the "mechanism of orality"; characterologically, they are all "injustice-collectors," stabilized on the masochistic level of the mechanism of orality. This mechanism consists of the unconscious creation of, or search for, defeat, as the first step; in the second step, memory of the provocation is repressed, and conscious perception of the opponent's "malice" is substituted. This "malice" must be resisted, righteously, and in self-defense (pseudo-aggression). The third and final step is conscious self-pity, and unconscious masochistic pleasure.

The homosexual's personality, therefore, is no more "normal" than his choice of sexual object, for injustice-collecting is a technique used only by neurotics. This technique, it should be noted, is characteristic of *all* neurotics who are orally regressed.[2]

The presence of the mechanism of orality in the homosexual's character indicates that he is orally regressed, and that the Oedipus complex is *not* decisive for him. But the mechanism of orality is not a characteristic exclusively possessed by the homosexual; it is visible in many entirely unrelated neuroses as well. The presence of the mechanism of orality is proof of oral regression, only. But only in the homosexual is this mechanism so extravagantly accentuated by the individual's narcissistic structure. No other neurotic even approaches the height of the megalomaniacal superciliousness possessed by the homosexual. It is this exaggerated narcissism in the children who later become homosexuals that explains why they are so severely wounded by their discovery that they cannot maintain the infantile fiction of omnipotence. Their recovery from the defeat of weaning is only partial, and even this half-recovery is accomplished only with the aid of narcissistic recompenses. The *"reduplication of one's own defense mechanism"* enters the picture here.

There is another proof of the existence of an oral substructure in male homosexuality, and this proof was first stressed by myself. Nearly all male homosexuals, when in analysis, pass through a period in which they produce the symptom of premature ejaculation with women. This symptom appears during the final stages of destruction of the perversion. Now, there is always an oral substructure in all complicated cases of premature ejaculation. The unconscious motto of these patients is to refuse the woman pleasure; they "spill the milk before it can reach the mouth." At the root of these manifestations is their al-

[2] In *The Basic Neurosis* (l.c.) twenty-seven clinical pictures of this type are described. To the general mechanism of orality a *specific* distinguishing and *additional* factor is added, constituting the specific and differing clinical entities.

leged hatred for the entire female sex, but they are so profoundly afraid of their own masochistic attachment that they take refuge in pseudo-aggression.

The notorious unreliability of the homosexual (in combination with psychopathic trends) is another of the end-results of the masochistic elaboration of the original oral trauma. On the surface, this unreliability seems to relate to the revenge fantasy, but it is actually a cover for deeply rooted self-damaging tendencies. And in the majority of homosexuals, this broad façade of pseudo-aggression is an unconvincing cover.

There is a very precise distinction between perversion and neurosis: the homosexual experiences conscious pleasure in living out his perversion, while the neurotic's pleasure gain is invariably unconscious. Moreover, there is never conscious acceptance of the *neurotic* symptom. The impotent man, to take an obvious example, is never proud of his impotence. By and large, however, the male homosexual willingly accepts his "difference," and even prides himself on it.

This pride and acceptance are the direct outgrowths of a complicated inner defense. The acceptance of the perversion is in itself a defense mechanism; the conscious approval is a screen for the homosexual's basic conflict, oral-masochistic regression. The homosexual who has not been analyzed is of course unaware of what is going on behind the scenes, and so he denies his defense mechanism. The desire to change is felt only when the individual's inner guilt is not appeased by the real difficulties (secrecy, extortion, social ostracism) confronting every homosexual.

The homosexual is a frightened fugitive from women, fleeing in sheer panic to "another continent." He wards off his repressed masochistic attachment to the pre-Oedipal mother with pseudo-aggression; he "rejects" women; he "hates" women. No matter how carefully it is disguised with hatred and anger, this inner fear is still visible in his homosexual relations, where his partner is used merely as sexual object and in most cases very soon discarded.

Nowhere is the *impersonal* element in human relationships so predominant as in homosexuality, as illustrated by the common practice of sharing masturbatory activities in baths and comfort stations, where neither participant either knows or even looks at his partner. And if "romantic" feelings develop among homosexuals, they are immediately followed by pathologic quarrels of the injustice-collecting type.

Genetically speaking, perversion homosexuality denotes a stabilization on the unconscious defensive level: "I cannot be masochistically attached to mother; I have nothing in common with her, and I am not even interested in women." The boy singles out the organ which has disappointed him (the breast or breast equivalent), finds a replica of it on his own body (the penis), and all his life, while his ostensible object is the penis of another man, he really pursues a duplicate of his own face-saving substitute for the disappointing breast.

On a secondary level, the homosexual strengthens his unconscious defense by clothing it in a "philosophy." He proudly accepts his homosexuality because it so well camouflages what he is trying to escape from: his oral masochistic regression. But this acceptance and approval cannot camouflage other reverberations of his fundamental conflict; the key to the riddle remains in plain sight in the form of his endless injustice collecting.

Homosexuals not infrequently claim that they are perfectly contented, or would be if only the outer world were more tolerant and less "unreasonable." This claim is easily refuted. The unconscious pattern of the homosexual, not the environment's attitude, is what rules out real conscious happiness. For the homosexual unconsciously *wants* to be thwarted and disappointed, a purpose he shares with every other adherent of the mechanism of orality. Conscious contentment cannot result from an unremitting unconscious search for disappointment. The worst heterosexual relationship cannot match the amount of conflict, of jealousy, back-biting and petty irritations commonly met with between homosexuals.

The basic conflict in every homosexual relation, stated as briefly and starkly as possible, is that of a baby wanting to prove that his mother is "mean" and unjust to him, while the pathologic mother refuses everything he asks for and plots to do him harm. The homosexual is inwardly sick, but he contrives to shift the blame for his illness to the malignant outside world. His method is indirect, but it guarantees him a steady supply of his staple diet: psychic masochism.

Usually, it is not until his late teens that a homosexual discovers and realizes his perversion. Under typical conditions, this age, or the early twenties, marks the end of the period during which the homosexual fights against conscious awareness of his defense mechanism, which he mistakenly believes must be his final destiny.

These precepts can be boiled down into a *genetic yardstick* to be applied in making a differential diagnosis: A *male homosexual is a person whose predominant means of fighting his repressed masochistic attachment to the pre-Oedipal mother is the unconsciously based defense mechanism of a man-man sexual relationship, and whose personality is predominantly that of an injustice-collector, governed by the mechanism of orality.* Both elements *must* be present.

The bitter paradox of the homosexual is his utter inability to "escape" from the mother whose rejection has been dictated by his inner fears, and whose entire sex has been included in the rejection. The homosexual's salient characteristic, that of injustice-collecting, genetically and historically belongs to *mother*. The homosexual's sexual aim, the penis of his partner, is actually the disguised breast, or breast equivalent; again the exiled *mother* appears in the center of the stage. And the short-lived nature of his sexual relationships, the unending list of sexual successions and rejections for which the homosexual is notorious, again points to the original offender; these rejections are pseudo-aggressive acts, intrapsychically directed at *mother*.

Homosexuals themselves are in general disinclined to any attempt to change them through psychoanalytic treatment. Two factors account for this reluctance. One is the strength of the homosexual's camouflaging defense; the other is the widespread pessimism which largely characterizes the psychiatric-psychoanalytic attitude towards the possibility that homosexuals can be changed through treatment. This pessimism has been the almost invariable attitude for decades; in my opinion, it is merely a reflection of the therapist's inability to cope with the specific problem. As a matter of fact, homosexuality has an excellent prognosis, provided the oral-masochistic basis is reached.[3]

Homosexuals who don't "wish to change" take full advantage of this prevailing anti-therapeutic attitude on the part of psychiatrists and psychoanalysts, and point to it gleefully. A good example is the recent book by Donald Webster Cory, *The Homosexual in America.*[4] The author is a homosexual, writing under a pseudonym. The book's subtitle, *A Subjective Approach*, is frank; in a review printed in *The Psychiatric Quarterly* it was correctly pointed out that the subtitle should have been "An Emo-

[3] For details, see my study, "Eight Prerequisites for the Psychoanalytic Treatment of Homosexuality," l.c.

[4] Greenberg Publisher, New York.

tional Approach." The reviewer (the reviews in this important journal are not signed) went on to say:

". . . The social conflict of homosexuals is described, an appeal for understanding made, but the technique is rather extravagant and slightly grotesque:

". . . The homosexual, thus, has two historic missions to perform. Whether he is a democrat or a totalitarian by political conviction, he is historically forced to enter the struggle for the widening of freedom of expression. And, whether his religious and ethical convictions are those of the continent or the libertarian, he is historically compelled to enlist in the legions fighting for liberalization of the sexual mores of modern civilization . . . And it is this inherent lack of assimilability that is the greatest historic value of homosexuality . . . Thus on three scores, homosexuality—fortunately but unwittingly—must inevitably play a progressive role in the scheme of things. It will broaden the basis of freedom of thought and communication, will be a banner-bearer in the struggle for liberalization of our sexual conventions, and will be a pillar of strength in the defense of our threatened democracy." (pp. 233-235)

"One should not judge the book on the basis of these, let us say, oddities alone. There are more serious misunderstandings. Homosexuality is taken as unity; the fact that it represents but an illness is more or less denied; as genesis exclusively older theories are adduced and newer findings neglected (Jones, H. Deutsch, Bergler), etc. Full credit for unchangeability is taken from the arsenal of psychiatric contradictions, and outdated pessimism. And when the author is forced to admit that, e.g., Bergler claims that homosexuality is curable, the "subjective approach" works this way:

"Bergler maintains that homosexuals can be cured—and that he had cured some, but upon examination the ex-homosexuals have become bisexual. (*Neurotic Counterfeit-Sex*, p. 189) He cites the fact that one of his patients has married, but this does not prove that he no longer craves sexual relations with men." (p. 185)

"Your reviewer looked up the alleged quotations, and found that the author misrepresents approximately 100% what Bergler really says.[5]

"All in all: The tearful appeal for "self-acceptance" (p. 258) and being accepted by the outer world miscarries, because of the partly extravagant, party mistaken assumptions, all presented with superciliousness, without real foundation."

There is a specific type of passive man—the Caspar Milquetoast—who is constantly accused—*and accuses himself*—of homosexual "tendencies." He is the innocent victim of a combination of rumors and misconceptions.

Here is the genetic history of the passive-feminine man:

Between the ages of two and a half and five, the boy develops a strong attachment to the Oedipal mother, and correspondingly, a strong, aggressive, and rejecting attitude towards the father. A typical "positive Oedipus complex" is erected. Fifty years ago Freud proved that this stage is typical for every child. In the course of normal development towards maturity, the child relinquishes these transitory wishes, with their libidinous-aggressive contents.

At the same time, however, parallelling the development of the "positive" Oedipus, every child builds up an attitude called the "negative" or "inverted" Oedipus complex (Freud). Although negligible in strength when compared with the positive Oedipus, the inverted Oedipus is an attitude of considerable importance. In this unconscious pattern, the boy's view of the father is not one of single-minded and aggressive rejection. The boy admires his father's supposed strength and power, and at the same time, in identification with the mother, wants to enjoy all the "cruel" and mysterious things his parents do together. In

[5] I fully subscribe to the reviewer's fact-finding; Cory's specious argument is a sentence taken out of context, and misunderstood to boot. Many (not one!) homosexuals were reported cured in *Neurotic Counterfeit-Sex*. And "cure" denotes not bisexuality, but real and unfaked heterosexuality.

effect, the father is loved and the mother rejected as competitor.

Under normal conditions, this leaning towards passivity disappears in time, and without ill-effect. (This phallic passivity is but recapitulation of previous oral-anal passivity; how strong the negative Oedipus is depends on these early contributaries.) But it is not uncommon for this generally harmless and passing phase to become predominant. The hysteric neurotic with the unconscious feminine identification is fixated on the level of the "negative" Oedipus.

The unconscious repercussions of such a fixation are decidedly unpleasant. The inner conscience (superego) constantly vetoes the individual's passive wishes. The passive-feminine man is inevitably driven to construct a series of unconscious defenses, which he hopes will disprove the accusations of conscience. In compensation, he produces a blatant He-Man attitude; later he chases after women and speaks disparagingly of them. His potency is weak and erratic. Sometimes it achieves a record-breaking level, but most of the time it is temperamental, and "won't work."

The compensatory attitude is not always satisfactory. When the defenses are weak, they produce the Caspar Milquetoast who is designated as "effeminate" by the outer world, and misjudged as a homosexual even in scientific literature. This unwarranted judgment of the Milquetoast, like the confusion attendant upon the term "castration complex," can be traced back to the order in which Freud made his discoveries. In the early days of psychoanalysis, when the oral level was either unknown or neglected, homosexuality was considered a specific aberration of the Oedipus complex, Freud's first discovery.

External behavior, the popular rule-of-thumb for identifying homosexuals, is an unreliable and completely misleading indicator. Caspar Milquetoast is not a homosexual. The markedly effeminate homosexual, on the other hand, is using camouflage to conceal his real conflict. It is essential to take cognizance of the fact that the so obvious feminine identification in homosexuals is inwardly but "*acceptance of the blame for the lesser crime.*" The real intrapsychic crime, again concealed by a smoke-screen, is psychic masochism.

The key to the problem of external behavior is found in the existence of two forms of unconscious identification, the "*leading*" and the "*misleading.*" The *leading* unconscious identification embodies those decisive wishes that were crystallized within the personality as the end-result of the infantile conflict. The *misleading* unconscious identification is an alliance for the sake of an alibi; it is a surface identification with persons whose traits might serve as an effective disclaimer when the neurotic is reproached by his superego for harboring his specific neurotic wishes. In the passive-feminine man, the *leading* identification pertains to the Oedipal mother; the *misleading,* alibi-identification is with a person of the He-Man type. In the homosexual pervert, however, the *leading* unconscious identification varies with his sexual role. If he is "active," the *leading* identification is with the pre-Oedipal mother; if he is "passive," he identifies with the baby of the earliest mother-child relationship. His *misleading* unconscious identification also depends on his sexual role. If he is "active," it pertains to the Oedipal father; if "passive," to the Oedipal mother.

Unless a clear distinction is made between the two types of identification, the problem of homosexuals and "effeminate men" remains a mass of unsolved contradictions. The very existence of the active variety of homosexual pervert becomes an inexplicable paradox to anyone who has been taken in by the fallacious formula: effeminacy equals homosexuality. The same unjustifiable formula brands as a homosexual every passive man who stays meekly married to a shrewish wife. Worst of all, its spurious authority often convinces poor Milquetoast himself that he is a homosexual, which he is not.

The alleged "bisexual" has been too well publicized to be omitted from this survey.

The homosexual in whom slight remnants of heterosexuality can be detected does exist. The pseudo-"bisexual" is capable of erection for some time in a lustless coitus. The coitus is necessarily lustless; the libidinous drive cannot be "divided" between homosexuality and heterosexuality because homosexuality is not a drive at all, but a defense mechanism, as proved in the preceding pages. A so-called "bisexual" is a homosexual who can at times be potent with women he does not love.

The homosexual's unconscious attitude towards woman is one of *deadly fear.* If one questions a homosexual directly, his answer is a barrage of pseudo-hatred and pseudo-irony that would delight any misogynist. The homosexual, of course, does not even suspect that his hatred and irony are but a defense.

There are times when homosexuals, retreating to another defensive level, boast that they do *not* despise women. They are merely "indifferent" to women, or even like some women in a "non-sexual" way. Looking into these friendships, one finds that the women are elderly, ugly, or socially undesirable for a variety of reasons. The homosexual consciously uses them as confidantes; unconsciously, they serve to strengthen his inner alibi that "women are impossible." [6]

The case of Oscar Wilde is an unusually explicit—and unusually well-documented—example of a homosexual for

[6] It is only fitting, of course, that "impossible" women should be draped in "impossible" clothes. Without knowing it, therefore, fashion-obsessed women live under the shadow of a peculiar conflict. The homosexual designer's unconscious defensive hatred of women is opposed by the wish—also an unconscious defense—to show that he is "one of them." Defensive hatred wins out.

whom clothing was a significant vehicle of neurotic expression. But then, all the mechanisms of the homosexual, as explained in the preceding pages, were near the surface in Wilde. In addition to his eccentric dandyism, he paraded his high-pitched narcissism, his irony towards women, and above all his unconscious self-damaging tendencies, as witness the foolhardly suit brought against the father of one of his homosexual friends, a suit which ended in a prison sentence for Wilde, followed by exile and poverty. Only a pronounced psychic masochist could have maneuvered himself into the position of undertaking a hopeless legal fight for the alleged purpose of saving the family "honor" —meaning his mother's reputation.

If Wilde is, as the old-fashioned phrase had it, in any sense a "household word" today, it is more as the author of some half-dozen superb wisecracks or as the central figure in a notorious "case" of the nineties than as critic, poet, playwright or novelist. And in the same way, his career as a literary figure was well launched long before he began to reach an appreciable audience in 1891[7] with the publication of *The Picture of Dorian Gray.* Gilbert and Sullivan's magnificent lampoon on Wilde and the aesthetic movement in general, *Patience,* was produced in 1881, when he had published only a badly reviewed but popular book of poems and an unsuccessful play. The immediately recognizable character of Bunthorne in *Patience,* therefore, was not a caricature of Wilde as a writer expressing ideas which could be made to appear ridiculous, but a reduction to absurdity of Wilde's deliberate dramatization of his "difference." He actually did "walk down Piccadilly with a poppy or a lily in his mediaeval hand." He actually did wear velvet coats, knee-breeches and silk stockings. He actually did wear flowing locks, flowing ties and a long cape over

[7] Publication dates in this section are as cited in *The Oxford Companion to English Literature.*

all. And the audiences he attracted on his American lecture tour in 1882 obviously came to see and not to listen, as the action of fifty or sixty Harvard students made clear. These students turned up at his Boston lecture dressed in knee-breeches like his, swallow-tail coats, and flowing wigs. They wore green ties around their necks, and large lilies in their lapels. Each one carried an enormous sunflower in his hand.[8]

I have called Wilde's way of dressing during this period a "deliberate dramatization of his 'difference,'" and it is quite clear that the reason for the costume was his calculated assessment of the value of notoriety to a rising young writer. But this was conscious reasoning; from contemporary descriptions of Oscar Wilde's mother we have more than a suggestion that other influences were, more obscurely, at work as well.

In a recent biography[9] Lady Wilde is described as wearing a red silk dress, floor-length and extravagantly full, flounced with lace. As a sash she wore an Oriental scarf embroidered in gold. Her head was crowned with laurels. Her bare neck and arms were covered with jewelry; small portraits of members of her family, set into brooches, were pinned across her bodice. In her white-gloved hands she held a bottle of scent, a fan and a lace handkerchief. Frank Harris, in his biography of Wilde, describes Lady Wilde sitting at a tea-table bundled into voluminous wrappings, looking like "a sort of female Buddha," and heavily painted and powdered.

Any description of a woman's costume, sixty years after it was put on, is apt to sound absurd, if not ugly. But any contemporary mention of Lady Wilde refers to her appearance as odd, eccentric, and over-decorated. Biographers

[8] This incident is recounted in Frank Harris' *Oscar Wilde: His Life and Confessions,* Brentano, New York, 1916.

[9] *The Paradox of Oscar Wilde,* by George Woodcock, The Macmillan Co., New York, 1950.

have called her son's dandyism an imitation of his mother, forgetting that Wilde's attitude towards clothing differed in different periods of his life. After he became definitely established as a social and literary success, he was a dandy within the accepted standard of dress. He was, as photographs taken in the nineties indicate, an extremely well-dressed man of his decade and social standing. This cannot be construed as imitation; it is more like a dramatized retort. It is success showing up failure. As for Wilde's Bunthorne period, when he appeared in velvet cloaks and breeches, this was an unmistakeable unconscious caricature of his mother, a method of revenge which might be called sartorial scurrility. The technique in general is discussed at greater length in Chapter Seven.

4 *Clothes Are a Masculine Invention*

MAN'S UNCONSCIOUS FEARS and women's punishment for being the innocent target are both inexhaustible. Fantastic rules governing conduct during the menstrual period are common to aborigines in all parts of the world; evidence of similar rules, and of the superstitions which are their aftermath, can be found in the classics of Western civilization. The adjurations in Leviticus 15 were literally interpreted by the Jews, and women "put apart seven days" until Rabbi Akiba's reinterpretation of the chapter in the second century of the modern era. Akiba ended the Jewish woman's ritual isolation, as well as the penalty of uncleanness" which adhered to any Jew who touched a woman during her period. In Pliny, we are told that wine turns to vinegar if touched by a woman who was menstruating, crops are blighted and seedlings killed by her touch, fruit loosened from trees, mirrors clouded, razors dulled, metal rusted, bees killed or driven from their hives, and so on. Similar superstitions are recorded from other sources.

Among aborigines the first appearance of menstruation is especially subject to taboos. In their practical effects, these elaborate restrictions transform the adolescent girls into biological lepers, in some cases *for years.* The girls are segregated, and the taboo often requires that they neither touch the ground nor see the sun. One needs hardly more than a touch of imagination to get a graphic picture of the torture imposed upon women by man's fear.

The details of these taboos vary from tribe to tribe. The

rules range from the very stringent and elaborate to the simple; isolation from men is invariable, but in some tribes seclusion in the menstrual hut, especially at the time of the first period, is made the occasion for social gatherings of the young girls of the tribe. The unchanging theme in all cases is the fact that menstrual blood is "dangerous," and in one way or another imperils the village. As a logical extension of this theme, food taboos are imposed; some of these continue for as long as a year after the initial menstrual period. Sir James G. Frazer, in *The Golden Bough*,[1] mentions the belief of the Dieri of Central Australia; these aborigines are convinced that all the fish in their river would die if a menstruous woman ate one, and the river dry up if she bathed in it. The Arunta, a nearby tribe, eat large quantities of a certain bulb; they forbid menstruating women to gather these bulbs on the theory that the crop would fail if the rule were broken.

Almost as widespread as the food taboos are the sun and fire taboos. There is a curious twist in some of these customs. It would seem almost logical, if one could grant the premise that a menstruating woman is extremely dangerous, to reason that the sight of her might weaken even so powerful a force as the sun; the preventive for this danger would be seclusion. But why the converse should be true, why she should be forbidden to *look at* either sunlight or firelight, is a puzzle which can be explained only by the assumption that the magical and malevolent power accompanying menstruation is an active force and not a passive contagion. Man's deeply rooted fear that injury will come to him through woman, especially during her menstrual period, is illustrated in Frazer's account of the Kolosh Indians of Alaska. In this tribe it is believed that a menstruating woman who so much as looks at a hunter, fisher

[1] Abridged edition, Macmillan, New York, 1949.

or gambler will destroy his luck. It is also believed that a woman can turn objects to stone at this period, merely by looking at them. The classical as well as the still persisting European parallels to these beliefs—the legends of Medusa and the Basilisk, and the evil eye—come immediately to mind.

A revealing sidelight on the purposes of the menstrual taboo is reported by Margaret Mead in one of her authoritative and understanding accounts of primitive life,[2] that of the Manus of New Guinea. These primitives make a cubbyhole of mats for the girl who is having her first menstrual period. For five days she must not stir from the cubbyhole. All her food—she has a special diet, since some staple foods are now taboo for her—is prepared in separate containers at a separate fire. She is forbidden to speak aloud, and must not be addressed audibly. Young girls of the village are allowed to visit her, however; they commonly sleep on the floor around her.

This is a more or less familiar body of taboos; it differs from the usual in that it marks what is ostensibly the only menstrual period the girl will have until she is married. The fact that all women menstruate regularly after puberty is kept a complete secret from the males of the tribe. One can conclude that the purpose is to lessen their fear of approaching young and therefore marriageable girls.

The Golden Bough contains extensive material on the elaborate restrictions imposed by primitive tribes at the time of menstruation.

The Ut Danoms of Borneo, for example, put their girls into solitary confinement in a small room of the house at the age of eight or ten. The cell is kept in almost total darkness. The girl may not leave it for any purpose whatever. She is attended by one slave woman in an isolation

[2] *From the South Seas,* Morrow, New York, 1939.

which may last for as long as *seven years*. She spends her time in weaving mats and doing other handiwork. At puberty, when she is allowed to emerge, she is pale and undersized. She is shown the world as if she had never seen it before. A feast is given for her and a slave is killed in her honor. She is then smeared with the slave's blood.

On the island of Yap, the girl who is having her first menstrual period is shut up in a small hut at some distance from her parents' home. She stays there for several days, and for one hundred nights afterwards sleeps in the tribe's special menstrual hut. She is forbidden to sit directly on the ground if she is overtaken by her first period while on a public road; she must beg for a cocoanut shell to sit on.

The girl of the Yarakaina tribe of Northern Queensland must spend a month or six weeks in a special hut unseen by men, though not by women. She must lie flat on her back on the floor of the hut. Sight of the sun is forbidden; as sunset approaches she must close her eyes and keep them closed until night. She may not eat anything that has lived in salt water; if she defies this taboo, she will be killed by a snake. She is waited on by an old woman. In some other Australian tribes the girls are partially buried in more or less shallow holes in the ground, presumably to make the sun taboo more effective.

The Aht or Nootka Indians of Vancouver Island impose solitary confinement on their girls. An enclosure within the house is made with mats; sunlight and firelight are entirely eliminated. The girl may drink but not eat while in the enclosure. There is no set period of isolation; she stays as long as she can, and the longer she endures the greater is the honor to her parents. For her to see the sun or fire during this period means disgrace for life. She must at all times remain in a squatting position. She is not allowed to put her hand to her hair, though she may use a comb or special piece of bone. She is not allowed to scratch any part of her body; it is believed that if she does, there will be a scar. Fresh food is forbidden her for eight months after puberty. During all this time she must eat alone, using her own cup and spoon.

The Tlingit Indians of Alaska used to put girls approaching puberty into a small cage which had one airhole but was otherwise completely closed up. The period of isolation, without heat, light, exercise or permission to communicate with others, lasted a full year. The girl could be fed only by her mother or a female slave. She wore a special headgear with large flaps to prevent her from polluting the sky by looking at it.

The Guaranis of Southern Brazil sewed the girl up in a hammock when she reached puberty. A small opening was left so that she could breathe. She remained in this hammock, fasting, until her period was over. After that, her hair was cut short. Eating flesh of any kind was then taboo until her hair was long enough to cover her ears.

The Macusis of British Guiana also use the hammock as an isolation cell for girls having their first menstrual periods. The hammock is hung near the roof of the hut, and the girl spends the day in it. At night, she leaves the hammock to sleep next to a fire which she lights herself. If this rule is broken, it is believed that the girl will get sores on her neck and other parts of her body. While menstruation continues, the girl must fast; afterwards she leaves the hammock and goes into a dark corner of the hut. She may eat, but the food must be cooked by herself at a separate fire and in her own container. In about ten days she is visited by a magician who frees her from the spell by saying charms and breathing on her body and on any valuable objects she may have touched. The cups and other containers she has used are broken and buried. She then bathes, and after bathing her mother beats her with thin rods; she must make no sound during this beating. She is beaten again after her second period, but is then considered clean, and allowed to associate with the rest of the tribe.

Other Indians of Guiana keep the girl in her hammock near the roof for a month, after which she is left near an anthill infested by ants whose bite is extremely painful. In some cases, the girl must fast during the *entire* period of isolation in the hammock.

The Guayquiries of the Orinoco believe that everything a woman steps on while menstruating will die, and that any man who walks in her footsteps will get a swelling of the legs. The married women of the Bri-bri Indians of Costa Rica use plates made of banana leaves during their periods; the banana leaves must be securely hidden after use lest a cow eat them and die. The women drink out of special cups as well; anyone drinking out of a cup used by a menstruating woman is sure to fall sick and die.

For our purposes, a detailed investigation of the unconscious reasons for these more than fantastic nightmares of suspicion and punishment for being a woman would lead too far afield.[3] It is sufficient to state that man's fear of the bleeding and "castrated" female genital is beyond question, and is clinically confirmed in every analysis.

Man's fear of the genitally "castrated" woman not only revives his phallic anxieties, but *the earliest infantile "septet of baby fears," as well.* In addition to the already described supercilious He-Man attitude, man has three ways of warding off these Hydra-like fears.

First, he flees the sight of horror—he forces woman to cover the "wound," and the body.

[3] There exists an extensive psychoanalytic literature on that topic, starting with Freud's *Totem and Taboo;* continued, e.g., by Reik's "Die Pubertätsriten der Wilden" (in *Probleme der Religions-Psychologie,* Internationaler Psychoanalytischer Verlag, 1919), Winterstein's "Die Pubertätsriten der Mädchen und Ihre Spuren in Märchen" (*Imago,* 14, 1928); and in many of the excellent analytic-anthropological studies of Geza Roheim.

Second, he declares woman "cruel." He-Man's deprecatory judgment: "She is *only* a weak woman," is typical, if not universal, but at the same time every man (I said *every* man!) harbors the opposite views as well, which is the fanstasy that woman is by nature cruel, and after man's scalp. Shakespeare's statement in *Twelfth Night* (Act I, Scene 5, line 259), "*Lady, you are the cruell'st she alive,*" is a tenet which man keeps in perpetual readiness in a hidden corner, and brings to life and illuminates when the "necessity" arises. And the "necessity" arises every time a *real* woman fails to correspond to man's infantile fantasies of a pretty doll. There is no reason to conceal the fact that women (especially when infuriated with the illogical amalgam of Baby and He-Man) have a good-sized aggression at their disposal. It is only man's silly fantasy, which tells him so authoritatively "what women are like," that causes the terrified "surprise" which is his reaction to such situations.

If further proof of the above statement is wanted, it may be found in Chapter Two, p. 28 ff., where the "septet of baby-fears" is listed, detailing all the evil intentions attributed by the immature ego to the giantess of the nursery. Or, if proofs drawn from folklore are more convincing, take the old (older than Grimm) tale of Hansel and Gretel, where the cruel step*mother* convinces the father that the children should be left to die of *starvation*, where the cruel *witch* lures the children into her chocolate cottage, and fattens them up to provide her a delicious *cannibalistic feast* . . .

When we consider how these unconscious fantasies influence man's sex life, we can see some of the reasons for impotence produced by castration fear,[4] and also some of

[4] Theodor Reik, in a study on wit written in 1929 ("Anspielung und Entblössung," included in *Lust und Leid in Witz*, Internationaler Psychoanalytischer Verlag, Vienna, 1929) connected the sexual interest in looking at female clothes with the pleasure of the alluding fantasy, origi-

the reasons for the fact that woman is more alluring to him dressed than nude.

Man's fear of women is not a modern invention; most likely it is as old as the relation of the sexes.[5] To quote but one authoritative example: the evil powers attributed to witches (hence women!) with respect to man's potency. *Malleus Maleficarum* (The Witch Hammer), the official law book governing ecclesiastic diagnosis and the punishment of witches, written in 1486 by the inquisitors Heinrich Kramer and James Sprenger and authorized by Innocent VIII, has this to say on the subject (Question IX): "*Whether Witches Can Create an Illusion by Trickery About the Male Genitals so that they Seem to be Wholly Absent from Bodies.*

"This truth is made manifest by the works of devils in respect to the male genitals when it is asked: whether witches have power over the male genitals by virtue of devils really and truly or whether they merely remove them through a deceiving apparition? And it is argued that they do so really and truly, by an argument *a fortiori*. For demons are able to do much more than this, such as kill men or transfer them from place to place, as is clear from the men killed in the stories of Job and Tobias. Therefore demons are able really and truly to carry off the genitals of a man.

"Moreover, here is the commentary of the Psalm "Punishment by Evil Angels." God punishes evil angels as he often punished the people of Israel by various illnesses and

---

nally directly connected with the culturally forbidden naked female body; he explained, as many others did, the fear of nakedness via the phallic castration complex. In this paper, Reik is mainly concerned with clarification of certain types of alluding witticism. For elaboration of sexual fears, see *Neurotic Counterfeit-Sex*, l.c.

[5] Ernest Crawley in *The Magic Rose* (Boni & Liveright, 1927, originally published 1902) collected extensive anthropological literature to show the segregation of sexes among primitive peoples, and attributed man's fear to mystical taboos.

by real and true attacks upon the body. Therefore it is possible to attack infirm persons in this about the genitals.

"It may be said that this is possible by divine permission because God allows the generative force to suffer evil the more due to the corruption of original sin which has come down to us through the generative act itself. And therefore he permits the genitals to be carried off in their totality.

"Moreover, the conversion of Lot's wife into a pillar of salt was a greater thing than to remove the genitals, but that was a true and real, not an apparent, conversion because the pillar remained visible. And this was done by bad angels, though forced to it by good angels who had previously driven them out of (Sodom) so that they might not come into (Lot's) house. There were also the other crimes of those at Gomorrah. Therefore the commentary asserts that she (Lot's wife) was infected with this same vice (sodomy), and therefore was punished.

"Furthermore, whoever is able to induce a natural form can take it away. Now demons can induce many natural forms as is clear from the magicians of Pharaoh who by virtue of devils made frogs and snakes. However, Augustine says that all things which are made visible, even by the inferior powers of the air, cannot be thought to be irrational. But this thing men can do, that is, by some art or incision take away the genital. Therefore demons can do that invisibly what others do visibly.

"On the other hand, Augustine in the *Civitate Dei* says that he does not believe that the body of a man can be changed into bestial form either by the power or art of devils, and therefore by a similar argument it would not be possible to take away from the human body that which truly pertains to it. Elsewhere he says that he does not think that the visible world is subject to the whims of transgressing angels, but only to God.

"In reply to this: There is no doubt that certain witches work wonders on the genitals. This has been both seen and heard of by many, and assuredly public knowledge asserts this because the truth concerning this organ is verified by the senses of sight and touch. However, it is possible to say that this thing can be done in a double sense, that is, really and truly as touched upon by our first arguments, and by the operation of trickery. That, however, which is done by witches in this manner is not done except by an illusion of trickery, though this illusion does not occur in the mind of the sufferer, because his imagination is able to assess in truth and in reality anything that is not present, granted that through the exercise of his exterior senses of sight and touch he perceives it as not present.

"From whence it is possible to say truthfully that in the sufferer's imagination the organ is gone, notwithstanding that it is not so in fact. Several things show how this comes about. First, the two modes by which the illusion is created. It is not surprising that the devil is able to deceive the exterior senses of man since he is able to confuse those interior forms which only make their appearance by abstracting from the sensory principle. He deceives them in their natural operation so that what is visible seems invisible, tangible intangible, audible inaudible, and so forth. This truth, however, says nothing about the organ itself since all these things result from the distortion of the perceptions of the genital which is itself unchanged. Thus the eyes, hands, etc., are deceived.

"We can demonstrate this from certain natural instances. Thus sweet wine seems bitter because of an infection in the tongue during fever. Hence the taste is deceived due to the humor of the body and not due to the wine. There is no deception with respect to things but only with respect to the senses of the organism.

"To return to what we were saying concerning the generative force. Demons hinder it through the imposition of another body of some other person of the same color and appearance. And they are able to interpose between the sight and touch of the eyes and hands a flat body painted in flesh color. So that the sufferer is able to see and feel nothing in his judgment except flatness in that part of his body and not the real member. See the similar remarks of St. Thomas and Augustine concerning illusory tricks. This evil work of demons creeps into all the openings of the senses, presents itself in figures, accommodates itself to colors, adheres to sounds, subjects itself to odors and fuses itself with tastes.

"Moreover, reason goes astray because not only is the trick illusion, by the interposition of the flatness of the body, of not having a male genital presented to sight and touch, whence certain spirits or residual species are brought to the interior sensitive principles, that is, imagination and fantasy; but it also may be elicited from the interior sense in the first place. For as was touched on in the preceding question, demons by their own virtue are able to move bodies from place to place and they corrupt by the transmutation of spirits and humors and even according to the operation of nature. I say that somehow a fecund imagination or sense is natural because the Philosopher (Aristotle) in *Som. et. Vig.*, in assigning the cause of apparitions in dreams, says that when the soul sleeps, much blood descending to the sensitive principle carries with it motions or impressions left over from sensory motions which are retained in the sensible spirits. (These terms have been explained above.) And thus they appear as if the sense had perceived them from the first as unchangeable external objects. And because nature is able to produce by the power of fantasy or imagination the form or appearance of the body as flat without the male genital, so much the more are devils able to do it as if it were so in truth." [6]

Man's third system of warding off his fear of woman is through sugar-coating it, by finding *unconscious* "pleasure in punishment and fear," by *psychic masochism.*

A psychic masochist is *the* "unbelievable character" of fiction and life. He is unconsciously a lover of defeat, humiliation, deprivation. He does not merely extend a passive welcome to misery; unconsciously, he actively engineers it. Since the whole process, and especially the perception of pleasure, lies below the level of consciousness, the psychic masochist does not wear a tag proclaiming, "I am a lover of the proverbial kick in the jaw." He just gets it.

How does such a distortion of inner feelings arise? Psychic masochism represents a faulty elaboration of two inborn factors, infantile megalomania and infantile aggression, which are confronted with an external factor, maternal (and later paternal) authority in the nursery. The child must accept—and with good grace—the fact that not all of his wishes can be fulfilled; many of the demands made by His Majesty the Child are denied, frowned upon, inhibited, and later are even punished with words and deeds. If the child tries to retaliate for this offense to his alleged "all-powerful" megalomania, and attempts to put to use some of his store of aggression, he finds, very soon, that a "triad of retribution" is set in tank-like motion against the transgressor of educational commands. This triad is composed of punishment, moral reproach, and later, inner guilt. The easiest way out is diplomatic adaptation to a stronger reality. This way leads to normality.

[6] The translation was furnished at my request by Dr. Arthur Wormhoudt, to whom I express my thanks.

Assuming, however, that a specific child does not take the easy way out, and in spite of punishment, moral reproach, inner guilt, persists in his "naughtiness." This child automatically comes into conflict with his own "pleasure principle"; every human being insists on *some* fun. What fun, it any, can be extracted from punishment, moral reproach, guilt? Obviously none; therefore the child whose later development follows the normal pattern adapts himself to the demands made by the rulers of his environment. The future candidate for psychic masochism, having rejected this compromise, finds a truly fantastic "solution" of his own. This pseudo-solution consists of *learning to love punishment, moral reproach, guilt.* In short, "by making pleasure out of displeasure," the child immunizes himself against pain and defeat. More than that, he unconsciously welcomes and prefers it.

The solution is ingenious and self-damaging; it is, however—and there is no doubt about it—a "solution." Unfortunately for the child who adopts the principle that "the only pleasure one can extract from displeasure is to make the displeasure a pleasure," new conflicts have a way of arising even after the establishment of this unconscious guide to living. This time the conflicts arise from an internal and not an external source. The inner conscience begrudges the child even this peculiar "pleasure in displeasure," with the result that the child embarks on a life-long and unending routine of hoodwinking conscience. The new technique consists of making oneself appear to be the innocent victim of outside malice. This outside malice is easily supplied: provoke your adversary, and he will kick you. A merciful fate obscures the psychic masochist's vision. He will never even guess that he was the provocateur; he considers himself the perpetually misunderstood victim.

The "masochistic schedule" is simple. Its triad of maneuvers is completely typical, and not subject to any variation.

Act I. *Unconsciously,* I provoke (or misuse) a situation in which someone refuses, denies, or inhibits my wishes;

Act II. Having *repressed* my own provocation, which started the ball rolling, I see only the inexplicable malice of the enemy, against whom I consciously fight in righteous indignation and in "self-defense."

Act III. Having achieved my juicy defeat, I *unconsciously* enjoy my misery; *consciously* I retire in the whining corner and wallow in self-pity, "Such an injustice! It could happen only to poor little me."

The technique is not patented; every psychic masochist invents it for himself—and is ignorant of his feat.[7]

Interestingly enough, Mark Twain had an inkling of the existence of psychic masochism when he wrote the following lines in his deeply pessimistic book, *The Mysterious Stranger:*

Every man is a *suffering-machine* and a *happiness-machine* combined. The two functions work together harmoniously, with a fine and delicate precision, on the give-and-take principle. For every happiness turned out in the one department, the other stands ready to modify it with sorrow or a pain—maybe a dozen . . . Sometimes a man's make-up and disposition are such that his *misery-machine* is able to do nearly all the business. Such a man goes through life almost ignorant of what happiness is. (p. 83)

[7] The three-part technique, the "triad of the mechanism of orality" (alluding to the time when it started, which was during the oral "gimme" phase), was first named and described by the author. Psychic masochism is not a new invention; Freud described the *genetic picture,* consisting of aggression—guilt—libidinization of guilt. What is new and my personal contribution is the elaboration of the secondary *clinical* picture embedded in the "injustice-collecting" technique of the "mechanism of orality," and its interconnection with the oral phase specifically. For further discussion, see *The Superego* and *The Basic Neurosis* (l.c.).

The "suffering-machine"—is psychic masochism. What Twain did not suspect was that the "misery-machine" is—unconsciously—producing "pleasure in pain."

One can, however, fully agree with Twain in this conclusion:

"Satan was accustomed to say that our race lived a life of continuous and uninterrupted self-deception. It duped itself *from the cradle to the grave* with shams and delusions which it mistook for realities, and this made its entire life a sham." (p. 141)

If one were to ask how neurotic man typically combines all these defenses, the answer would be: he marries a shrew, acts the He-Man with her, is slapped down, complains about her cruelty, and unconsciously enjoys his masochistic suffering, heightened by his poor potency.

Numerous theories have been put forward in the attempt to explain the origin of sexual modesty. To name a few:

1. *The religious theory*, proclaimed by St. Augustine (*De Civitate Dei*), explains why solitude is sought even for conjugal intercourse: "Because that which is by nature fitting is so done as to be accompanied with a shame-begetting penalty of sin." St. Augustine also declares that sex and lust were orginially distinct from each other, and that the taint of lust in sex was the result of punishment.

Religious beliefs are not an object of scientific scrutiny. Religion is the most personal affair of man's life, and works on a psychic level entirely different from that of science. There is no contradiction between the two approaches, as is visible in the fact that some scientists are devoutly religious.[8]

2. *The theory of protection*, promoted by Stendhal, among others. As Stendhal put it in *De l'Amour*, this is the argument: "People have noticed that birds of prey

[8] For elaboration, see *The Battle of the Conscience*, p. 1, and *The Basic Neurosis*, p. 104.

hide themselves to drink; the reason being that, obliged to plunge their heads into the water, they are at that moment defenseless." Westermarck correctly objected that sleep is even more dangerous.

3. *The theory of guarding against disturbance by rivals* also fails to explain why sex is so discreet a matter. Ward, in his *Dynamic Sociology*, argued that "where there are several cocks, they seek to separate their chosen mates from the rest in order to enjoy complete immunity." To which Westermarck, in *The History of Human Marriage*, ironically objected, "The cock avoids the presence of other cocks, but not the presence of other hens besides its mate. So also the fear of rivals might have inclined men to avoid intercourse in the presence of other men, not in the presence of women. But how, then, could such fear have been the originating cause of sexual modesty, considering that men exhibit this feeling chiefly towards *women*, and that it is even more marked in women than in men, or at least in young virgins compared with young men of the same age."

The "cock argument" is also senseless because psychological facts from the animal kingdom, when applied *directly* to human beings, are always misleading. We have recently witnessed the one-sidedness which results from the use of this biological fallacy. Kinsey, in his by now notorious *Report*, calls man the "male animal" and rejects the existence of the most prevalent form of psychogenic potency disturbance (premature ejaculation) on the basis of the fact that duration of intercourse in mammals is short. Obviously, observation of animals is more convincing to the biologist than to the psychiatrist, especially if the latter also objects to the rather naive idea, promoted by Kinsey, that neurotic facts can be established or verified by statistics alone. Kinsey's findings showed that most of the men he "investigated" suffered from premature ejaculation; applying the principle of majority rule, Kinsey declared that this constituted a state of normality in the male. Here is what Kinsey says about premature ejaculation:

Far from being abnormal, the human male who is quick in his sexual response is quite normal among the mammals, and usual in his own species. It is curious that the term "impotence" should have been applied to such rapid response. It would be difficult to find another situation in which an individual who was quick and intense in his response was labelled anything but superior, and that, in most instances, is exactly what the rapidly ejaculating male probably is.[9]

Applying this same principle, it would be the solemn duty of the historians to record that tuberculosis was at one time "normal" in the slums of our big cities. And to top all this, Kinsey's anti-psychiatric bias also leads him to adduce inadmissible "evidence" through the use of inadmissible "analogies."

4. The "*domestication theory*" of modesty seems to have been prompted by a study of the habits of the elephant and the camel. The elephant is said to retire to the deepest part of the jungle, and the camel to the loneliest solitude of the desert, before copulating. Confronted with the obvious contradiction offered by domestic animals' lack of reticence, the proponent of this theory, L. Tillier,[10] argued that domestication teaches animals that they may feel safe without taking the precaution of secreting themselves during intercourse. This sophism only washes out the argument, since it is unclear why homo sapiens should be less domesticated than his—dog.

5. The "*disgust theory*" of the genesis of modesty has found many adherents, although nobody has ever been able to explain why urinary and anal functions are disgusting. At one and the same time, sexual acts are declared disgusting because of anatomic proximity to the anal and

[9] *The Kinsey Report*, p. 580.
[10] *L'Instinct Sexuel Chez L'Homme et Chez Les Animaux*, Paris, 1889.

urethral orifices ("Inter urinas et faeces homo nascitur"), and anality and urethrality are adduced as argument to prove why sex proper is "dirty" and "beastly." The inherent contradiction is invisible to the proponents, or ignored by them.

The contradiction reaches rather grotesque proportions when one observes the concern and concentration with which the mistresses of the nursery (mother, nurse) judge the amount, color, consistency, frequency, etc. of the baby's bowel movements. It is only at a later period that anal and urethral functions become taboo, to be mentioned not at all or with circumlocution. It seems that adults are permitted to have a rational approach to excretory matters only during the first few months of their children's lives. During the fifties and sixties again, when prostatitis in men, cancer of the rectum in both sexes, or at least digestive troubles may appear, some kind of rational aspect is reintroduced, with medical blessings. In between, there are only taboos.

On the other hand, scatological jokes and allusions are, statistically, no less frequent than those pertaining to sex proper. The official taboo seems to be counteracted by a strong inner "attraction."

It may be, as some aesthetes claim, that humanity tends to progress in the direction of purification from "animal functions." In putting this claim forward the aesthetes have failed to clarify either reason or purpose. They have not explained why so strong a weapon as shame has to be mobilized as penalty, nor have they suggested any reasonable substitutes for the mechanisms of excretion and elimination. And finally, they have never informed their adherents why they consider a new car beautiful, and the motor pipes and exhaust—"dirty."

6. *The "evil-spirit" theory* bases its assumptions on primitive peoples' numerous fears of magic influences affect-

ing the male genitals.[11] The most pronounced example is probably that of the natives in Tanna (New Hebrides), where, as Summerville reports, "the closest secrecy is adopted with regard to the penis, not at all from a sense of decency, but to avoid the Narak (that is, bewitching force), the sight even of that of another man being considered dangerous." Therefore the natives use rather fantastic protective measures; they wrap the organ in many yards of calico, "winding and folding them until a preposterous bundle eighteen inches or two feet long and two inches or more in diameter is formed.[12]

Tannaits have never been analyzed: experience with

[11] J. C. Flugel in *The Psychology of Clothes* (Hogarth Press, London, 1930) cites Wundt as inclining to the belief that the real reason for the invention of clothing grew out of the custom of carrying articles on the person for the purpose of magic, and that the ornamental purpose followed, instead of preceding, the magical purpose. (p. 72) There is no doubt that magical elements enter the pre-history; a great deal of work—so far not accomplished—will be needed to clarify that point. Otherwise, according to Flugel, the authorities are in general agreed that there are three main purposes served by clothing: decoration, modesty and protection. Some authorities have given first place to modesty, on purely anthropological grounds (Schurtz). The majority opinion holds, however, that the basic motive for the adoption of clothing was *decoration*, and that clothing's usefulness as protection from the weather and as preserver of modesty was a discovery which followed after wearing clothes had become habitual. The anthropological basis for this conclusion is mainly the fact that unclothed primitive tribes are known, but there are no tribes which do not use bodily decoration.

Flugel's book is the only valuable work attempting a psychological approach to the problem. It contains excellent material; its conclusions, however, are nearly exclusively based on repressed exhibitionism and defenses against exhibitionism and phallic castration fear.

Our Argentine colleague, Dr. Angel Garma, recently promoted the theory that clothes are considered necessary and comfortable because unconsciously they repeat the sheltered existence of the embryo in his foetal membranes. I doubt the theory, although the argument at first seems convincing. I also doubt the theory, suggested by an ironical patient of mine, to the effect that the first masculine clothes are provided by nature: man's foreskin. Though Nature is not in the habit of informing us of its aims, this "theory" seems most convincing when it is used to prove this patient's possession of a sense of humor.

[12] These protective measures go far beyond the otherwise stressed necessity of covering the genitals to keep them from the animal and insect attacks encountered in warm climates.

Western neurotics leads to my suspicion that the evil spirit is probably the bad castrating mother (later father) of their early babyhood, conveniently shifted outside.[13]

7. The "*woman as property*" theory injects economic factors into the psychological discussion, and is almost invariably linked by its proponents with the argument of masculine jealousy. Jealousy is a complicated phenomenon, which may explain why the layman prefers taking it for granted to inquiring about its psychology, or trying to dissect his own reactions. The husband in the *New Yorker* cartoon who flies into a rage at the sight of his undressed wife sitting before the television set, watching (and presumably watched by) the man on the screen, is more than a merely ridiculous figure; he has, also, a psychology of his own, which is not included in the joke. Without a discussion of the psychology of jealousy (see Chapter Ten) it is impossible to point out why the "woman as property" theory is entirely inadequate as an explanation of the genesis of modesty.

8. *The "olfactory theory"* suggested by Lombroso and Ferrerro stresses the decomposition of the vaginal secretions, and the consequent reaction of disgust on the part of men. Other theorists go so far as to claim that the artificial waistline in clothing, which separates the upper from the lower part of the feminine body, has the same precautionary origin. No one, as far as I know, has attempted to reconcile this theory with the fact that extremely tight waists were in vogue during the notoriously odor-impervious eighteenth century, nor with the fact that in the finicky twentieth century there was one period of almost a decade when women's dresses were made without any waistline whatever. Obviously, no purely hygienic measure can be

[13] These fears are frequently thinly veiled (leading to segregation of sexes and even to taboos on men and women eating together). Sometimes they are directly connected with women. See also Crawley's *The Magic Rose* (l.c.).

so inconsistent as fashion, nor produce so deeply rooted an emotion as modesty or shame.

9. The most reasonable theory promoted by earlier anthropologists in explanation of the genesis of modesty is the *"anti-incest" hypothesis.* This theory still has some validity, even though the real depth of the problem did not become clear until after Freud's psychoanalytical investigations and Roheim's anthropological fieldwork. There is no doubt that shame is also the second line of defense where originally there was wish and prohibition. Every child goes through a period of incestuous wishes, not because of the attraction of common blood but only because the parents are "just around" and sexually inaccessible. A child born in Paris and transported immediately afterwards to a South Sea island would probably weave around the figures of his foster-mother and foster-father the same net of misconceptions, fantasies and wishes he would have attached to his real parents if he had remained in Paris.

Freud pointed out that under most favorable conditions the woman chosen by an adult is but the second edition of the Oedipal mother. On the other hand, inner renunciation of early infantile attachments is a sign of emotional normality. The emphasis at one time placed on all this lost much of its impact when Freud discovered the pre-Oedipal phase; clinical experience proves that many neurotics, under an Oedipal palimpsest, are fighting fantasies which date from a period preceding the establishment of the full-fledged Oedipus.[14]

These and similar theories hardly begin to explain the genesis of modesty, and cast no light whatever on who "created" that strange though familiar feeling. Most of

[14] In my opinion, the Oedipus complex represents an unavoidable "rescue station" from more deeply repressed baby fears. For a discussion of the problem, see *The Basic Neurosis* (l.c.).

the theories promoted disregard unconscious mechanisms altogether. In all of them, there is exclusive concentration on rational factors—an inevitable dead end when the problem to be solved is one of irrational feelings.

One example would be the "theory of protection," alluding to reality dangers. He-Man is indeed in need of protection, and consequently wants privacy in sex, *because he is mortally afraid that his sex technique, the size of his organ, his general clumsiness, his partial or real impotence, will be ridiculed.* Nearly thirty years ago Ferenczi described "the complex of the small penis," the fantasy, common to many neurotic men, that the sex organs are too small. This fantasy does not necessarily have a realistic basis.[15] The absurdity (again, realistically speaking) of the whole problem becomes even more marked when one takes into consideration the widespread misunderstanding which leads boys and men to compare the sizes of their sex organs when they are not in the erect state. The differences, which are great, are no indication whatever of the size of the erect organs. And since the usable length of the vagina is no more than two and a half to three inches, everything above three inches is just "window-dressing."

A woman with strong leanings towards prostitution once told me in analysis that she had devised a simple but never-failing method of keeping lovers as long as she wanted them—by exclaiming about their "enormous" erections. "Men are suckers for that," she said disparagingly. She did not know why her "method" was so successful; pragmatically, "it worked."

Since every man labors—more or less—under this pecul-

[15] Much has been said in anthropological literature about the theory that modesty is but "acute self-consciousness about appearing unusual." Time and again the literature adduces man's feeling of discomfort when he appears in street clothes at a formal gathering.

The whole assumption confuses surface-reverberations with unconscious connotations. The feeling of self-consciousness pertains to—castration fears. The latter, being repressed, find a hitching post in—conventions.

iar fear, the question arises: why and when was this infantilism acquired?

The "improbable" but clinically provable answer to the riddle of every man's admitted or unadmitted qualms about his sex organ is the "unfortunate" comparison he made in infancy between the very same organ and his mother's breasts. All analysts are accustomed to the constant irony of the average layman's remarks in psychological discussions. Pre-disposed to doubt all answers, the typical layman is sure to seize on what appears to be a flaw in this one, and point out with an air of triumphant finality that the majority of babies in progressive countries are bottle-fed, and therefore do not have the opportunity to make the "tragic" comparison. An obvious fallacy postpones the psychologist's downfall: the baby does not distinguish between breast and bottle. For him, "something enormous" is pushed, by "something enormous," into his mouth. And later he learns to call that giantess "mother."

Nobody can deny the fact that all children are "gimmes" and jealously want whatever they see in another person's possession. This was clinically established early in the history of analysis, on the example of the girl's "penis envy." She too wants what the boy has, or something similar. What has been frequently overlooked is the fact that the boy's "penis pride" (enabling him, in the phallic phase, to look askance at the "castrated" female) has a precursor—breast envy. Thus the ridiculous overstressing of his penis pride by the boy is but a compensatory defense, covering the never-healed narcissistic wound inflicted when he was "deprived" of the—breast.

In sex, the now grown-up He-Man is asked to perform with the sex organ which he has so over-valued as a compensatory defense. The result is that again the unhappy comparison is made—only unconsciously, of course. Nevertheless, there is an evident effect, "the complex of the small penis." This uncomfortable feeling, in my opinion, is one of the contributary factors in man-made "modesty."

Man's fear of being exposed as possessor of an inadequate organ in adult sex makes secrecy and absence of witnesses imperative. As a result, children are given the impression that adult sex is "uncanny" and "mysterious." Repeat this experience over the course of many generations, and one of the pillars of sexual modesty is firmly established.

Clinically, we are well acquainted with the havoc played among neurotics by the fantasy, "sex is forbidden." In *Neurotic Counterfeit-Sex*[16] I gave an account of the results.

In Freud's phrase, "sex loses its value" for some neurotics if the sex act is not accompanied by the condition of the forbidden. The poet Heinrich Heine was acute enough to observe this, and he has the honor of having been the first to do so.[17] In his book on Boerne, written in 1840, Heine wrote:

". . . We, Boerne and I, also visited Boernheim . . . There were beautiful girls . . . Boerne's eyes twinkled. In this mysterious twinkle, in his insecure lewd blinking, afraid of the inner voice, the whole difference in our feelings was enclosed. Boerne was, though not in thought, but therefore more in his feelings, a slave of Nazarene abstinence. As usual with all people of that sort, who accept sensual abstinence as the highest virtue, but are incapable of living up to that ideal, *he dared only in the secretive twinkling and blushing, like a gluttonous boy, to taste of Eve's forbidden apples. I know not whether the enjoyment of these people is more intense than with us who miss the allurement of the secret absconding and moral contraband.* On the other hand, it is said that Mohammed forbade wine to his Turks only for that purpose: that it should taste sweeter to them . . ."

[16] L.c.

[17] As I pointed out in *Divorce Won't Help*, Harper & Bros., 1948. (pp. 38-39)

This prerequisite was linked by Freud with the unsolved infantile connotation of sex: in the neurotic and *not* in the normal adult, sex and the forbidden are still intertwined in the unconscious. In this concept the *aggressive* defiance of Oedipal prohibitions not only contributes to the enjoyment of sex, but actually becomes an indispensable requirement.

Through the study of a long series of cases in which this peculiar partnership of sex and the forbidden was evident, I have become convinced that the aggressive layer conceals a more deeply repressed, pre-Oedipal structure. For these neurotics do not simply "enjoy" sex within the atmosphere of taboos they create for themselves. The "enjoyment" is accompanied by deep anxieties, fear of being caught, found out, punished, involved in a "scandal" leading to loss of social standing. Often the element of fear becomes so intense that it assumes the quality of the *uncanny.*

In my opinion,[18] the feeling of uncanniness is a specific form of psychic masochism, in which is embodied in capsule form the whole history of infantile megalomania, including its eventual and painful end.

In 1919 Freud described the uncanny as a special variety of the fearful, and distinguished between two types of uncanny feelings. One is produced when some impression brings repressed infantile complexes to the surface once more; the other emerges when the primitive beliefs we believed we had overcome seem once more to be confirmed.

In practical experience, Freud declares, the two types of uncanny feeling cannot always be distinguished from each other, since primitive convictions are most intimately connected with infantile complexes and are in fact derived

[18] See *Neurotic Counterfeit-Sex,* l.c.; also "Psychology of the Uncanny," *International Journal of Psychoanalysis,* London, 1934. This study is a continuation of Freud's famous paper, "The Uncanny," *Collected Papers IV.*

from them. The uncanny is a hidden but familiar thing that has undergone repression, but bursts out upon occasion.

In dissecting the feeling of uncanniness, each stage of psychic development leading to psychic masochism can, in my opinion, be clearly discerned: megalomania, fury, subduing of megalomania through one or another branch of the septet of danger (later subsumed under the "septet of baby fears"), the turning of aggression against oneself, and finally the libidinization of fear. Perhaps the most powerful of all the fears which beset the human being is the feeling of uncanniness. To a large extent this accounts for the tendency to capitalize on its "game" quality, and enjoy uncanniness in the theatre, in movies, "thrillers," ghost stories, and of course in spiritualism. Thus masochistic pleasure is combined with the comforting reassurance that it is all "just child's play."

It is the element of condensation in uncanniness that differentiates it from other types of fear. The entire aftermath of infantile megalomania—the victory *and* the dreariness—is passed in review in an instant. To begin with, the aggressive contents of infantile megalomania are reaffirmed, in a brief repetition of the fantasy of omnipotence which prevailed in infancy. This explains the megalomaniacal, though repressed, pleasure derived from uncanniness.

The recapitulation continues, passing on to a later stage in the history of infantile megalomania: its masochistic end. It should not be forgotten that both the clinical *and* genetic pictures of psychic masochism include remnants of megalomania. The unconscious process which, when complete, is psychic masochism, begins: "*I* create, unconsciously, a situation in which somebody refuses, denies, inhibits *my* wishes." These defeats—self-selected, self-determined, self-perpetuated—contain visible if pale traces of the original megalomaniacal glow.

The feeling of uncanniness is therefore seen to have a double purpose. It reaffirms the aggressive component in the first of all human fantasies, that of absolute power, and at the same time emphasizes the masochistic elaborations which amend and weaken that fantasy later on. The unconscious pleasure derived from the feeling of uncanniness may seem to pertain to the aggressive connotation, but it does not. Since the aggressive and the masochistic elements are superimposed on each other, it is clear that it is the combination, and not one or the other individual element, that makes uncanniness so alluring.

As in all fear phenomena, there is over-emphasis on the aggressive connotation, and willingness to accept blame for aggressiveness as a disguise for the more deeply rooted, more serious offense: that of psychic masochism. Here again, there is resort to the familiar ruse in which aggression is used as unconscious defense against the accusation of psychic masochism.

One can compare the situation with that of a dethroned king who consoles himself in his exile with fantasies in which he is still in power and still signing death warrants. Behind that false, megalomaniacal daydream of aggression is hidden the whole history of defeat: his unconsciously self-damaging tactics, his acceptance of his overthrow, his unconscious pleasure in his own "pain and humiliation."

The feeling of uncanniness is actually an asset, if judged from another point of view. The lightning stroke of this emotion saves a person from the prolonged discomfort which would otherwise accompany the memory of his first defeat: the realization that his cherished belief in his own omnipotence was a myth. Uncanniness therefore prevents protracted anxiety and much psychic work.

The adult is not capable of the intensity of feeling which characterizes the emotions of the child. I believe that the profound terror which accompanies the feeling of uncanniness is only a reflection of the child's original reaction when he encountered situations which contradicted his fantasy of omnipotence. The most extreme terror experienced in uncanniness, multiplied by one thousand, is still only an approximation of the child's emotions during the period of the septet of baby fears.

The element of condensation in uncanniness has the effect of partially reviving that infantile terror. The intensity of the shock experience, plus the fact that it is all over in an instant, has the paradoxical effect of cushioning the blow. In this sense, uncanniness is a "fear to end a fear." It can be only momentarily successful in this aim, however, because of the connection with "pleasure in fear."

Like all other fears, that embodied in uncanniness also serves as a warning signal. The human being's unlimited capacity for suffering explains the tendency to run the whole gamut of terror in uncanniness. Terror is conquered by the device of "pleasure in pain," and then the signal, warning of even greater damage, cuts the masochistic pleasure short, at the same time ending the uncanny feeling.

In analyzing neurotics whose prerequisite for sex[19] is the "condition of uncanniness," I have observed that their fears are more closely connected with the septet of baby fears than with simple castration anxiety. Only on the surface is the aggressive component dominant. Actually this surface component is a defensive layer concealing the more deeply repressed masochistic temptation. It therefore represents pseudo-aggression.

It is of course granted that, even in our presumably outspoken culture, every child links sex with the forbidden. The child sees sex as a great mystery, discussed hesitantly in fumbling terms or not discussed at all. This does not explain why one individual is capable of adjusting his inner

[19] See *Neurotic Counterfeit-Sex* (l.c.), Chapter 3, #1.

views to the requirements of objective reality, and another individual cannot. In my opinion, the individual who is more deeply involved in the tangles of masochism cannot make the requisite inner adaptation because of the allure of uncanniness.

This neurotic connotation of sex can become the source of an imposing series of difficulties. Most important is its effect in devaluating marital sex; the result is that the husband is impotent with his wife, the wife frigid with her husband, since the essential atmosphere of the "forbidden" is lacking. The consequence may be divorce,[20] in which case the identical process of depreciation will ruin the second, third or nth marriage. More frequently a solution is sought in sexual escapades, which become increasingly risky. The social consequences can be damaging indeed—not to mention the financial ones.

In attenuated form, the fantasy of the forbidden, with all its masochistic connotations, is one of the primary reasons for man's attraction to feminine clothes. It is in fact symbolized by this attraction. Nevertheless, the frequently heard statement, "women attract men with their clothes," is only a simplification. *It is not with their clothing, but with the unconscious revival of the infantile fantasy of the forbidden hinted at by clothes, that women attract men.* Thus fashion is more than a succession of absurdities, changing with the seasons; it is a game of half-exposure and half-concealment, *gaining its power from a universal infantile experience.* Man's eternal complaint, "You can never tell what fashion stylists will come up with, or what the 'gals' will go for," is consequently slightly out of focus. They will "come up with," and they will "go for" one of the modifications of the seven basic elements in fashion

[20] See *Divorce Won't Help* (l.c.), and *Conflict in Marriage*, Harper & Bros., 1949.

(see Chapter Six), and the attraction will come from the unconscious reactions of the stunned man, and not from the new style.

Expressed differently: feminine clothes help to restore for the child in the grown-up man one of his infantile and repressed connotations in sex. Moreover, clothes make it possible for man to "progress" from the *frightened* pre-school boy who peeps at the forbidden to the *would-be-superior* pre-school boy. The latter, now dressed up as an adult, is no longer aware that the former is still within him. The would-be-superior "adult" is still the frightened pre-school boy, which accounts for the typical He-Man attitude of aggressive peeping and undressing in thought. If, as some men complain, they pay "through the nose" for their wives' extravagance in dressing, they have only themselves to blame. They should adjust their bookkeeping systems, and charge these bills up to a special account called "My Unconscious Alibis."

In any case, man's main attraction to feminine clothes can be attributed to the *constant oscillation between the "uncanny-forbidden," masochistically tinged, and the would-be-superior attitudes of the frightened and seemingly heroic pre-school boy, respectively.*

Feminine clothes unconsciously activate the infantile "situation of the forbidden." More than this, they act as catalyst for another subdivision of infantile fantasy. "The thoughts of youth are long, long thoughts," as Longfellow observed. These "long thoughts" have the quality of being endlessly protracted, the quality of durability and endurance.[21] Children's characteristic insistence on hearing the same story, told in exactly the same way, again and again, is a case in point. This consistent and *protracted* pleasure

[21] Our Hungarian colleague, Dr. S. Pfeiffer, later killed by the Nazis in an extermination camp, called this quality "Dauerlust," permanent pleasure.

with children derive from their erotic, aggressive and narcissistic fantasies is not experienced by adults, whose pleasure is of the short, *orgastic* type, as far as the direct sexual-erotic component goes. The sexy titillation provided by looking at women "dressed to be undressed" (at least in thoughts) establishes contact with the infantile fantasy of the forbidden *and* durable. And this type of titillation involves no obligations, requires no performance. Thus is established one of the pillars of masculine attraction to feminine clothes, especially since the familiar child's excuse is offered, "I didn't do anything, I was just—looking."

We have adduced two reasons leading to the requirement of privacy in sex: one, for the sake of inner reassurance, to hide man's fear of comparisons of the size of his sex organs, and two, clinging to the "situation of the forbidden" in sex. There exists a third reason which is also not mentioned in the existing literature on the subject. That third constituent in the requirement of sexual privacy has intimate though repressed connection with the *infant's autarchic desire to be the center of the universe.* The first relation of the infant includes only one other person: mother. Attentions from anyone else are considered by him "unwanted intrusion." That, in turn, produces the fantasy of a duality which is not to be disturbed by the environment. Later, the duality-unity is repeated in sex.

One could speak of a *triad of reasons* for *privacy in sex*, and point out that these fearful masochistic and megalomaniacal fantasies are all below the level of consciousness.

The problem of male modesty and shame can be studied from another angle—the simple physiological one. Too little attention has been paid to the fact that the process of erection, and the experience of being, literally, shamefaced, both involve an accumulation of blood. Of course, analysts long ago learned from analyses of blushers that these neurotics shift "from downwards upwards," blushing having the symbolic meaning of an erection. In superficial layers,[22] it is also a denial of castration executed exhibitionistically, though on unsuitable—and sexually unusable—organs: cheeks. Still, the erection is a triumph in certain situations, blushing a defeat. Thus the classical "You should be ashamed of yourself" is—psychosomatically—a "negative erection." And we hear frequently enough from impotent men that they leave the woman "shamefaced," having experienced "heat" on the whole body, with the exception of the organ suitable for the occasion.

Summarizing, one can state that female modesty, in clothing and attitudes, is a masculine "invention,"[23] secondarily enforced by man in woman's conduct, for the purpose of protecting the He-Man from:

a. recollection of the unfavorable comparison between his miniature organ and the "enormous" breast;
b. recollection of hopeless attempts, in the Oedipal period, to win the mother sexually;
c. recollections of the sight of the "castrated" and bleed-female genitalia (menstruation);
d. recollections of the "complex of the small penis," with consequent fears of ridicule because of impotence, faulty technique, etc.

[22] See *The Basic Neurosis*, Chapter 6, #6, "Pathologic Blushing."

[23] To repeat, there is no theorist or authority of any standing who claims that clothing was invented to fill the need for additional warmth or protection. This "common-sense" solution to the puzzle is rejected in favor of less obvious explanations. Clothing's function in protecting the body from the elements, it is agreed by these investigators, is a byproduct only. This pertains especially to "fancy" fashions.

5 *The Paradox Unfolds: Contradictions of the "Improved Skin"*

FEMININE CLOTHES, according to our definition, constitute improved skin, minus the frightening genitals. Man, reassured by concealment of the cause of fear, proceeds to prove to himself that he still is the great He-Man, sexually titillated by women. Never having outgrown the concupiscent peeping urge of his infancy, he stares at the fully clothed woman in order to undress her mentally. No human situation proves more conclusively that the child in the man controls the man than does the adult male's consistent peeping. Casual observation in any bus, train, subway, restaurant shows that no man passes up the opportunity of staring at the slightest exposure or hint of exposure in women's dress.

Now, both of the attitudes described—that of purported sexual "attraction" by innuendo, as conveyed by feminine dresses, and that of sexy peeping—have an *aggressive* connotation. The infantile taboo has been violated by indulgence in either attitude. But by overemphasizing the activity of peeping, the *inner fear*—that of being *passively forced into the corner* and confronted with the frightening female genitalia—is *negated.* That is the crux of the matter, and paradox No. I.

The joker in the pack is the amazing hoax: the conscious aim of peeping is purportedly to see the woman naked. The real—*unconscious*—aim is to run away from precisely that sight. The two horns of the dilemma which makes up paradox No. II are conveniently resolved by woman's clothing, which makes it possible for man to glory in his conscious aims, achieve them in conscious fantasy, and avoid the danger of being put to the test. If he achieves his full aim, he too frequently finds himself in the position of having "captured" something he cannot use because of inner inhibitions.

The next paradox—No. III—is the popular assumption that the nude female body is sexually more attractive to men than the illusion of half-nakedness promoted by clothes. This, too, is a mirage. The anthropologists tell us that "concealment affords greater stimulus than revelation." If "revelation" were the real aim, the "stimulus" would increase in due proportion to the increase of "revelation." What happens instead—and too frequently—is only an anticlimax: the sexual desire, even if present and usable, is far less intense or enjoyable than the anticipated pleasure promised by the imagination. Analytic authors have stressed this fact and explained it in terms of man's castration fear.

Paradox No. IV is the wild illogic which forbids to the *skin* the identical attitudes which are approved for the *substitute skin,* or clothing. To expose the breasts is taboo in our culture; to accent the breasts through the use of the brassière, with semi-décolletage, high waistlines, "plunging necklines," etc., is generally accepted. *The magic of the intervening layer of thin material* seems to make the moral difference.[1] The distinction, once it is queried and not merely accepted, is laughable; when the key is provided, in

[1] The potency of this magic layer can be judged from the announcement, in June, 1952, of a series of new bras visualized as double purpose items, to be worn either as under- or outer-clothing at the caprice of the owner. A "cocktail bra" created by Lilly Daché was described: ". . . long, strapless . . . ablaze with emerald green stones set amid black leaves . . ."

the fact that "the magic of the intervening layer" pertains to man's infantile fears, it can be understood.

Paradox No. V concerns what Flugel (in *The Psychology of Clothes*) calls "clothes ambivalence," by which is meant the never-ending conflict between modesty and display. His term is not too well chosen; what he describes is rather a "return of the superficially repressed material." (Freud) Flugel adduces the attitude of hiding the body, and showing it off in clothes, and compares it with pathological blushing, which in his opinion represents exaggeration of the "normal symptom of shame" on the one hand, while on the other hand and at the same time it involuntarily draws attention to the blusher, thus gratifying his unconscious exhibitionism.[2]

Whenever exhibitionistic-voyeuristic elements enter the picture, one must guard against the danger of overlooking the masochistic component. This is well exemplified in Arthur Schnitzler's well-known book, *Fräulein Else.* Schnitzler's novelette describes the plight of a young girl who is confronted with a moral problem while on her vacation, without her parents, at a resort hotel. Her father's business is threatened with bankruptcy; an elderly financier, who could save the day, is by chance staying at Else's hotel. Else's father telephones, asking her to approach the financier and request his help. Else complies; the old roué agrees, on condition that she show herself to him, naked. Her father, of course, is to know nothing of the financier's terms. The heroine cannot make up her mind. At last she makes her appearance, nude, in the crowded lobby of the fashionable hotel. Shortly afterwards she commits suicide.

In Flugel's opinion, the core of the emotional situation

[2] The problem of blushing is far more complex than Flugel's assumption would make it appear. See "A New Approach to the Therapy of Erythrophobia," paper read at the XV Intern. Psychoanalytic Convention in Paris (France), August, 1938. Reprinted in *The Psychoanalytic Quarterly* (New York), 13:1, 1944, and in *The Basic Neurosis* (l.c.), pp. 175-186.

here is the unconscious appeal of the financier's outrageous request. Else's modesty cannot compete with her repressed exhibitionistic tendencies, which now are provided with a rationalization in the form of her father's urgent need for funds. Flugel believes that Else's solution is the use of the unconscious mechanism of "over-determination"; in her "over-reaction" to the request, she is at the same time satisfying her exhibitionism, and so shaming herself that suicide is inevitable.

I am of the belief that Flugel missed the point. Else's action is a reduction to absurdity of her father's request, and typical for masochistic injustice-collectors. By increasing the stakes, Else seems to be saying to her parents, "Why don't you ask me to do *that?*" It is the neurotic masochism, and not the superficial exhibitionistic conflict, veiled by pseudo-aggression, which drives poor Else to her death.[3] The pseudo-aggressive camouflage is also visible in another way: by creating a scandal, Else ruins her parents' prospect of financial help. The fact that her parents are entirely ignorant of the real conflict—the financier's immoral request—strengthens this assumption: Else's masochistic conflict is repressed and infantile; when provoked by an incident which happens to fill the bill, it erupts like a volcano.

Paradox No. VI has been well established, analytically; it is the sexual symbolism of some articles of dress. For instance, the shoe, the tie, the hat, the collar, coat, and trousers are considered phallic symbols; the shoe, the garter, the girdle, and jewels, represent the feminine symbols.[4] All this can be studied in dream-symbolism—and in fashion

[3] Flugel explains Else's suicide in terms of "public shame," which I believe is insufficient to serve as the real unconscious reason for self-destruction. See "Problems of Suicide," *The Psychiatric Quarterly*, 1946, reprinted in *The Battle of the Conscience*, Chapter V; the extensive literature on the topic is also included.

[4] Compilation in Flugel's "Clothes Symbolism and Clothes Ambivalence," *International Journal of Psychoanalysis*, X, pp. 205 ff., 1929.

reality. Once more, the innuendo is tolerated and the actual model rejected because of its fear-inspiring quality.

Paradox No. VII is the seemingly senseless succession of prudish and "shameless" styles and customs which prevail in any particular social level at different epochs. The history of fashions and morals in England is a pertinent example. In the second half of the nineteenth, and the first quarter of the twentieth century, the British created a fantastic bogey of moral stuffiness, snobbishness, and hyper-puritanism, a bogey as inclusive and as uncompromising as the religious fanaticism of an earlier day. A typical late Victorian, or his children with their rigid acceptance of the code of their times, would have been very likely to burst the traditional blood-vessel if suddenly confronted with a preview of our current fashions. But this very same late Victorian, given a family tree with deep enough roots, could have had in his "lumber-room" a portrait of one of his Tudor forbears, in full panoply of *his* day's fashion. And for the Tudor fashion-plate, "the tightness of male nether garments necessitated the housing of the genitals in a special bulging portion of the hose (the cod-piece)—a portion to which attention was sometimes gratuitously drawn by a vivid contrasting color, and which was further sometimes embellished by padding in such a way as to simulate a perpetual erection." (Flugel) And even preceding the cod-piece wearer of the Tudor period, there was undoubtedly an ancestor who wore the *poulaine* of the Middle Ages—the obviously phallic-shaped shoe which aroused indignation and led to pitched battles on the moral issue over all of Western Europe.[5]

[5] See Havelock Ellis, *Studies in the Psychology of Sex,* chapter on "Erotic Symbolism," p. 25:

Ellis quoted Dufour: "At the first glance it is not easy to see why these shoes—terminating in a lion's claw, an eagle's beak, the prow of a ship, or other metal appendage—should be so scandalous. The excommunica-

Paradox No. VIII is connected with the peculiar fact that morality and modesty—at least according to the professional moralist—are determined by time and place. A "sundress," revealing naked shoulders, may be worn when a woman goes to the supermarket, but a covering jacket is added in the office. The same yardstick applies to the beach; with sand as a background a mere brassière and panties achieve decency for a female, but anywhere else the same attire is "shocking." The contradictions of time-and-place morality have never been explained by the censors—unless the melancholy, inevitable, "it cannot be helped" is accepted as an explanation.

Paradox No. IX is a modification of time-and-place morality: the same girl who is so self-assured when she parades, nine-tenths naked, on the beach, loses all her poise when her dress flies up above her knees in a subway, bus, or restaurant.

Paradox No. X has been stressed with amazement by a number of authors. If clothes have the alleged purpose of serving morality (translate: of promoting anti-sex), why is there such strict insistence on the distinction between masculine and feminine attire? Logically, the moralist should do everything possible to diminish the sex distinction in clothes. In reality, hc does exactly the opposite.

Even people who no longer believe that women must dress differently from men in order to warn men away from the devil's receptacle, which they supposedly represent, are quite adamant on this score. Their certainty is

---

tion inflicted on this kind of footgear preceded the impudent invention of some libertine, who wore poulaines in the shape of a phallus, a custom adopted also by women. This kind of poulaine was denounced as maudite de Dieu and prohibited by royal ordinances. Great lords and ladies continued to wear poulaines."

Ellis adds: "In Louis XI's court days they were still worn a quarter of an ell in length."

entirely unshaken by their inability to explain their "conviction."

It is easy enough to take the bundles of contradictions which are part and parcel of moralistic sartorial attitudes, and reduce them to absurdity. It is an amusing, but a one-sided, sport; the victim cannot defend himself. Caught in an invisible psychological net, and thoroughly unaware that he is caught, the victim can do no more than reiterate his statements, forgetting (as the old saying goes) that he can still be wrong, even at the top of his lungs.

The sartorial purist cannot resolve the paradoxes that have been listed, nor can he explain such historical curiosities as the fact that the identical fashion has been, at different times, the sign of social elevation or of degradation. In his history of prostitution,[6] Dufour states:

> In old Rome, matrons have appropriated the use of the shoe (soccus); prostitutes were not allowed to use it, and were obliged to have their feet always naked in sandals or slippers (crepida and solva), which they fastened over the instep with gilt bands. Tribullus delighted to describe his mistress's little foot, compressed by the band that imprisoned it: Ansaque compressos calligat arcta pedes. Nudity of the foot in woman was a sign of prostitution, and its brilliant whiteness acted afar as a lure to attract looks and desires.

Fortunately, modern women, walking about in toeless, heel-less shoes or sandals, over naked or nylon-clad feet, are ignorant of old Roman customs and history.

Feminine vanity, like the half-score of paradoxes in fashion, has always been conveniently taken for granted. Long ago, analysis proved that this narcissistic self-adoration hides a duality of phenomena. The narcissism is compen-

[6] *Histoire de la Prostitution,* II, xviii.

satory, overlying the deeper wound of alleged castration (Freud); moreover, what appears to be simple narcissism is frequently but disguised exhibitionism. Thus the simple formula, "women are conceited show-offs," no longer appears simple when the psychological substructure is examined.

In my opinion, exhibitionism is not a primary instinct. I believe that exhibitionism is an inner defense mechanism installed *after* the original drive of peeping (voyeurism) came to a dead end in the course of the educational process.

Can anyone in his right senses, observing a baby, claim that he is conscious of his nakedness? Or that he enjoys exhibiting? Observe him again, a few months later. The baby has begun to show some curiosity about his own body; he will examine his hand or foot for minutes at a time. Still later, this interest is extended to the nutritional apparatus (breast or bottle), and the bearer of the breast or transmitter of the bottle. Here the child meets with mild prohibitions, which later become more severe when, in the adult's opinion, "real sexual curiosity" develops in the child. Finally, sexual peeping at oneself (masturbation!) and at others is inhibited by *all* educators, whether severe or mild, whether explicit or inadvertent in their teaching, for the child assumes that mere failure to participate in his active and passive sexual games constitutes disapproval.[7] (Anna Freud) The empathy of the child is greater than obtuse adults suppose; frequently adults credit themselves with "never having intimidated the child," unaware that their shocked or disapproving facial expressions, or even reflex gestures, have done exactly that. The moral connotations and superstitions of adults invariably penetrate even

[7] For elaboration, see my contribution to the symposium "Theory of Therapeutic Results," held at the XIV International Psychoanalytic Convention, Marienbad, August, 1936. Published in *Int. Journal of Psychoanalysis* (London), 23:6-18, 1937.

into the most "modern" of our systems of education, that which reverses the old roles, so that parents are now in awe of their children and not children of their parents. As far as future neurotic possibilities are concerned, the results of the new system are hardly different from those of the old. The trouble is that the educator has far less control over a developing, or not-developing, neurosis than he naively imagines. The decisive factor always is how well or how tragically the child accepts the unavoidable blows dealt to his fantasy that he is the center of the universe (infantile megalomania).

In any case, objective observation shows that exhibitionism develops in the child *after* serious and *unavoidable* voyeuristic disappointments. The inner defense installed by the big psychologist in swaddling clothes reads: "I do not wish to peep, I wish to show myself."

This observation has practical and therapeutic value; it clarifies many otherwise inexplicable human actions in the sphere of peeping and exhibitionism. Here are three examples:[8]

A patient suffering from erythrophobia (pathological blushing) stated that in childhood it was very distressing for him to sleep in the same room with his mother. He said that even at the age of three and a half he felt ashamed. He clearly remembered the following scene: The outer wall of his bed, made of netting and therefore permitting a full view through the interstices, was turned towards his mother's bed. He would always cover this outer wall with his top sheet and the other covers given him for the night. Officially, this was a proof that he was not watching his mother undress; nor by inference, in the Oedipal period, was he watching parental coitus. At the same time, exhibitionism—lying half naked without cover—was here

[8] First pointed out in "Further Contributions to the Therapy of Erythrophobia," l.c.

used as a defense against the original voyeurism. In the third layer, the exhibitionistic defense too was warded off: he felt ashamed whenever his mother would cover him in the morning.

While being analyzed, another erythrophobic patient had the following experience. At a mountain cottage, he met a lady whom he thought he knew. He stared at her, against his usual custom, but could not remember where he had seen her face before. Suddenly it occurred to him that she might be a patient he had frequently seen at my office on leaving. The thought was distressing to him. He looked away but in the next few minutes behaved very exhibitionistically: he spoke loudly, began to sing, opened his shirt, put on another sweater, etc. The lady, not understanding what was going on, reported to me: "The man behaved as if he desired to attract attention, although at the same time he was rather embarrassed and quite red." Again we see the same set of facts: the primary desire to stare is secondarily warded off by means of exhibitionism ("as if he desired to attract attention to himself"), and at a tertiary stage the exhibitionism itself is warded off ("rather embarrassed and quite red").

Another patient occupied a box one evening at a circus performance. While watching two woman trapeze artists demonstrate their skill she suddenly became "dizzy," covered her face with her hands and cried out very loudly, "I can't look at it; please tell me when it's over." Voyeurism was warded off by means of exhibitionism; by attracting the attention of those about her, the patient exhibited herself. But this defensive exhibitionism was itself warded off as the patient blushed, grew ashamed and self-conscious, because the scene she provoked was consciously very painful to her.

The connection between exhibitionism-voyeurism and fashion becomes quite clear when one studies the *six inner defenses* which are served by adult women's sometimes ridiculous preoccupation with clothes.

1. This preoccupation embodies the end results of unsolved infantile peeping conflicts, *shifted to exhibitionism as defense.* The paradoxical result is that clothes-exhibitionism has—as far as the inner conscience is concerned—a moral connotation: the "lesser crime" of exhibitionism is admitted, to ward off the more serious crime of peeping.[9]

2. It embodies attempts to *solve* the problems of alleged "castration"; clothes-exhibitionism contains the unspoken feminine invitation: Look at every part of my body *but* the 'mutilated' genital!"

3. The inner defense against the girl's infantile idea of alleged castration is also visible, this time in a negative fact: *there exists no perverted vulva-exhibitionism in women* comparable to perverted penis-exhibitionism in men. The parks in large cities harbor many male exhibitionists; no man has ever reported a case of vulva exhibitionism.

4. Moreover, female "vanity" also serves *narcissistic attempts at reparation,* the unspoken reproach being, "Nobody loves me, so I am forced to love myself." Analytic experience proves that exaggerated narcissism in some women can be diminished only *after* solution of the problem of the masochistic complaint against the enshrined image of the mother.

5. Still another factor must be considered—one which Freud described in an entirely different connection: there is a constant *flow of mutual identification* between the peeper and the show-off. The exhibitionist unconsciously experiences double pleasure: he satisfies his—as I believe,

[9] In my opinion, the psychic apparatus works after the principle of "admission of the lesser crime": accused by the inner conscience of a specific misdeed, the unconscious ego defends itself by admitting to another but lesser crime. Unfortunately, the external and internal moral codes are by no means identical. For elaboration see *The Basic Neurosis* (l.c.) and *The Superego* (l.c.).

defensive—exhibitionism, and at the same time, unconsciously, identifies with the spectator. Thus, via the spectator, he peeps at himself. The same process, in reverse order, applies to the voyeur. From the viewpoint of infantile prohibitions, this system of mirror-peeping (using the other person as a mirror) is a triumph over the educational authorities, and their specific taboo on self-examination, even with the eyes.

This much-delayed unconscious triumph over the educational authorities—meaning, at bottom, the mother—amounts not so much to a real aggression as to a pseudo-aggression, in which the ultimate purpose is self-damage, rather than damage to the enemy. At the same time, however, it accounts for the malicious byword: "women dress as they do to anger other women."

6. Fashion and its *details* have grown so complicated that they can be judged only by a female connoisseur; the average man gets no more from a costume than a "*general impression.*" By unconsciously identifying the female spectator with the (allegedly) refusing mother of infancy, the masochistic child in the woman manages to record still another triumph.[10]

The literature on the subject fails to mention an additional point, directly related to the question of shame and modesty: there are men who enjoy forcing women to overcome that feeling of shame in intimate situations. This is an additional proof that a man-made institution, secondarily imposed upon women, becomes an additional source

[10] "I do not understand chiffons," regretfully admitted the hero of Anatole France's *The Red Lily*. Today's clothes and accessories are even more difficult to "understand." A patient reported that she met an acquaintance whom she had not seen for several years. The acquaintance, a woman, looked at her contemptuously, and said, with some jealousy, "I gather from the way you are dressed that you have a lot of time—you must have given up your job." The diagnosis was correct. Time, even more than money, seems essential.

of allure, for isn't the man "active" in forcing the woman? In general, one can safely say that women, in their private thoughts, are more rational about modesty-taboos than are men. It goes without saying that there are some women who believe that they have to play-act before men.

The perversion coprophemia has at its core the pleasure which some men take in actively causing women embarrassment through the use of obscene language. The technique used by these sick people consists of muttering obscene words to unknown women on the street, and enjoying their subsequent shame-reaction. To exemplify the complexity of unconscious reasons:[10]

A kleptomaniac of twenty-six entered analysis at his uncle's insistence. The uncle, incidentally, also paid the initial fees. The young man regarded his pilfering as rather a practical joke, and was "tickled to death that that old hypocrite of an uncle was socially embarrassed." In addition to his kleptomania, the patient was a check forger, a pathologic gambler, and a sufferer from a potency disturbance. He also had coprophemia; he would habitually approach well-dressed women on the street and whisper obscene words to them.

"It is really superb," mused the patient, "how I am able to embarrass such a high-class lady with one well-chosen word or short epigrammatic sentence. These women either blush, pretend not to hear, or are silently furious . . . It is enough for me to see their faces redden in embarrassment or fury. *I feel like an omnipotent sorcerer with inexhaustible power.*"

Asked whether any of his victims ever denounced him to a police officer, he laughed and said that only a very few out of "hundreds of these women" ever threatened to do so and even they were too embarrassed to go any fur-

[10] First published in "Psychology of Gambling," *Imago*, 1936. For psychology of gambling, see *Money and Emotional Conflicts*, Part V (l.c.).

ther. Once a "bitch" had denounced him, but his uncle's lawyer was able to convince the investigating officers that the lady must have misunderstood "something." In any case, no prosecution followed.

Superficially, the patient presented the picture of a constantly amused psychopath. He ridiculed accepted moral standards, claimed that "bourgeois values" were good only for "idiots," and considered himself a "superior person." He quoted Napoleon: "The usual moral laws do not apply to me."

I asked him whether he was aware of the risk he was running with his check forging, kleptomania, and coprophemia. He shrugged his shoulders and replied: "Until now, nothing has happened. For his own protection, my uncle covers me up." Pressed further, he said, "One has to take chances. Take for example my gambling . . ." This was the way his gambling was brought into the discussion, tangentially and accidentally. The patient did not consider his gambling a pathological phenomenon and was rather amused that I was of a different opinion. He used gambling as a "moral alibi." His argument was: gambling, compared to kleptomania, is a socially acceptable way of getting money. What's wrong with that? If, as I claimed, both his gambling and coprophemia were based on the fantasy of child-like omnipotence, masochistically colored, why not tolerate gambling, since society tolerates it?

The next day he reversed the argument: "Isn't gambling 'morally' inferior to coprophemia, since the former is more 'materialistic'?" Thus, shifting his argument illogically, he proved one day that gambling was "moral," and the next day that coprophemia was "moral." The common denominator was the old trick of reducing bourgeois standards to absurdity.

The patient was the only and posthumous child of a short-lived marriage; the father was accidentally drowned before the child was born. His mother was an obstinate, illiterate, aggressive, and "half-wild" person. She owned a canteen near an army camp, and promiscuously changed lovers every few weeks. The child was frequently present during intercourse. One scene he remembered especially clearly during analysis: an "enormous" soldier forced the mother to have intercourse by squeezing her breast until she nearly fainted from pain. That incident was repressed and came to consciousness in connection with the analysis of a strange habit the patient had developed during puberty: he believed that squeezing girls' buttocks was the surest technique for seducing them. It became apparent that this "squeezing technique" represented the precursor of his coprophemia. The reason was twofold. The progress of his neurosis necessitated stronger repression (in squeezing he repeated the soldier's technique but shifted from the forbidden breast to the more harmless buttocks); and, at the same time, coprophemia represented a megalomaniacal "improvement." The soldier had to resort to an action, but he could get the same results with a word. This explains the previously quoted boast: "It is really superb how I can embarrass a lady[11] with *one single word* . . . I feel like an *omnipotent* sorcerer . . ."

The next step was the shift from coprophemia to kleptomania. The patient began stealing electric light bulbs, for no apparent practical purpose. He did not sell them but destroyed them in the lavatory. Later, when he began to steal other things, he sold his loot and lost the money gambling. A series of dreams proved that in the symbolism of the patient's unconscious vocabulary the bulbs represented breasts.

[11] Once more, unconscious ridicule of bourgeois values. Since he did not consider his mother a "lady," he even debased those on a higher social level. Considering his mother a "low-grade type," he demonstrated his superiority and megalomania by "seducing" upper-class women. The neurosis manifested itself in exhibitionism and Peeping-Tom activities, too.

We see that the patient went through a series of pseudo-aggressive acts aimed against the consciously hated mother: the "squeezing technique"—later projected upon women in general—coprophemia, and kleptomania. When his mother reproached him, he stated that all his actions were for the purpose of "taking revenge on her." This conscious hatred was then shifted to the family; he embarrassed his uncle socially by stealing, and by forging the latter's signature.

This pseudo-aggression was only a cover, however, for psychic masochism. The erotic and "sadistic" elements served as a defense against the more deeply embedded masochistic tendency. This became clear the moment this question was put to the patient: "Don't you see that you are damaging yourself more seriously than your mother and uncle?"

One could argue that all these self-damaging acts were only belated revenge-aggressions, carried out under self-damaging conditions because of inner guilt. But this was not true, as proved by the fact that he later sought these self-damaging conditions because they satisfied his desire for psychic-masochistic pleasure. The perfect proof of this was his attitude towards gambling. He stated very precisely that during gambling he experienced a thrill "not comparable to any other sensation known to me. Only once, when a lady whom I'd insulted with an obscene word called the police, did I experience anything similar to that thrill. Why, an orgasm in sex is nothing compared to it. After all, sex is not forbidden . . ."

And here is a literary example, in which some of the points made in this chapter are illustrated with, as they say, "live models." This is from the night-club scene in Charles Yale Harrison's brilliant novel, *Nobody's Fool:*

"There have been hundreds of striptease acts in the cultural history of America, but none was more simple and provocative than Gloria Dale's routine:

"SET: The bedroom of a girl's boarding school. College pennants on walls. Pin-up photographs of movie stars and crooners. A daybed, left, a table, right, on which there is a photograph; two easy chairs, a bridge lamp. A curtained window, rear. This is a fancy school, the script writer will have you know, where the tuition alone costs twelve hundred dollars a year.

"GLORIA, *who has made sleep possible for more young men than sheep-counting, hot milk, or seconal; a cute trick who's read all the books on Sumner's Index and has come through unscathed.*

"MUSIC: *Mood Indigo*, first straight, and toward the end, gutbucket.

"AT RISE: An empty stage, music pianissimo, then:

"Gloria enters, right, straight from the campus. She is wearing blue jeans, moccasins, anklets, a leather golf jacket, and under that you see, when she starts peeling, a sloppy pullover sweater. (*"Lissen, Lou, I tell ya this is sumpin diffrent, a bran' new routine"*) She carries some books which she tosses on the daybed after she enters. She climbs out of her jacket, lights a cigarette and goes over to the gramophone, puts a record on it and starts playing. The machine is dead, the music comes from the orchestra. Then she starts to undress. She takes a yellow ribbon out of her hair, shaking her hair free, then the sloppy sweater comes off and underneath it, instead of Sloppy Joe underwear she's wearing delicate, feminine underthings. (*"Get the idea, Lou? Suspense. First ya think maybe she's wearing BVD's, but underneath she's a smart chick who knows her business. Wait'll I tell ya . . ."*) She unhooks her brassiere and regards her breasts with innocent curiosity, she caresses first her shoulders, then her breasts. She is completely oblivious to her audience. (*"This ain't no cheap burlycu strip routine like Kelly's where the broad has a red heart light up near her G-string when she sings 'My Heart Belongs to Daddy.' She's alone in her room, see? She's a school girl!"*) Then, off come the jeans, the lazy way, with one soft rolling wriggle to shake them below her hips, and instead of a pair of dollar shorts you see the finest pair of Vogue panties you ever set eyes on, they're cut smart and brief, hand-stitched. And so right until the end where the music is up and throaty until just as she's about to slip out of her panties. Then, socko, she suddenly looks out at the audience in the dark, looking indignantly, as though they were so many lecherous voyeurs. (*"Kin ya see it, Lou? Kin ya hear the cash customers breathin' hard? It's like she didn't know they wuz lookin'!"*) And now right here the music is away in the background, hardly audible. There's a horrified look of girlish outrage on Gloria's face. Eyes wide open, mouth rounded. Why, you nasty men! (*Blackout.*)

"There was a pause after the curtain while the men in the audience adjusted themselves to reality, made a long journey in a few seconds and quickly saw that the deeply forbidden thing was still forbidden. And then there was a wild applause . . ."

6 *The Seven Ingredients of Haute Couture*

STRIPPED TO ITS ESSENTIALS, fashion is no more than a series of permutations of seven given themes, each theme being a part of the female body: the breasts (neckline), waist (abdomen), hips, buttocks, legs, arms, and length (or circumference) of the body itself. Organs "appear" and "disappear" as the theme of fashion changes, and one and then another part of the body is emphasized by succeeding styles. Thus breasts and legs are "opposites" in fashion; if, in one season, the neckline plunges and breasts consequently become the center of attraction, one can be sure that in subsequent seasons breasts will be covered and the spotlight will be on legs. And so on, in endless variations.

One can demonstrate this factor by means of a painting of Picasso's dated 1923, one of his series called *Women*. Three women appear in this painting; the one of importance to us in the left background. She is lifting one enormously elongated leg; the leg is longer than the other leg, plus torso and head. The painting is merely one of Picasso's many attempts to achieve three-dimensionality via distortion; it happens to be usable for our purposes. Just as Picasso grotesquely enlarges one limb in this picture, fashion over-emphasizes successive "details" of the body, and so focuses attention on them. The fact itself was recognized long ago; Flugel, in his *Psychology of Clothes*, presents an admirable summary of the results.

According to Flugel, fashion constantly shifts its emphasis from one part of the body to another, with the shift reflecting to a greater or a lesser extent the prevailing mood of the period. In an era of modesty, for example, the part of the body which at other times may be considered the primary physical attraction is played down in dress, and made inconspicuous. Flugel gives as an example the Middle Ages, when the general tone of feminine fashion was ascetic, and the function of the corset was to conceal the contour of the breasts. Asceticism in women's dress vanished with the Renaissance, and the shape of the corset was changed so that it revealed instead of concealing the breasts.

Emphasis on the bosom has been a major theme ever since the Renaissance, but it has not been the only center of interest. The abdomen was given special importance during the later Middle Ages and the Renaissance, when the pregnant woman was idealized, and the walk and stance characteristic of pregnancy were fashionable. The pictures of the period clearly illustrate this trend. By the eighteenth century, this theme was outmoded (it reappeared briefly from time to time in modified form). The emphasis now was shifted to the breasts and the hips. The breasts were now brought into still greater relief by the introduction of tight-laced waists, and by high heels. High heels, which push the weight of the body forward, make the Holbein-Botticelli carriage, with protruding abdomen, impossible; the body must be held erect, which makes the bosom more prominent.

Flugel comments, here, on the seeming anomaly between the retention of high heels in the nineteen-twenties and the abandonment of the bosom theme during the same period. He postulates four reasons for the apparent contradiction:

1. High heels contribute to the desired flat-stomach look.
2. There is an apparent increase in both height and slenderness, so that the total effect is youthful.

3. The heel itself may be an unconscious phallic symbol, thus fitting into the general "boyishness" of the style, with its short hair and straight lines.

4. High heels make the foot look smaller.

The styles of the Empire period stressed the bosom, through the extremely high waistline, but otherwise clothed the whole of the body rather than any part of it. Subsequently, however, fashions again centered around one or another part of the body. The latter half of the nineteenth century saw a succession of styles emphasizing the hips; the medium was the crinoline, a name first applied to a mass of horse-hair puffing out the full skirt, then to a wire frame over which the skirts billowed. Following the full and rounded skirt came the bustle,[1] which accented the posterior rather than the hips.

Summing up the styles of 1930, the date of his book, Flugel notes that the emphasis is on legs and arms; dresses are sleeveless, or the sleeves are tight-fitting, since the ideal is a long and graceful arm. Legs are of major importance, and this for the first time in centuries. ("Centuries" is Flugel's estimate; surely "millennia" would be more accurate.) The long-limbed, narrow-torsoed look, Flugel de-

[1] Flugel remarks: "That the bustle is really symbolized, and served to draw attention to the buttocks is of course clearly evident to all who give a little attention to modes of the time. Cf. the amusing rhyme then current:

Die letzte Kleidermode war,
Noch immer nur so so;
Jetzt erst sind wir gar und gar
Ein wandelnder P. . ."

Flugel's British reticence leads him to substitute a row of dots for the word "Popo," which is German vernacular for buttocks. The stanza is difficult to translate literally; I have heard it rather freely paraphrased as follows:

The style before the last could pass,
But what's been done this year?
They've made of every stylish lass
A peripatetic rear.

In the last few years, by the way, there have been tentative and unsuccessful attempts to revive this fashion.

clares, is the look of immaturity, and to accord with this look all the characteristics of the mature figure are frowned on, including the full bosom. In Flugel's opinion, women lost as well as gained by the shift. When modesty abandoned the once-shrouded region of the legs and veiled the bosom, women were asserting their freedom, which was all to the good; at the same time, they relinquished some of the "erotic privileges" of femininity. All in all, the fashions of the twenties accentuated the body rather than the styles, idealized youth and not maturity, and substituted the limbs for the trunk as the center of erotic value.[2] In Flugel's opinion, a reaction from these styles would come very soon; signs of approaching change were already visible.

Flugel was of course correct. It took hardly less than a year, at the end of the twenties, for skirts to drop from close to the knees to a length almost touching the ankle. This was a change so abrupt, so radical, that it drew from the late William Bolitho the gloomy prediction that the new style would lead to obvious class distinctions among

[2] A series of futile attempts has been made by sociologists to construct a correlation between fashion and woman's social setting in various epochs of history. The argument that a crinoline is not a fashion of dress suited for work, but rather for luxury, may be correct, but does not explain why, even today, women's entry into the working world has not prevented their admiration for—and purchase of—evening dresses of the luxury type, and the 1951-52 versions of the crinoline. Certainly this last admits of no logical explanation; it was both inconvenient and expensive, and to dismiss it as a college-girl fashion only brings up additional unanswerable questions, such as: "What is the sociological distinction between the genus College-girl in Dungarees and the genus College-girl in Crinoline?" Neither does the argument explain why working women (surely not ladies of leisure) follow fashions which in succession expose different parts of the body.

Nor is fashion's emphasis on youth a purely sociological problem. Flugel calls this stress another form of variation in style, and points out that it has eliminated that rather strict boundary which once divided the child from the woman. Lengthening one's skirts, putting up one's hair, was once a privilege awaited with as much enthusiasm as mature women now put into the attempt to keep themselves looking like adolescents. The sexual and social value of maturity is low today, Flugel declares.

Sociology is simply not a substitute for psychology.

women, since only the daughters of the very rich could afford the leisurely—and incidentally more alluring—postures necessitated by the new skirts, and stenographers, housewives and factory girls would be forced for efficiency's sake to retain the practical short skirt. He was thoroughly wrong, but not in essence, for the distinction between evening and street lengths which was virtually standard practice in the thirties and forties and still exists today makes the same concession, if not really to efficiency, at least to the "proclamation of freedom" expressed in the modes of the twenties.

With the lengthened skirt came the "natural" waistline, which at first, while skirts remained long and moderately slim, was barely indicated. Succeeding fashions tightened the waist, introduced the flared (and again shortened) skirt, and in about the middle thirties brought the midriff, and consequently the breasts, into the spotlight. This emphasis on the midriff, borrowed from the Empire period, was an ingenious touch. It enabled fashion to transform the full-breasted look of maturity into the high-breasted look of youth, the "youthfulness" of a fashion seemingly having become a permanent requirement. The emphasized bosom and the small waist revived the corset and the brassière, articles which had fallen into comparative disuse during the flapper period. (Practically speaking, women renounced the idea of such artificial aids to the figure rather than the articles themselves; in a tactful advertisement dating from 1926 customers were offered "bandeaux" and "hip confiners" on the apparent theory that no one would recognize the symbols of bygone fashion under a new alias.)

Gradually, the flared skirt became both fuller and shorter, until by the outbreak of the second World War it was practically at knee length again. The return of the leg to the front of the stage brought a new nudity—that of the foot—via the open toe (symbolic?) and the skeleton sandal. There the fashion was forced to remain throughout the war-time period.

The "new look" followed almost immediately after the end of the war. Skirts dropped again, to a new low; necklines "plunged" accordingly; waistlines were smaller than ever. But nothing lasts; the violent upheaval in silhouette which changed women's outer appearance almost overnight began to undergo modification almost as soon as it was established. Skirts were shortened to a conservative mid-calf length, where they still remain. More than that, a diversity of silhouette became acceptable. The last few years in women's fashions might even be called the era of co-existence. The "pyramid," the pencil and the crinoline shapes, far from warring for supremacy, appear side by side under their ever-changing names in the pages of the fashion magazines and of course on the streets. So far from rigorous is style these days (1952) that at times the only requirements for a well-dressed woman seem to be a small waist, a full bosom, and a silly hat.

There have been some curious minor developments in the last few years, however. What would have been called "nakedness" a decade ago has done an excellent job of encroachment into formerly conservative locations, such as the city in the summer. The blouse that begins at the breasts—though usually paired with a jacket, more as a concession to etiquette than to morality—is a commonplace. The arm naked to the shoulder, once "wrong" except in the country, is now standard.

The "poodle" haircut is also a fashion of interest to our theme. The short hair of the flapper period was "masculine"; the equally short hair that is smart today is not. The difference, of course, is a matter of silhouette, both of head and of body; the flapper's Eton crop was straight-haired as well as short, while the girl of today wears her hair softly curled; the flapper's small head topped a straight, curveless body, while today's classic figure is all curves. The paradox here lies in the fact that the woman of this decade does without thinking twice about it what the flapper would have viewed as a "masculine prerogative" to be seized, and wears as a matter of course fashions the flapper would have thought "daringly immodest." To take an obvious example, compare today's stockingless legs with the rolled stockings of the twenties!

Flugel is quite correct—as far as he goes. My reservation pertains to the fact that he makes no distinction between "*appositional*" and "*constrictive*" elements in these fashions. I would define an appositional element in fashion thus: by emphasizing a rounded female organ (breast, buttocks or arm, as in the leg-of-mutton or puffed sleeve), or an oblong (legs), man's fear of the "castrated" horror is diminished. In direct contra-distinction, a constrictive element in fashion artificially *creates* something akin to castration. The wasp waistline of the Western woman, the bound foot of the Chinese woman,[3] are examples.

The question arises: Why should woman's fear-inspiring "castration" be artificially duplicated in fashion? If the premise is correct, and clothes are sexually attractive to man because of their fear-diminishing effect (upon their inventors!), then the synthetic *demonstratio ad oculos* of exactly that which inspired the fear is inexplicable. The seeming contradiction resolves itself when we remind ourselves of the unconscious repetition compulsion which plays so important a part in the establishment of the He-Man attitude. *Active* repetition of what has been *passively* endured in reality or in fantasy is the formula for eradication of a wound to self-esteem. Therefore, actively impos-

[3] There exists additional evidence that the constrictive quality of this Chinese fashion had direct sexual connotations. Havelock Ellis' correspondents claim that the contact between the crippled foot and the male sex organ is one of the most acute of pleasures.

ing an artificial symbolic castration, and passive subjection to its sight or threat, have quite different effects in man's unconscious.

A mixture of appositional and constrictive elements is seen in the "metal collar" worn by some African women and by the women of some hill tribes in upper Burma: artificial constriction of the throat is combined with creation of an artificial and unconsciously reassuring female penis. Flugel quotes Stanley as reporting on the ornaments worn by the wife of an African King: metal rings weighing between forty and eighty pounds encircled their necks. Weight was not the only discomfort involved. The metal rings absorbed the intense heat of the tropical climate, and in order to make them bearable water had to be poured on them at frequent intervals.

It is rather amusing to observe the mental contortions, both scientific and popular, which accompany attempts to explain *constrictive* fashions. The theorists have recognized, however, that this type of foolishness in fashion poses a problem. Havelock Ellis offers a typical interpretation in his *Psychology of Sex* (p. 21). He traces the custom of binding the feet of Chinese women back to the fact that the Chinese foot is characteristically small to begin with. The bound foot, therefore, exemplifies the familiar tendency to accentuate (and even exaggerate to the point of deformity) the beauty of racial characteristics. It is also an indication of the high sexual value put on the Chinese woman's naturally small foot. The basis of the practice is sexual attractiveness, he declares. So, too, the naturally small waist of the European woman becomes still more enticing to the European man when still further constricted by a tight corset.

Beauty, claimed Stendhal, is a promise of happiness. But what happiness (or, as Ellis has it, "sexual attractiveness") is to be found in constriction? Ellis was on the right track, partly, but all he could do was register rather than explain the peculiar fact that constrictive fashions are sexually attractive.

The popular explanation of the identical phenomenon is rather naive. Tradition has it that a Chinese Empress, reigning in about 1100 B.C., had a club foot. Not wanting to be unique in her deformity, she initiated the practice of binding women's feet.

I have not uncovered a corresponding "tradition" of a fat European Empress who wanted to torture her entourage by forcing them to wear corsets. But perhaps my search of the material was not sufficiently thorough.

The significance of both appositional and constrictive elements is confirmed by universal dreams, by some dances, and even, directly, by some of the fashions of old and extinct cultures.

A universal dream of *all* men (normal, neurotic and what not) is the appearance of a woman with a penis. Every analyst of experience has analyzed thousands of such dreams. The purpose of this type of dream is reassurance against castration fears: if woman has a penis of her own, the poor man can sleep contented, or at least unafraid. The woman will not castrate *him!*

The great popularity of the cancan—aside from its attraction as multiple exhibitionism—was primarily based on the *unconscious* "reassurance" provided by frequent glimpses of the buttocks, and the continuing sight of one leg waving in the air. Symbolically, the dance attested to man that woman "possesses" a penis.

And, to go back a few thousand years, the Minoan snake goddess offers the identical reassurance: she shows her breasts, has a snake in her hands, and boasts an artificial waistline so thoroughly constricted that it could rouse the professional jealousy of a modern corsetière.

Finally, perverse fetishism in males points in the same

direction. Fetishism[4] is a word with many connotations; in a strict sense, it means that an article of feminine *clothing* is singled out as the only sexual attraction. The real fetishist dispenses with the woman. He is quite satisfied with a shoe,[5] a stocking, a garter, a skirt, a slip, a brassière, etc. With these as his model, he masturbates; with women, he is impotent. Years ago, Freud found that the male's fetish unconsciously represents the fantasy of the female penis. Thus, the fetishist reassures himself against his own castration fears!

What happens to a woman when high fashion shuffles its seven basic ingredients, and chooses for emphasis a region which, in that woman's body, is not attractive? Or, even worse, what happens when a specific woman is too "fat" for the slim fashion line? The problem of "how to reduce" becomes subjectively all-important. Not only does the overweight woman look slightly out of place; to quote a patient, her weight, or the faulty distribution of her weight, is a hazard for the eye and purse, since most ready-made dresses are sized for slim women.

Reducing means sacrifice of the type of food which is subjectively most appreciated. That is hard enough, but there are women who are completely incapable of sticking

[4] The term, fetishism, is sometimes loosely used as denoting predilection for specific *parts* of the female body, e.g., "breast-fetishists," etc. These "half-fetishists" are only half-fugitives from the real woman. See an example of this type in Chapter Nine, in the case history of the half-fetishist for the color white. (pp. 214 et seq.)

[5] Ellis states (l.c., p. 17): "Among leading English novelists Hardy shows an unusual but by no means predominant interest in the feet and shoes of his heroines; see, e.g., the observations of the cobbler in *Under the Greenwood Tree,* Chapter III. A chapter in Goethe's *Wahlverwandtschaften* (Part I, Chapter II) contains an episode involving the charm of the foot and the kissing of the beloved's shoe."

The latter episode has been analytically explained in Dr. Eduard Hitschmann's well-known study on Goethe: "Goethe may have been a fetishist; once he wrote to his wife that she should send him her dance-torn shoes. 'A pretty foot,' he once declared, 'is a great gift of Nature!' "

to a prescribed diet. There has been a great deal of talk, recently, about the psychological reasons which prevent some women from reducing. Although most of these discussions point in the right direction, the reasons adduced are rather naive and confused.

It is pointless to speak of emotional conflicts in general, unless one goes on from there to point to specific ones. The motif most frequently adduced of late is the equation: love equals getting food from mother. Under normal conditions, this is true enough. But when dealing with neurotic women who cannot reduce, this formula bypasses a vital consideration. In these women, there has not been a simple substitution; there has been an unconscious masochistic elaboration. The wish to be refused is therefore paramount; the wish to get in superabundance is installed merely as secondary defense. These women overeat because their secondary defense is their modus vivendi. For this reason, the interpretation that they "want to get" in order to make up for infantile disappointments is both ineffectual and misleading. The penalty follows the mistake: these allegedly "cured" women revert to their old pattern of overeating.

There is another reason for the confusion that characterizes the prevailing interpretations. They mistake overlying strata for fundamental ones. Of course, the unconscious fantasy of being a barrel of fat may also (in specific cases) mean imitation of the mother's pregnancy. The same applies to other superficial motives.

This fact is decisive: Without analysis of the masochistic-oral wish to be refused, only secondarily warded off with the wish to get food in superabundance, the neurotic reaction cannot be permanently removed. How pronounced the masochistic substructure is can be seen in the ambiguity of the "getting" defense: these women make themselves into the kind of "spectacle" that people automatically avoid looking at.

It should be remembered that the child's gustatory history starts with one bland food—milk. By the time he is an adult, he is a gourmet or at least a lover of a *variety* of foods; rightly or wrongly, everyone considers his own taste exquisite. At least mentally, he smacks his lips and "enjoys good food," whatever that means.

How and why is that transition accomplished? Besides the obvious role played by the taste buds, a psychological factor enters the picture: exactly *because* milk was "tasteless" (or more or less neutral in taste) a desire for an exaggerated variety of tasty foods is later cultivated. Once more, what is accomplished is deflation of the value of what mother had to offer. That bit of pseudo-aggression helps support the culinary industries, besides making for "delicious cooking."

This can best be studied in cases of neurotic "simplicity" in eating.

A young girl from a wealthy Western family, in New York alone to take violin lessons, used to get her allowance by mail on the first and fifteenth of every month. By the third and by the seventeenth of each month, she had spent the bulk of her money, foolishly, and for the remaining twenty-six days of the month "starved" on a diet of cottage cheese and milk. In this simple way, she managed to prove how "unjust" her family (mother) really was.

A wealthy young man had for years been eating only one dish—tuna-fish salad. "It is nourishing and inexpensive," he said. His whole life, however, had also been unconsciously devoted to proving his belief that "mother starves me."

Another man went through a series of food fads only to end up with the following routine: he lived for three days on nothing but black coffee ("I'm not hungry,") and waited for "real appetite." After the third day, he became "really hungry," overate, and discovered that the food "did not agree" with him. Then the same cycle was repeated. He, too, was elaborating on the theme: "bad mother starves me."

The opposite extreme is represented by people with "exquisite" culinary tastes: they prepare their own food, thus "proving" that they are "autarchic." This is especially pronounced in men who are good cooks.

The masochistic pseudo-aggressive refinement is not always so pronounced. Some of these neurotics are simply overeaters ("He eats like a pig," complained the wife of such a patient.) Preventively, they counteract the starvation which their mothers allegedly imposed and which they still expect. This is apparent in small details: they cannot wait until their portion is meted out, they eat from the salad bowl and the meat platter.

Vegetarians and food-faddists in general are a special subdivision of that group. Using some foolish rationalization as cover, they concoct a list of foods to be shunned, mostly meat. They are opposed to the slaughter of animals; via unconscious identification, they are the slaughtered animals. Accused by their inner conscience of overdimensional psychic masochism, they defend themselves with cannibalistic fantasies, secondarily warded off with humanitarian protestations. Other neurotics restrict their food intake according to hypochondriacal principles. The results are identical: "someone" refuses them their favorite dishes. Whether this "someone" is an organ of the body "placed by some freak of nature (mother) inside," or the basis of restraint is "ideological," as it is with the food faddists, the point is the same. It is the "bad mother" who is denying the child, and not the poor masochist who is being masochistic. A perfect alibi!

Every reducing cure, regardless of whether it is self-elected or recommended by a physician for aesthetic or medical reasons, puts the patient's "willpower" to a severe test. Invariably, the candidate for reducing discovers that he must abstain from his favorite foods. He is constantly tempted by the "forbidden" food, and therefore fights a never-ending battle.

Lord Byron's famous "thinning campaign," a well-known literary example, is apropos here. The poet started taking reducing cures while he was at Cambridge; when he conceived the idea that he could not bear to see a woman eating at his table is not known. Byron was quite consistent in this rejection of the mother-image, and either dined alone or in male company. The connection with "injustices" can also be established: he interrupted his strict diet immediately after his ostracism in England, at the time he was living in exile in Venice. Only in the last year, when his fame returned, did he resume his diet.[6]

In studying patients who are losing the battle "on the reducing front," as a witty patient expressed it, it is clear that these people do not consider abstinence from a specific food as a rational measure during reducing, but as a deep "injustice." Superficially, they react as do children when they are denied or forbidden candy. Unconsciously, they concoct an infantile neurotic situation of denial, and react with fury, or transgress the prescribed diatetic rules.

The most convincing example I have observed was that of a very good-looking woman in the early twenties who made herself unattractive by overweight. At the same time, she had irrational conflicts with her child, a girl of four, all about—food. The child was a poor eater; capitalizing on her mother's loud and furious insistence that the undernourished-looking child eat, the little girl made it a fighting point, simply by refusing. Their battle, in turn, infuriated

[6] For elaboration, see Dr. Arthur Wormhoudt's excellent book *The Demon Lover* (Exposition Press, New York, 1949, pp. 141 ff.), where the author applies, with great skill, my clinical results on writers, summarized in my book *The Writer and Psychoanalysis*, Doubleday, New York, 1950.

the husband, who took the child's part, yelling, "Leave her alone!"

The patient's technique in achieving overweight was simplicity itself. She ate too much. Her overeating was an inner defense against the reproach of conscience: "You want to be refused." The inner defense read: "Quite the contrary. I want to get. I eat voraciously." [7] In the relation to her child the woman *unconsciously* performed a peculiar "negative magic gesture." This was in answer to another reproach of conscience, to the effect that her masochistic accusations of her mother, on the score of alleged starvation, were unjustified. Unconsciously, she retorted: "Quite true, but the food was given without love, and as a mere bothersome duty." Two decades after the event, the child in the patient reverses the roles in the dining-room scene: *she* acts the "bad" mother, with her own *daughter* representing—*herself!*

A woman of thirty-eight stated, in analytic treatment, that she could never muster enough "willpower" to carry on a reducing diet. "I have a marked tendency towards obesity and must reduce. I tried at least twenty times—always in vain. First I get depressed, then furious. The end result is that after a few days I eat more than before. I seem to be incapable of carrying out my decision, though I am rather concerned with my appearance."

Another woman, aged twenty-six, observed that when reducing she became deeply depressed. "I avoid reducing, since at such times life seems void of pleasure and I am really a candidate for suicide. Not only is everything colorless but I start thinking about all my defeats in life, all the lost possibilities. The only way out is—eating."

In all these, and a long series of other cases, I observed that orally regressed neurotics are incapable of reducing

[7] The woman lost twenty pounds in short order, once she "digested" the interpretation.

exactly because they are still unconsciously confusing the *rational* and consciously approved act of reducing with the *irrational* equation: lack of food equals starvation imposed by the cruel, pre-Oedipal mother. Eating has for these neurotics the unconscious meaning of a new "slave rebellion" defense: "I'm independent of mother, and don't want to be masochistically refused."

The conclusion is clear: some neurotics are incapable of reducing their weight without first having "straightened out," analytically, their unsettled infantile accounts with the first provider of food, mother.[8]

[8] For elaboration, see *Basic Neurosis,* Chapter VII.

7 Dresses and Three Types of Reputation

NOBLESSE OBLIGE—nobility involves duties—was the slogan of the old aristocracy. It was a moral slogan, promising fidelity to moral duties, but in actual performance it was more often a self-imposed obligation to dress with splendor than to act with charity. In any case, until modern times, the clothes worn by the higher brackets were designed to make immediately evident their membership in a self-appointed elite. The *reputation of belonging* had to be sartorially expressed, and sartorially certified. This also applied to the members of the guilds.

The aristocracy of birth was displaced by the aristocracy of capital, and the outward symbol of belonging to the new elite, the elite of power, was again expressed sartorially. Charles Lamb alluded to it: "In the indication of female poverty there can be no disguise; no woman dresses below herself from caprice."

But this was only the beginning. Wealth, after all, is of two kinds: either inherited, or self-made. How were the members of the entrenched "aristocracy of money" to distinguish themselves from the nouveau riche? The answer to the nouveau riche was the development of the "second generation" type. In *Money and Emotional Conflicts,* I described the difference between the two types:

This . . . neurotic (the "second generation" type), out of principle, dresses in a shabby fashion (leading "idiosyncrasy" is in the matter of dress; one often mistakes the millionaire for the beggar). He lives frugally, watching his necessary expenses with great care. Careful, cautious, he is proud of his meagre way of life and looks with contempt upon the nouveau riche. He constantly uses the phrase, "I cannot afford it." He is pathologically suspicious lest someone "take advantage of him." He worships the very act of not spending money. His fear mounts close to panic at the thought of losing his money. He constantly claims that both government expenditure and taxes are ruinous (March is his worst month). His pride is concentrated in the conviction that only a fool spends money without long deliberation: (he, of course, thank God, is not such a fool). If one listens to him: the pleasure in life consists of disguising the fact of possession of money, of looking askance at spendthrifts and their extravagances (to him, practically the whole world), and, finally, of warding off the repeated, never-ceasing attempts of rascals desirous of exploiting him. He never offers more than forty to fifty per cent of any stated purchase price. He is a firm believer in the act of impressing and intimidating one with the sheer weight of the *reputation* of possessing money. The moment a person allows himself to be intimidated or impressed by his money, he despises the person as a nonentity and, given the opportunity, squeezes him mercilessly.

The only way in which one can hold one's own with this type of neurotic is to call his "bluff," thus showing him that you are *not* impressed. But to call his bluff with a bluff of your own will prove of no avail; it is useless to fake or pretend with him, for, like a child, he has a very acute sense of whether a person actually sees through him or not.

The "parvenue type": This type lives in constant fear that people might not believe he is well-off. The phrase "I cannot afford it" never comes to his lips. He is a "flashy" dresser, buys only the very latest, overpays, overtips. He looks down upon, really despises, the unsuccessful person, takes considerable pleasure in poking fun at him. In general, he comes from the "wrong side of the railroad tracks," but always attempts to disguise the fact (exceptions being the overstressing of the "self-made" attitude). His ambitions are conventional; he is a social climber and a snob. Easily impressed, especially by the static wealth of the second generation type, he admires money and has to prove constantly to himself and others that he possesses it, and can afford to spend it. Inwardly he is as stingy as the second generation type, however his inner necessity of proving that he is financially a "big shot" overshadows his greed.

The parvenue type is a free spender for display purposes in public; in private, at home, we find him to be a merciless miser. If you are not impressed by his public display, the bubble of pretense collapses almost immediately and the primitive unadulterated personality comes to the fore.

Once I analyzed a man and his wife simultaneously; he came from the "right" side, she from the borderline of the "wrong" side, of the tracks. He had inherited a great deal of money; she, in her profession, earned quite large sums. At one time, they received a worthless unframed painting as a gift from a stingy relative. The painful irony of the situation was the fact that they both felt the necessity of displaying the painting in their apartment (neither wished to "insult" the wealthy relative). But even more painful than this was the fact that they had to buy a frame for the worthless canvas. At the framer's the following scene took place: the dealer quoted them a price of twelve dollars. At the mention of the sum, the husband immediately told the dealer with great indignation: "We cannot afford to pay twelve dollars for the frame."

His wife, relating the incident to me in analysis, said: "I nearly died of shame. I have known this dealer for years. He respects me for my social position. Why must my husband make a show of our financial circumstances in front of him?"

Here, in a nutshell, we see the differing approach to the phrase: "I cannot afford it." He, being wealthy from early childhood on, simply meant, "I can, of course, afford it, but I don't want to be made into a sucker." She, in her parvenue manner, was shamed by his use of the phrase, and could think of it only as an admission of poverty to the dealer. In fact, I am sure that under no circumstances would the phrase "I cannot afford it" ever come from her lips.

The distinction between these two types sometimes leads to amusing misunderstandings. A dress manufacturer of the parvenue variety had his analytic appointment just before the hour of a middle-aged New England millionaire. One day the manufacturer, whose constant complaint was that I was exploiting him financially, met this wealthy New Englander in the elevator. At his next appointment he stormed into my office, exclaiming indignantly: "Don't tell me that this shabby, dilapidated school teacher can afford your fee!"—"We would both be very well satisfied if we had to share the interest on the interest on the money of that shabbily dressed man," was my deflating answer.

Clothing plays a part even in the establishment of that indefinable essential, reputation. Reputation can be divided into three categories; category No. I is the conscious feeling that one "belongs." An example is the familiar phenomenon of the woman who identifies with members of a higher social stratum by imitating their way of dressing. More complicated is the reputation built on the *conscious mental picture* every person has of himself. That picture has *unconscious motivations*, but the reverberations are conscious. In women, they lead to Reputation No. II—that of the mental impression every woman wants to convey via her clothes.

Some years ago, Jeanne Singer, the excellent novelist and author of *This Festive Season*, published an amusing study on seven types of "feminine clothes as hieroglyphs." [1] These seven types are: 1) the chic, 2) the would-be chic, 3) the expensive dowdy, 4) the careless dowdy, 5) the pretty-pretty, 6) the arty, and 7) the well-dressed.

To be chic, Miss Singer declares, calls for competence to begin with, but also for self-discipline (for the sake of her figure), for ruthlessness (she can allow herself no leeway in what she acquires or discards), for alertness (she must

[1] "One Woman's Hat," *Harper's Magazine*, May, 1946.

be among the first to spot a trend). Her motto, like the late Mayor La Guardia's, must be "patience and fortitude": patience for interminable fittings and matchings, fortitude not only in diet but in wearing fashions unsuited to either climate or anatomy.

The "would-be chic" are failures because they select the wrong models; their hats are too smart, they wear too many jewels. To this group belongs, also, the weak and sweet imitator, who is always on her way but never arrives at her goal.

There are three main subdivisions of dowdiness, according to Miss Singer's survey. There is the *expensively dowdy* woman who shies away from beauty in clothes, and substitutes quality. Her aim is to appear unmistakeably as "a lady," one who need neither please nor advertise, and who is above pleasure. This type ignores both color and the shape of the human body. The *careless dowdy* woman may own clothes that are either in the best of taste or the worst, but the effect is always the effect of her sloppiness—the slip or shoulder-strap showing, the torn stocking or the spot on the skirt—and not the effect of the costume itself. The *indifferent dowdy*, the woman who buys clothes only when she needs them for warmth or covering, and who then purchases the first article that fits, is extremely rare.

The "pretty-pretty" category dresses to play up her favorite feature, her hair or eyes or complexion, instead of dressing to suit the fashion.

The "arty" woman is the one whose hair is long when everyone's hair is worn short, whose skirts are full when the fashionable silhouette is slim, who wears Chinese jackets and Russian hats when nobody else does. Miss Singer considers this a way of emphasizing intellectuality, individuality and emancipation, and points out that for an ugly woman there is "strong justification" in such a way of dressing, for flaunting physical unattractiveness can make it enticing rather than repellent.

The last (seventh) category is, in Miss Singer's euphemism, the "well-dressed." She is full of praise for the ideal, but no psychological evaluation is supplied.

In *Reputation No. III,* the decisive point is fully unconscious, and its reverberations are highly misleading to the bearer.

In my opinion, the way a woman dresses has intimate connections with the unconscious impression of herself which she wishes to convey, first to her inner conscience, and later to the environment. This is a complex picture, based on *infantile repressed ideas of oneself, narcissistic identifications* dating from early childhood, *inner defenses, guilt, compromises, renunciations.* To repeat the formulation, dress is an unconscious technique used in the manufacture of "reputation." *The onlooker is asked to attest to the efficiency of the inner hoax.*[2]

[2] Whether or not this "third type of reputation" which every person must maintain for his own benefit is connected with mechanisms which have become known as "body-image" is problematical. Schilder (*The Image and Appearance of the Human Body*) defines the latter as "the picture of our own body which we form in our mind, that is to say the way in which the body appears to ourselves." What I have in mind is obviously a consequence of the infantile ego ideal. The "body-image" may or may not use some of these features; the point is unclarified. On the other hand, Schilder claims that the "body-image can shrink or expand . . . It is a new proof of the lability of the body-image that whatever comes into connection with the surface of the body is more or less incorporated into the body . . . Whatever article of clothing we put on immediately becomes a part of the body-image and is filled with narcissistic libido . . . Since clothes are a part of the body schema, they gain the same significance as part of the body and can have the same significance as part of the body." (pp. 202-3)

As far as the individual is concerned, the picture built up of oneself by the ego ideal (one's own picture of one's real self) is a distorted one. The picture is composed of—sit venia verbo—unreal material: infantile megalomania, plus infantile expectations growing out of this infantile megalomania, plus filtered images of infantile identifications. This triad naturally conflicts with reality, even in the best of cases. Since clothes are *also*

The initial thought which prompted my deductions and conclusions on unconscious reputation in general[3] came from an amusing incident involving a friend. This friend, while staying at his country cottage, was given charge of a few letters, to be delivered to the postoffice two miles away. Again and again before he left he was reminded of the letters. As an added precaution, they were not handed to him, but deposited in the car. When he returned, he was repeatedly asked by his whole family whether he had forgotten to mail the letters. Ironically, the defendant remarked: "I don't know why I have the reputation of forgetting to mail letters. I also had the reputation of being an 'unmarriageable person,' and I've been married exactly twenty-four years. Perhaps I ought to divorce my wife to live up to my reputation." More seriously, he concluded: "Which all goes to show that all reputation is the bunk."

Well, what is a "reputation"? It is, first of all, a simplification—and one made by simpletons. The result is a superficiality clothed in an exaggeration.

No one who appreciates the infinite diversity of the human psyche can think of a person's reputation as an assessment of his total character. At best, it is a convenient method of pigeonholing—a method favored by "simple" people with a strong streak of malice, people who feel the constant need to sort and classify and label complicated phenomena. The label, which strips the phenomenon of both mystery and depth, is a reassurance against the inner discomfiture which arises from fear and ignorance. Out of

---

chosen in accordance with the dictates of this unconscious triad, ridiculous discrepancies between intention and effect are common. If one goes further, and takes into account the problems of inner guilt and inner defenses, e.g., psychic masochism, it becomes obvious that there is a substantial difference between the custom tailor's appraisal of his customer and the very same customer's image of himself.

[3] "Psychology of Reputation in Neurotics," *The Psychiatric Quarterly*, 22:680-684, 1948.

inner necessity, the label must represent a distortion and an exaggeration.

Reputation, therefore, can be defined as an inflated simplification, manufactured by simpletons. Is that all?

The entire concept of reputation contains a decisive error: the assumption that an individual's "real self" can be *directly* revealed by his actions and failures to act. The knowledge that unconscious mechanisms prompt these actions refutes that naive assumption.

Taking actions and omissions of actions at face value is an ingenuous technique long ago discarded by psychiatrists. But the advent of modern psychiatry, profoundly influenced by Freud's discoveries, substituted for it still another assumption, which holds that the unconsciousness enters consciousness in a direct form, thinly covered by a defense. In my opinion, *an unconscious wish never enters consciousness directly: only the secondary defense against the unconscious content appears on the psychic surface.*

The problem hinges on a difference of opinion regarding the structure of the neurotic symptom in particular and personality traits in general. The older and accepted formulation postulated a three-layer structure: an unconscious wish (layer 1), meeting the veto of the superego (layer 2), is cloaked in a defense mechanism (layer 3), which then reaches consciousness in the form of a rationalization. According to my clinical experience, the structure has *five layers.* The process begins when an unconscious wish (layer 1) is warded off by a superego reproach (layer 2); as a result the unconscious ego institutes a defense (layer 3). This first defense—which invariably changes the original wish into its opposite, thus constituting "admission of the lesser intrapsychic crime"—is in its turn always warded off once more with a second veto from the superego (layer 4). It then becomes necessary for the unconscious ego to put forward a second defense (layer 5). This final layer consists of a denial and an alibi, plus acceptance of punishment for the "lesser crime" previously admitted to. Only the reverberations of the second defense (layer 5) become visible (covered with rationalizations) in the neurotic symptom, sign, personality structure.

The problem is elaborated at length in *The Basic Neurosis* and *The Superego.* To prove the universality of my formulation, the latter book contains an analysis of fifty human reactions, deliberately chosen at random.

Taking the complexity of these scientific differences of opinion into consideration, one can easily imagine the confusion produced in laymen by *their* misinterpretations of the whole subject. Benjamin Stolberg's witty definition of an expert as "a person who avoids the small errors as he sweeps on to the grand fallacy" precisely describes those hopeful interpreters whose proving grounds are cocktail parties. On the amateur level at least, these "experts" are responsible for perpetuating the confusion of unconscious wishes with the double sentinel of inner alibis and defenses.

And that is precisely the pitfall that yawns before the manufacturers of reputation. In the most illustrative of cases, they confuse wish and double defense, thus arriving at precisely the conclusions *unconsciously* desired by the object of their observation. They are like detectives who fall for the false clue planted by the criminal.

A patient of mine, a scientist, was reputed by his colleagues to be arrogant, megalomaniacal and unsociable. The man was intolerant of criticism; unconsciously, he interpreted every objection as an accusation of passivity. Since he had a good-sized stock of inner passivity, this quality provided the inner conscience with an excellent means of torture. Instead of realistically accepting human aggression as inevitable, the scientist unconsciously considered it "injustice." To counteract this inner danger, he created (also unconsciously) a defense mechanism consisting of an attitude of boredom, aggression and aloofness. He provoked people's anger, refused their invitations, and separated himself from them. He then complained about his isolation. Inwardly, he preferred to take the secondary blame for his pseudo-aggression—the "lesser crime"—in order to disguise his real "crime"—psychic masochism. His colleagues, of course, took his behavior at face value. Because his opinion of them seemed deprecating, they countered by calling him supercilious and slightly paranoiac. The man's behavior was obviously self-damaging—for who can afford to provoke and reject his environment in toto? —nevertheless, this tendency was not remarked. Complaints centered on his "aggression." In short, the patient had managed to imbue the outer world with the precise impression of himself he wished to use as a defense before his inner tribunal and its "presiding officer," his superego. His colleagues, who obligingly endowed him with a bad reputation and completely overlooked the fact that his pseudo-aggression covered a deeper layer of masochism, became weapons in his intrapsychic battle.

His colleagues' narcissism, which led them to misjudge the situation, added not a little to the margin of error in this patient's reputation.

Another patient, reputedly a dangerous fellow, made frequent appearances in the headlines. Even his enemies tended to surrender to him when they were faced with open controversy; his biting sarcasm and his ability to pin the adversary down were intimidating. His very presence made even his collaborators uneasy. This man came into analysis because of pathological jealousy. Behind this, it soon became evident, was a strong *feminine* unconscious identification. But that, too, was merely a defense; his "real" crime was psychic masochism and therefore oral regression.

The margin of error between reputation and reality in

this case was the confusion between unconscious repressed wish and double unconscious defense mechanism.

A third patient, a well-known writer, was noted for his understanding of the psychology of love. He had achieved this reputation through the publication of a series of books in which the theme of love predominated. He entered analysis because of *homosexuality!*

His reputation was built on a flimsy foundation, but hardly more so than that of writers on love in general. Such writers are neurotics of a specific type;[4] they produce a "self-cure" as long as they retain the ability to write. Their self-cure is the artistic product itself, for it is a secondary defense mechanism. Although they have no suspicion of the fact, their work directly expresses, not their conscious or unconscious wishes, but their *secondary defenses against* unconscious wishes. These people do not experience tender love;[5] they are capable only of a deep masochistic attachment to an object invariably "unworthy" or unattainable. The rationalization follows: "I am not incapable of love; love is too small for me." The result is that such writers produce books extolling exaggerated pictures of romanticized love, or they go to the other extreme, making their heroines nymphomaniacs and their heroes neurotic wolves.

"O, love will make a dog howl in rhyme," wrote the Elizabethan dramatist, John Fletcher in *Queen of Corinth.* But the cause of the howling is not love but lack of it; the howling is a masochistic complaint at a situation of lovelessness unconsciously self-created. When a poet or an artist speaks of "love," he is referring to the palimpsest which overlies that repressed desire.

The prevailing monumental confusion about the psychol-

[4] See *The Writer and Psychoanalysis* (l.c.).
[5] See *Unhappy Marriage and Divorce,* International Universities Press, New York, 1946.

ogy of writers accounted for a good deal of the margin of error in evaluating the third patient's reputation.

A reputation is not easy to shake off, once it is firmly established. No action is admitted by the environment to be out of character; if the action is contrary to the stereotype, it is explained away as a conscious and therefore false effort on the part of the victim. The effect of human malice should not be forgotten; "reputation" is primarily a word with negative connotations. "Good" reputations are decidedly rare; even evidence of virtue tends to be taken with a grain of salt, while rumors of dishonorable traits tend to be accepted as evidence.

There is one exception to the empirical fact that reputation pertains exclusively to the inner defense mechanism. This is "correct" conduct in finance and in sexual relations. Abiding by the accepted standards of conduct in these matters may be the result of a normally functioning conscience; it may also be due to the realization that it is an obvious advantage to conform to the norm.

Reputation is not automatically and effortlessly acquired; it results from the successful—though *unconscious*—imposition of a specific inner defense on the environment. In accepting these superficial trappings at face value, the environment renders a real service to the pseudo-victim.

Reputation is an act of unconscious misconception, unconsciously imposed on the environment in order to strengthen one's own inner defenses. The purpose of this unconsciously determined technique is to produce a smokescreen which will shut the inner self away from the view of others, and from one's own view. Reputation is an external reinforcement put to use in the inner battle of the conscience.

The malicious outsider, to whom "He acts that way, so he must be that way" is irrefutable logic, cannot know that he has been the dupe of his victim's inner defenses.

Nor can he know that the external disadvantage of bad reputation may sometimes be outweighed by intrapsychic advantage to the victim. "Bad" reputation helps many psychic masochists to maintain their psychic balance.[6]

Merely because feminine clothes are a weapon in a subdivision of unconsciously self-created "reputation" does not mean that one can say, "Her clothes show she is that kind of person." This direct conclusion, since it confuses the inner wish with the double inner defense, is entirely misleading.

The real interconnections are extremely complicated, as clinical experience proves. The following examples have been gathered from observations of analytic patients.

Case 1: Mrs. A., a three-time loser in marriage,[7] was one of the "would-be chic," to use Miss Singer's classification. Her expensive ensembles were always marred by one ornament too many. Her peculiar lack of taste, it developed, was an *unconscious attempt to caricature her mother.* The "would-be" quality thus represented a pseudo-aggressive accusation against her long-dead mother; the accusation covered a more deeply repressed masochistic attachment. Her "real self," obviously, was not expressed in her dress; the caricature which she executed by means of her clothes was an anachronistic *secondary defense* against her deep masochistic attachment to her mother.

Case 2: Miss B., a girl of seventeen, and daughter of a wealthy family, always came to her appointments shabbily dressed. (She was in treatment because of a personality

[6] Reputation should not be confused with the results of advertising. A wit has defined the difference: "Reputation is something you get without pay, but later have to pay dearly for; advertising must be paid for from the start." It should also be clear that this analysis applies only to people who are accepted in their specific communities with at least a minimum of objectivity. It does not apply to situations in which specific prejudices obscure the picture from first to last.

[7] See *Divorce Won't Help* and *Conflict in Marriage* (l.c.).

neurosis, manifesting itself in constant injustice-collecting.) Her "careless-dowdy" appearance was explained with the blunt statement: "I have nothing to wear." In a meeting with the girl *and* her parents, the truth was revealed. The girl had literally dozens of expensive dresses in her closet. She wore none of them. Indeed, she had torn and soiled some of them so that they could not be worn, in order to back up her complaint that her parents would not give her any clothes. In other words, this was the masochistic mechanism of injustice-collecting, used overtime.[8]

Her shabby clothes expressed, not her real personality, but her secondary defense mechanism, covering the masochistic substructure.

Case 3: Mrs. C. was the daughter of a famous beauty and fashion "queen." Mother and daughter were frequently taken for sisters. The mother was cosmetically ageless; the daughter, sartorially, was in the ranks of the "indifferent dowdy." She was "disinterested in clothes." She made herself artificially unattractive; for instance, she wore thick glasses in spite of having normal vision. This infuriated the mother and the husband.

An unconscious guilt, it appeared, was involved here. Since Mrs. C. had been in Oedipal competition with her mother in early childhood, she "solved" her aggressive problem with *inner guilt and renunciation:* "You have no right to be like mother, and replace her." Her drab clothing represented only the outward appearance of that guilt, plus the defensive inner irony: "Only a stupid woman like mother pays so much attention to clothes." Behind these defenses, the more deeply buried masochistic layer could be found.

Case 4: Mrs. D. wore "masculine" clothes; her suits and topcoats looked as if they had been borrowed from the

[8] See *The Basic Neurosis* (l.c.).

Police Department. She hated furs and feminine touches. Her exterior was that of a thoroughly masculine woman. Analysis revealed nothing of that kind. Nothing in her way of dressing was her own choice. Her *husband*—unconsciously a passive-feminine weakling—"*dressed her.*" Mrs. D.'s clothes reflected her husband's struggle with unconscious femininity. And to this husband Mrs. D. was frantically (and masochistically) submissive.

Case 5: Miss E. came to a consultation in the company of her fiancé. The first impression made by this good-looking girl was that she was color-blind. She was a walking color wheel, showing all the colors of the spectrum and all possible combinations of these colors. She wore Tyrolean red stockings with green embroidery, an orange dress, a loud green blouse, a bright yellow belt, etc. One might have guessed that besides being color-blind, she was trying to imitate the magnificent colors of the jungle, but had combined them badly. Very soon it became obvious that her "arty" way of dressing was an *inner accusation* against her upbringers. She was the daughter of an American missionary in Burma, and had spent the first twelve years of her life in the Far East. Clearly, masochistic-exhibitionistic tendencies were involved in her caricature of fashion, which more superficially had a pseudo-aggressive cover.

Case 6: Mrs. F. represented a variant Miss Singer missed in her subdivision under "indifferent dowdy": the woman who has *resigned from the feminine sex*. Though only in her early thirties, Mrs. F. was a partner in an "inactive" marriage. Both she and her husband, years before, had retired from sex, and tortured each other with violent reproaches of the masochistic injustice-collecting type. Mrs. F.'s dresses were impersonal, indifferent, timeless. Her appearance combined resignation with the reproach, "Nobody loves me," directed against the duality, husband-mother.

Once more, the pseudo-aggressive defense was executed via dress. In inner reality, Mrs. F. did not wish to be loved, but to be rejected.

Case 7: Mrs. G., a gold-digger[9] if there ever was one, had satisfied her early ambitions by finally achieving a mink coat, a penthouse, and a substantial bank account. Now she wished to devote her life to higher aims. Her idea was to become a successful actress. She had some small talent, but her plans did not include any attempt to develop it. Instead, she looked for "short cuts" to the stage, and started a series of "directed affairs" with influential personages in and around the theater. All this strategy got her was a succession of bed parties, frequently with impotent men, and promises of "connections." During one of these affairs, in which one of these men kept her on tenterhooks for months, she entered analysis.

The first impression was that of a good-looking woman, expensively dressed, but obviously taking a *demi-mondaine as prototype.* Behind this was discernible an unconscious accusation directed against the mother. After the masochistic substructure had been worked out, the patient's appearance changed. She began to "hate" everything "cheap" and "low." During this transitory phase, the patient adopted a new "rolc," to which, again, she fitted her actions and her clothes. This time her rather naive notions of the "lady as prototype" were in the foreground. Interestingly enough, Mrs. G. did *not* imitate real people in either her demi-mondaine or lady period. Each time, she followed her *distorted narcissistic fantasies of the chosen prototype.*

The "really well-dressed woman," although comparatively rare, should not escape scrutiny. These women, roughly speaking, fall into two types: the *normal,* and the *pseudo-normal.*

[9] See *Money and Emotional Conflicts* (l.c.).

The pseudo-normal type may be a neurotic (generally suffering from masochistic personality neurosis) with a normal corner in her ego which has not been submerged by neurosis, or she may be maintaining the prototype of the well-dressed woman for unconscious reasons. When the masochistic "defendant" is accused by conscience of psychic masochistic "crimes," either identification, or counter-identification with mother can be used to answer the reproach.

Last but not least, there *are* normal women with good taste.

An anonymous wit once defined a diplomat as a man who remembers a lady's birthday but forgets her age. *Mutatis mutandis*, feminine sartorial taste can be defined as the ability to achieve an effect that is visible without being conspicuous. In the great majority of neurotic women, the whole problem of clothes is subsumed in the neurotic process. For these women, the styles do not really change. Regardless of the year or the season, they go right on dressing themselves in their unconscious defense mechanisms.

8 *Clothes, Children of Man's Fear, Become Independent*

In the remote past, clothes were forced upon women—by men. There is a Latin proverb warning the buyer to beware; there is another familiar tag (Timeo Danaos et dona ferentes), to put the beneficiary of a gift on the alert; there was no proverb to warn man of the consequences—to themselves—of the dubious gift they presented to women. The average man unconsciously paraphrases an old saying every day of his life, and tells himself, "Clothes break—not make—the man." Some of his bitterest complaints center about his wife's extravagance in dress, and her "silly" preoccupation with fashion. It is a far cry from man's repressed genetic-historic viewpoint on clothes to his actual, practical opinion of them. And, to add a final ironic touch, he is of course unaware that he himself (meaning his forebears) was the inventor of this instrument of marital discord.

To make the situation more difficult all around, his invention became "independent," and clothes now seem to have a life of their own. "My wife," said a patient, "has a more intimate affair with fashion than she has with her husband. Why, if I ask her to change even a detail, she starts a violent quarrel because I am trying to infringe on her personality. If there's some idiotic fashion change, she is the first to follow it, like a willing slave. I've quoted

Oscar Wilde to her again and again: 'Fashion is a form of ugliness so intolerable that women have to alter it every six months.' As you can well imagine, my darling wife is not impressed."

Fashion has become a *science, though one which cannot be defined.* When I started to gather information on fashion, styles, and colors, I was surprised by a duality of factors: every well-dressed woman had very precise ideas on the subject; not one of these well-dressed women was capable of expressing her ideas. Practically speaking, all their formulations amounted to was the commonplace dead end: "You just feel it." I had been meeting this identical exasperating statement—"I just feel it"—in the course of my clinical investigations of writers. Where writers were concerned, I finally decided the answer was quite reasonable; since writers create from their unconscious, it is more intelligent for them to have recourse to "feelings" than to resort to silly rationalizations. The question then arose: In the case of the average fashion-obsessed woman, are we confronted with the identical—though not creative—circumstances?

The following guides to the mysterious "rules of fashion" were requested and obtained under most favorable conditions: I approached the problem with humility, admitting my complete ignorance, and thus excluding any possible competition. I made it clear, as well, that I was familiar only with some of the unconscious reasons for fashion, and that my judgments of good or bad taste in women's clothes were based on the familiar naïveté, "I know nothing about it, but I know what I like." To make the experiment even more propitious, my informants were exclusively women to whom even their female enemies conceded "sartorial taste." Moreover, they were all women of above-average intelligence and culture. Finally, I was consulting not only amateurs, but professionals and semi-professionals, for many of those questioned were editors, designers, or were artistically-sartorially creative women.

In spite of all these paper advantages, the story still boiled down to: "There are no rules; you just feel it." [1]

Having accepted this rule, with resignation, I asked whether—within the framework of the inexplicable—it was not possible to outline some minor but explicit pointers. This, the Board of Experts conceded, could be done. Unfortunately, when the results were in, no two informants agreed on "explicit rules."

I asked each of these women (and three men, for good measure) to answer the following general questions:

1. What is your definition of today's well-dressed woman?

2. What are the typical mistakes in dress, made by "lack of taste"?

3. What regulates a woman's choice of color combinations in the dress-ensemble?

Answers to these questions brought out some limited areas of agreement. One must distinguish between the "fashion-apes" who automatically accept every new decree and the discerning "fashion-habituées," who selectively adapt "what is good for them," I was told. The informants considered that only the latter group was worthy of serious consideration. The guiding principle, it appeared, was always to make the best of one's physical possibilities by covering up the "poor points" and stressing the good. A well-dressed woman is one who combines these three prerequisites: she must be completely honest with herself about her anatomic possibilities and her age; she must

[1] One of the features in the July, 1952 issue of *Vogue* was a complicated puzzle called a "double-crostic," in which some twenty words or phrases are defined and must be correctly guessed, and placed in appropriate places in a diagram. In this puzzle, all the definitions were in one way or another related to fashion; the definition for "good taste" was: "Arbitrary, often inborn sense of what is smartest, best, most suitable."

know what kind of personality she wants to impress on the world; she must have "taste" in executing these designs. Taste was mostly defined as indefinable; if pressed and coaxed, the most which could be elicted from my informants was: "Don't shriek in your clothes. Be discreet."

The typical sartorial mistakes were very simply defined. A woman becomes a "sartorial misfit" when she lacks any one of the three prerequisites to good taste mentioned above: when she is dishonest about her age or her anatomic possibilities; when she is uncertain of the picture she wishes to present; when she lacks color reticence or makes mistakes in combining colors.

On the color question, there was complete disagreement. It was admitted that "everything is possible," and that no rules exist which are not ephemeral and subject to repeated change. As a typical example, the inveterate enmity between black and brown was adduced: these colors had once been "impossible," but in the last few years their use in one ensemble has become high fashion.

The old rule, "a fashionable woman wears black," was contemptuously dismissed as cowardly. This, I was told, was the old French safety system, "the easiest way to avoid mistakes." With one exception, all my informants claimed that it was essential to have "the courage to combine shades and colors properly."

A well-dressed woman, according to my informants, must begin her deliberations with a correct evaluation of her hair and complexion (and some included with this the color of the eyes),[2] so that her general color-scheme may be built around these. The most ridiculous mistakes in color selection are made when a woman blindly follows the fashion, without considering whether the new color will

[2] Women with light-colored iris seem to have an advantage over those with dark: intense blues in dress will make their eyes look darker blue than they ordinarily do, and even give them, as some claim, "a new personality."

make her face look sallow, greenish, apoplectic, or "impossible."

Partly regretfully, sometimes triumphantly, this fact was emphasized: the old, simple rule of complementary colors (red and green, blue and orange, purple and yellow) has been endlessly complicated by the innumerable shades of these hues which are now commercially produced. "In the choice of the matching shades, the woman triumphs—or is hopelessly defeated." As a tentative rule, some of my informants referred each specific shade back to its original colors, and then accepted as "possible" any combinations derived from the original colors. I remember with amusement a specific example given at that time. To go with an orchid hat, either red or blue was allowed, since the color of the hat was produced by combining red with blue. But immediately a series of restrictions were stipulated. The orchid hat could be worn with a blue transparent veil, but not with a red veil, because a red veil would be unbecoming to the complexion of its wearer, and thus the entire ensemble would look "ridiculous." Moreover, although it is true that red or blue, as the parent colors, are correct with orchid, this orchid hat could not be worn with either a red or a blue dress. The veil is "good," since it is nearly transparent, and delicate in shading. The dress is not; it would underscore the original colors "too much." The several women working on the knotty problem of the orchid hat finally decided that its luckless owner would have to purchase a black dress to wear with it, and limit the orchid "lead" to her accessories. And why black? "All pastel shades go nicely with black." Some of the participants in the discussion pointed out that the decision on black was merely "the surest way out"; navy blue, dark brown or even lighter brown were also "possible"—providing that an adequate shade of any of these colors could be found by an expert. Stress was laid on the fact that any medium color (light blue, different shades of red, etc.) if it is to be combined with orchid, must be chosen by an expert. And this rule, it was declared, is applicable to all "difficult" colors.[3]

I asked why such a problem should arise at all: why should a woman, in assembling an outfit, start with the hat, knowing that later she would be faced with the almost insoluble problem of matching its color to the rest of her ensemble? Wasn't it like putting the cart before the horse? With a politely disguised mixture of malice and superciliousness, I was told that logic was of no help in the typical situation. A middle-income woman is frequently confronted with either an unexpected sale or bargain, too good

[3] Sometimes a single item, especially if it is a gift, can reveal itself as a Trojan horse. A patient had entertained a French manufacturer and his wife at dinner at his home several times. When the French couple returned to Paris, they sent their hostess, the patient's wife, a handsome tan calf handbag. As soon as she received the gift, she demanded that they reciprocate by sending a $50 present to Paris. The patient objected furiously, fighting for $50 and completely oblivious to the *real* consequences of the gift. The handbag, it turned out, was the starting point for a whole new outfit. The lady bought matching shoes ($35) and gloves ($10). Shopping around, she saw a "lovely tweed suit." In its pattern, it repeated the color of the bag. She could not resist the temptation especially as it was a "bargain" at $150. Of course, a matching hat and two blouses had to be found as well. These were purchased for the "ridiculous" sum of $105. Thus, the gift cost the husband an adequate amount of fury, plus $300, and the wife got a sports outfit which the husband never intended to buy.

What most violently infuriated my patient was his inability to shake his wife's profound allegiance to the theory of "matching colors." In his opinion, he pointed out, she could have used the bag with her nice brown outfit. His wife declared him a decided ignoramus. Whereupon the patient remarked acidly that high schools should teach their pupils the ABC's of "matching colors" in fashion, as preventive of future marital quarrels. To which his wife replied, no less acidly, that it was too late for him, and suggested ironically that he take an evening course in some institute for adult education. As an afterthought, she added that in her opinion culture and good taste (although they represent a real science) cannot be learned so simply, but need long training and experience.

The husband concluded the argument by saying that it was blasphemous to term as a science a technique of throwing away money in a systematic fashion.

to pass up, or an accidentally discovered (window-shopped) item which fits into her favorite, or dreamed of, outfit, and is in her most becoming color. She cannot begin assembling the outfit logically; she must match shades to the bargain reality, or the "matching predilection" that has accidentally presented itself.

Obviously, my informants had all been through this routine again and again. It was remarkable that none of them saw the irony of the situation; the combination of industry and ability required for the delicate matching of sometimes unusual shades made them very nearly half-artists, if only at the technique of building a house from the roof down. In any case, I got a glimpse of the brain-work, and the foot-work, involved in the banal phrase, "a well-dressed woman."

Taste also includes, they told me, "harmony of accessories." Two principles are accepted; the accessories may match the main color of the outfit, or take their lead from a detail. The standard combination, a navy blue dress with navy blue accessories, follows the first principle. An example of the second principle would be the identical navy blue dress with a white vestee, "asking" for white accessories. The same holds true for a gray suit with a pink pin-stripe, and pink accessories. The science of accessories, I learned, is not only complicated, but a "chronic heartache."

I asked what determines the partiality for specific hues in specific women. Experience, plus the surprised approval of the environment (the reactions of female enemies were the most valued), were judged the determining factors. And couldn't a naive woman be misled by the female enemy's hypocritical approval? Decidedly not; a woman knows —she "feels" it—whether the glimmer in the enemy's eye is true or false. Finally, this formula was arrived at: predilection for colors is based on "experimentation, experience, and—taste."

The fifteen[4] statements which follow are in answer to the three standard questions enumerated previously: definition of a well-dressed woman; typical mistakes in dress; choice of colors. I hope it is superfluous to state that I am in no way responsible for, or identifiable with, these answers. The number of contradictions they contain is remarkable—blame the theorists. To clarify the contradictions, the majority of the statements were submitted for comment to two of the informants, and their remarks are also included. I limited myself to printing thirty-one opinions (original replies, and comments); I believe that a fair cross-section of opinion in 1950 (the year of the questionnaire) is presented.

The following statement from a leading fashion editor may be taken as a guiding pattern:

"1. Today's well-dressed woman, to my mind, is one who gears her dressing to the specific type of life she leads. She dresses for coolness in summer, warmth in winter. She chooses clothes which involve the least possible upkeep, washable if she has access to washing machines, easy to move around in, drive a car, etc. She takes advantage of all the feminine prerogatives in dressing—sunbacks and short sleeves in summer, feminine cocktail sheer top styles for after five, colorful flattering hats which convey to everyone that she's a woman even if she's a business woman. She's got over feeling that to do a man's job she has to dress in the mannish way. Even her practical tweed and tailored suits are soft.

"2. Perhaps the most conspicuous mistake in dress made by lack of taste is the combination of ill-suited accessories, i.e., a *too-frivolous* hat with tailored clothes, a tailored handbag with dressy afternoon things, etc. Second might

[4] I interviewed approximately a hundred people, mostly women, and recorded approximately fifty answers. The final selection of fifteen statements is based on the fact that most of the others were only a collection of generalities and banalities.

be the tendency to overdress for specific occasions; for example, such as wearing clothes appropriate to dressy country wear in town. In the country, perhaps the most conspicuous mistake might be the tendency to be over-casual, i.e., the blue jeans set. I'm really not prepared to answer this one. I thing the level of taste has strongly improved via consumer papers, radio, consumer fashion magazines of which we have so many now.

"3. I feel that subconsciously a woman's choice of colors is regulated by color which looks well on her. There's a sort of response one gets at seeing a color which "does something" for the hair, the skin, the eyes, etc., which prejudices a woman to certain tones. Of course, if she sees enough of any color in all fashions, I feel she's apt to experiment with it where she might not have thought of it if she hadn't had the fashion impetus. Here again, I think education has greatly improved women's selection of colors for their own use.

"You realize that most of the women I see have some sort of contact with fashion, which gives them this background needed to select suitably and becomingly."

Here are the answers to the questionnaire:

From Miss A., associate editor of a national fashion magazine:

There is no common denominator for what a well-dressed woman should be. Neither ornateness nor simplicity can be used as a descriptive term for being "well-dressed," for both have been "in fashion" at different periods. Colors or color combinations likewise must be ruled out on the same historical grounds, as must the varying length and shape of the garment or accessories. The question must resolve itself into whether the *individual* woman, within the framework allotted to her by "the fashion" of the moment as to degree of ornateness, color, length and shape, successfully adapts those styles which conform best with her physical size, posture, coloring, and personality.

In short, the moment one gets down to "specific rules," one simply parades one's own prejudices in fashion.

Comment by Miss D., poet.

It would be captious to disagree with the point made in this statement. One cannot quarrel with the content of the statement, but when content is linked with source, one question becomes inescapable. Is this all that a member of the ruling group of the dictatorship, Fashion, can offer in the way of guidance to a loyal, if bewildered, subject? The "framework is allotted" by fashion; that is (in extreme cases), an unbecoming skirt-length, emphasis on a particular part of the body which the subject would like to underplay, unsuitable colors, are "recommended"—and beyond that point the subject is told to shift for herself. The dictatorship evidently has no faith in its Guidance Bureaus, its out-patient clinics, or even in its enormous body of common law, in which the populace (evidentally unlike the governing groups) devoutly believes.

One "specific rule" does suggest itself: since the framework of fashion is clearly a way of complicating the problem of finding suitable and becoming clothing, it should be much easier for a woman to be well-dressed if she ignores fashion instead of following it.

Comment by Mrs. C., a prominent photographer.

It is remarkable how carefully Miss A. avoids anything which is not commonplace. This reticence is very much in contradiction to the specific rules dictated by fashion journals. With slight exaggeration, the viewpoint promoted in the statement could very well be called nihilistic. Nobody denies the banality that each individual woman has to choose eclectically within the framework of fashion. But to say, as Miss A. does, that this is all, simply means shifting the responsibility to the very people who ask for "guidance." It may be that Miss A. suffers under the handicap of all specialists: the more they know, the more careful they are to generalize.[5] Or, to consider for a moment the dreadful possibility: Is there *really* nothing to say? Is fashion today but a constant variation and permutation, necessary because the "public demands it" and—business is business?

From Mrs. B., well-known professional fashion artist and painter:

I. I want to avoid the usual redundancy, "a well-dressed woman is a tastefully dressed woman." Your *Question No. I* involves the riddle: What constitutes taste in fashion? I would name two constituents:

First, suitability of clothing to the occasion; that is, one does not appear in street dress, but in formal dress, at a formal occasion. Nor should a full-length mink coat, worn over a cocktail dress, be considered suitable attire for a morning shopping expedition. Nor should a woman wear an afternoon dress, high heels, and a hat with ostrich feathers when she is pushing a shopping cart. Understanding of purpose is essential in choosing what is to be worn.

Second, harmony. Harmony includes not only the combination of colors in a costume, but also the proper matching of dress with accessories, a certain feeling for style, and

[5] Author's note: It is possible that Prof. Butler's definition of a specialist, "a person who knows more and more about less and less," is responsible for Miss A.'s monosyllabism. The same applies to the answer I received from a famous fashion designer:

"1. My definition of a well-dressed woman is one who is beautifully groomed at all times. Her dress should be harmonious with her own character, regardless of the dictation of fashion. Her dress should always fit the time of the day and the occasion, and never be conspicuous.

"2. The answer to the second question is almost answered in the negative of the first question.

"3. Becomingness of color or the dictates of fashion, or both."

the correct evaluation of age and personality. "A feeling for style," will inevitably make for a congruity of the outfit as a whole, and prevent such errors as high heels worn with sport dress, or an elaborate hat with slacks.

II. If purpose is not understood, and harmony not achieved, one automatically arrives at a point where the worst mistakes in dress are perpetrated.

III. There are no inflexible rules in color. Experience and tradition substitute for the non-existent rules. The classical example in support of this statement is the tradition, going back thousands of years, of Chinese art; the Chinese artist's feeling for delicate color-combination and effects is admired in the artists' world, and in the fashion world. Some periods in Chinese art are used as models even today, although the fashionable woman, hearing of the new decree in fashionable color, may not know the source of the new "inspiration."

The well-dressed woman does not require the exact knowledge of the textile printer, who must be an expert in complementary shades, and must be able to match one hundred and twenty-five shades in aniline dyes. The well-dressed customer, drawing on her own experience, or well advised by fashion stylists and designers, needs to know only the main color-combinations—e.g., nearly all pastel shades go well with black; white and black combine well, as does white and navy blue, light blue and dusty pink, gray and pink; all colors go with white, etc., etc. This is as far as knowledge can take one. The examples given, correct as they are, can become meaningless in a specific case, because personality, complexion and hair color must be taken into account. Besides this, the proper combination of colors may become ridiculous when purpose is disregarded. Bright and even violent colors are beautiful in bathing suits or play suits designed for the bright sunshine of Florida's or

California's beaches, but they seem merely garish in the delicate candlelight of a dinner table or a dance floor's subdued lighting.

For street wear in the daytime, the well-dressed woman of today is well-advised to use a suit in a neutral-delicate color (beige or sand) with bright-colored accessories (warm red, blue, brown, even the ominous orange). If tweed is chosen as the basic material, the ensemble necessarily takes on a sports-like tone, and a classical shirt-blouse is always good. For a woman who wishes to add a sophisticated touch, a jacket in "masculine" cut, with shoes, belt, handbag of solid leather and of good craftsmanship, is recommended.

As to evening dress, any occasion for which evening dress is to be worn is either formal or festive. Therefore, one's appearance should underline the purpose. A head-dress arrangement of flowers, ribbons or feathers, suitable for the hairstyle, is always "permissible." For such occasions, one's best pieces of jewelry should be reclaimed from the safe-deposit box. A stole of ermine or of precious lace can be counted on to evoke a fine first impression. Make-up, unlike daylight make-up, can be more pronounced, and should be expert. Because the lighting is always brighter than usual on festive occasions, colors that are too delicate are ineffective, even when these colors are favorites for daytime wear.

It is remarkable, by the way, that all colors and all shades combine perfectly well in nature, while similar colors in textiles would be sure to drive the manufacturer into bankruptcy. I remember that when I was a child I went for an hour's walk in the woods with my father, who was a naturalist. During this walk we counted two hundred and fifty shades of green. Not one of these shades of green offended its "neighbor." Try this in a dress, and if you are not very careful when choosing even two shades of green, your result will be "horrible."

Comment by Miss D., poet.

These opinions, laid down as a general scheme, are unexceptionable. But the specific examples chosen to illustrate the principles are open to some question. The examples are all extreme, and therefore immediately convincing. But if, to quote a well-known fashion designer, "mink is for football," [6] why is it not also suitable for a "morning shopping expedition?" And to come down to a less rarefied atmosphere, how is one to distinguish between clothing suitable for festive, and clothing suitable for utilitarian, pursuits? Expense, as in the case of the mink coat or the ostrich feathers, cannot be the only answer. Elaborateness, in periods of fashionable simplicity, is of no help at all. The cut of the item of clothing, and the material of which it is made, are the traditional gauges. But what is to guide a woman in a period like this, when house-dresses, sun-dresses, and evening dresses are all made with strapless bodices and little matching jackets, and are all made of thin cottons? This leaves "a feeling for style" as the only answer, but it seems to me that "a feeling for style," except in a stable fashion period, must be largely composed of

[6] Author's note: At this point the ladies' discussion gets slightly out of hand, and Miss D.'s sense of humor gets the upper hand. Miss D. who writes *satiric* poetry, is alluding to an interview which Valentina gave to the New York Herald Tribune on May 25, 1950. The newspaper describes the interviewed as "New York's most expensive high-fashion designer." The interview contains this passage:

"All ideas that crackle from the quick wit of Valentina are regally and explosively positive. An authority on dresses, she doesn't hesitate to pronounce also "edicts" for other fields, for instance, furs. Sable is for her the only fur. To a celebrated customer, just fitted with a new Valentina dress, she said: 'It will go nice with sable.'

"The customer shrank from the confession, but felt she might as well face it right then and there: 'Ah . . . Valentina, I have just bought a new *mink* coat.'

" 'Mink!' wailed the wounded Valentina. 'Mink is for football!' "

For other mortal and less millionaire-minded women, mink is still the epitome of fur-elegance. Hence, Miss D.'s objection to Mrs. B.'s statement is more satirical than factual. These facts, of course, are time-bound.

reliance on some professional advice (from a saleswoman, or a fashion magazine, for instance), and as such may be easily misunderstood. And in addition, such gauges as these, like the average bathroom scale, are characteristically more accurate in the higher brackets than in the lower.

As to the examples given for color harmony in dress, they seem to me to reflect personal preferences rather than general rules.

Comment by Miss A., fashion editor.

I agree with Mrs. B. on her first paragraph, that suitability to the occasion is one constituent to a well-dressed woman. However, I question a part of her second paragraph. I do not believe that if a woman has a "feeling for style" she will necessarily dress tastefully. There are many women in the fashion field who most certainly have a "feeling for style" but who would not be classified as well-dressed.

As to the third answer: I agree, of course, that there are no inflexible rules in color. Mrs. B. states that *nearly* all pastel shades go well with black. I will go so far as to say that *all colors* go well with black, just as all colors go well with white. I can go no further on other combinations, as it would be an endless list. And, as I said above, there is no basic rule. Mrs. B. goes on to say that bright colors are garish in candle light, or subdued lighting. I have never considered red or orange out of place in the evening.

In her paragraph on streetwear, Mrs. B. advises beige with bright accessories—why not beige with black? She goes on to say that tweed automatically takes on a sport-like tone. She wrote this answer a month too soon, I am afraid, as many of the manufacturers this Fall (1950) are showing tweed, flannel and plaid wool dinner dresses.

I agree with her paragraph on evening dress except when she says that too delicate colors are ineffective in the evening. What colors?

From Mrs. C., prominent photographer:

No woman can be well-dressed unless she has honestly evaluated her own appearance, and knows how old she really looks, what her good and bad points are, and so on. A woman cannot be well-dressed if she is perpetually attempting to convince other people—and especially herself—that her idealized picture of herself is the true one. But if she has an accurate picture of her own appearance, she will be able to choose clothes and wear colors—not always strictly according to the latest fashion—that suit her specific need. Provided, of course, that she has the right judgment and taste to "know" what to wear and when.

The typical mistakes in dress are pitifully clear to the photographer. When a woman is going to be photographed she wears clothes chosen to transmit a certain impression, and usually her face freezes into a mask, which emphasizes the impression made by her clothes. The photographer's eye is trained, which is bad enough, but the camera's eye is merciless. The artistic photographer tries to bring out what are, objectively, the "victim's" best points; the subject insists on being photographed as she apparently sees herself. Sometimes the only solution is to make two sets of pictures; one set as the woman sees herself, the other as the photographer sees her. A photographer of standing has more than a mere technical advantage over others in the field; his "name" gives him the authority to impress his more objective taste upon his subjects.

The situation is often ironic; a woman appears in the studio with a large suitcase full of clothing, and is finally photographed in a close-up and in a scarf draping, because all her clothes are hopelessly unbecoming. And even at this point the game continues; a woman with a wrinkled or ugly throat, unshapely hands or legs, resists every attempt to minimize these faults.

Where colors and styles are concerned, the most important factor is proper combination. Contrary to the popular assumption, expensive clothing and Parisian couture are not essential. I know a number of women whose clothes come from the most expensive houses, and who are much less tastefully turned out than others who spend less but choose better. American mass-production clothing is so well-cut, so tastefully executed, that a normally built "girl" (meaning anyone from fifteen to seventy) can look chic in quite inexpensive clothes. Of course, the quality and choice of accessories complicates the picture. These must be of superior quality, or they cheapen the entire outfit. Frequently shoes, hat or handbag are more expensive than the dress they are worn with, and it is the accessories, not the dress, that make the impression. Of course, it is absurd that these apparently minor items should be so expensive, but they are durable, and can be worn with different outfits and over a period of several seasons.

Through clever variations in her accessories—if the woman knows what colors suit her—the entire appearance of the outfit can be changed. To mention a typical example: a blue gabardine suit, worn with a white blouse and gloves, a blue hat, shoes and handbag, will be right for lunch or cocktail dates; the same suit worn with a white hat, colored scarf, red shoes and handbag, can be used as an informal spring outfit.

Naturally, the complexion, hair color (and color of the eyes), and type of figure, must all be considered when deciding on a basic color.

Comment by Mrs. E., distinguished interior decorator.

First, I would like to say that I am basically a *designer:* definition, one who creates the right thing for the right person at the right time; and a decorator: definition, one who shops for the hoped-for right thing in the available market.

Your photographer seems to me to be (sorry, there is no other word for it) cockeyed in her descriptions. She is completely subjective. She assumes that her opinion of the woman's appearance is correct. She doesn't understand that her job is to *serve,* and she has no function other than that of successful service. Her job is to take the most successful portrait she can, which means the finished job ought to resemble, as nearly as possible, the subject as she wishes she were, and not as she really is, and as the photographer sees her. Any deviation is just conceit on her part.

Her word "victim" is a dead give-away. Because she is in a position of dominance, she assumes her 100% proficiency. It never occurs to her that nobody wants to be stripped absolutely naked, figuratively speaking. People want to preserve an *almost pathetic fantasy,* and it's the photographer's job to help.

She uses the words "hopelessly unbecoming"—to whom? To her? She has never seen the woman before—how can she possibly know? It seems to me that she hates women, and doesn't know it.

I consider her description of accessories, colors, etc., pretty superficial. Craftsmanship shows in shoes, bags, gloves, jewelry. Sometimes one is lucky enough to find them for little, mostly they cost a lot. Therefore, one must decide on basic outfits, blue, black or brown, and build accessories accordingly. My basic color happens to be black, therefore I "play games" on black. Reasons: slimming, complement to hair, easier to maneuver, because I hate shopping.

Comment by Mrs. K., a well-known fashion consultant.

I admire Mrs. C.'s courage. She put into black and white something that is true but not generally admitted. My own experience coincides completely with the photographer's opinion. It may be regrettable that so many women don't know what clothes are suitable and becoming to them; on the other hand, I owe my profession to exactly this insecurity on the part of my customers. Perhaps it looks presumptuous to claim that a specialist, who frequently sees the woman just once, should be a better judge of her possibilities than the woman herself. Still, that is our skill and maybe talent. We are only too happy when we come across a woman with real taste, who knows her limits. This happens—once in a while, unfortunately, not often.

However, it is very satisfying—and I see from Mrs. C.'s statement that she feels this, too—to bring out the most favorable possibilities in our clients, and thus develop undiscovered charms.

Such frank statements as Mrs. C.'s are seldom made; it is more fashionable to pretend to be just the client's benevolent servant. This seems to me a hypocritical official attitude, covering something which is not willingly admitted.

From Miss D., poet:

To be really well-dressed, not merely acceptably well-dressed, or pleasantly well-dressed, a woman needs to have enough confidence in her own taste to choose clothes which neither follow the fashion exactly nor flagrantly precede it. She should be slightly outside the fashion, wearing clothes which in cut and color harmonize with what is currently accepted, but do not clash with it.

It is curious that with the enormous variety of items of dress which are offered to women in the shops, the mass impression that they give is still one of uniformity, but with the signals somehow crossed, as if half a dozen girls' schools had got together for a conference, and the uniformed pupils had been mixed together indiscriminately. It is curious, too, that one should so frequently overhear women saying, "I must get one of those . . . ," or "She was wearing one of those . . . ," with an undertone of envy or admiration, as if possession of a certain style were a ticket of admission to a favored circle, and consequently of identification with it.

I do not think this is a result of mass production; Jane Austen's heroines followed the fashion in the same anxious way. Income is of course a consideration; one needs money to dress "individually." But just as the earnest listeners at certain lectures all seem to have bought the same blouses and decided on the same hair-dos, so do most of one well-known designer's customers (according to a reliable authority) seem to wear coolie hats. Since they are so exclusive a circle, the designer's patrons remain well-dressed according to my definition, but only when they are not all gathered together under one roof.

The most common mistake made by women in attempting to dress attractively is failure to conceive of their costume as a whole, as far as line is concerned. Sometimes there is a wholesale failure on this point, when, with what seems like deliberate malice on the part of the designers, the coats offered for sale clash violently in line with the skirts that are in fashion, and the shapes of the hats exhibited for sale have nothing to do with either. This was true, in an especially flagrant way, during the early part of the New Look, when excessively full skirts were commonly joined with full-cut, three-quarter length coats, making for a bunchy, lumpy, layer-on-layer effect which could only have been justified by a Russian winter. This was of course complicated by the fact that in lower-income groups coats are generally two years behind dresses, and therefore can have little if any relation to a changing style.[7]

Most women are oddly insensitive to this detail, although it has been the subject of innumerable "dress-well" articles and columns; "Always look in a full-length mirror when you are buying a hat," is one of the related clichés. It is a much less important detail, seemingly, than the

[7] "Two years after this comment was written, the designers seem to have caught up with Miss D. The full skirt, still very much in evidence, can now be paired with the "spencer," a waist-length, tight-fitting coat which is a modification of a standard style of the past." (Comment of Mrs. K.)

question of color harmony, which rates a good deal of attention, even if it is not too frequently solved with success. And perhaps for financial reasons, it is the kind of failure in dress which is more tolerantly treated than any other.

There are not, and cannot be, any hard and fast rules governing what is allowed and what is not allowed in color choices for women's clothes. Any arbitrary rule adduced will be found to have its exception. And even if the exceptions are noted, a set of rules can be formulated only on the basis of a theory of "good taste," and "good dressing."

Assuming that the individual articles of clothing are pleasing in themselves, in good condition, and that in shape and cut they suit the wearer reasonably well, the well-dressed woman will be found to have chosen her colors on the basis of one of the following rules:

1. Harmony. The major theme will be relieved by variations, all complementing one another. As: a brown costume will be relieved by stripes in another shade of brown, by a touch of recessive color, by accessories in a weaker neutral color, such as gray or beige. The accessories in themselves must harmonize; if they do not form a unit, the effect is nondescript rather than harmonious. Here is where the rule, "don't mix black and brown," applies.

Or, 2. Contrast. Here the major theme is varied by deliberate surprise, or even disharmony. As, black and a saffron brown, for deliberate surprise, the correct shades of blue and green, for deliberate disharmony. But again, there must be relief in the form of a neutral color, both for the sake of avoiding spottiness, and of avoiding extreme. You can be loud, but don't shriek. Therefore, a red suit might very well be worn with a yellow blouse, and even a hat matching either suit or blouse, but to add yellow gloves, red bag and shoes, would be revolting. Bag, gloves and shoes in a soft, deep brown would be excellent.

Or, 3. Single-mindedness. This is the classic "black relieved with touches of white at the throat," carried through the entire costume, with perhaps other minor touches (very minor) in jewels, a flower, etc. This works only with neutrals or pastels. Beige or gray from head to foot, summer pinks, blues, whites, etc., are all perfectly good. In Christmas red or green the effect is horrible (perhaps because the attempt is too startling, perhaps because the color smothers the wearer); in ordinary black, dark blues or browns the end result is nondescript. There are some definite rules covering the wearing of stripes, plaids, prints, dots. Only one of these variations on the solid color should be worn, although a well-designed print can combine a plaid with a figure, a stripe or a dot with a figure. Accessory colors, when many colors are combined in the material itself, should echo one of those used in the cloth, and should generally be as unobtrusive as possible. A standard neutral, such as black, used even if it does not appear in the figure, is permissible but not advisable. It is not in "bad taste," but decidedly not in "good."

As I said above, there are always exceptions. Some of them are temporary, in the sense that they are passing dictates of fashion. I have read that in the 1890's, for instance, it was good form to wear "tan walking boots" with pastel evening clothes, a notion which would be considered pure madness today. Fashionable ensembles, off and on, are composed of a suit in a small plaid and a coat in a different plaid of larger size but in the same color. In general, plaids must not be mixed, although in this design there is a family resemblance between the two weaves.

This leaves quite a large question: what makes one color "go" with another? The only reliable rule-of-thumb seems to be that which governs the artist: do not mix your palettes. This means: all "hot" colors harmonize; all "cold" colors harmonize. The "hot" end of the spectrum is red, yellow, orange; the "cold" colors are blue, green, purple. Therefore, a green in which blue has been mixed becomes a "cold green," and will harmonize with any cold colors, or any warm colors which have been given a cold cast by shading with a cold color. As another example: a blue-red, which is cold, can be worn with a greenish yellow, which is also cold, but not with a red-yellow, which is orange and hot. A yellow-red, which is hot, can theoretically be worn with orange, but not with the cold green-yellow. Complementary colors: red and green, orange and blue, purple and yellow, always combine well.

A tentative conclusion can be drawn from this. Women are supposed to dress "to suit their personalities"; the woman who chooses her colors badly, so that she gives an effect of "bad taste," is really exhibiting confused taste, since she is unable to choose her side, hot or cold. Retiring to a safety zone, she becomes entirely neutral, or nondescript.

Comment by Mrs. B., fashion artist.

I disagree with the proposition that "cold" colors and "hot" colors cannot be mixed successfully, because of disregard for the shades in between. Moreover, the rule may be important for the painter; it cannot be used by the fashion artist. Otherwise, the rule, as stated by Miss D., is misleading for the average woman, who is not a color expert. For instance, Miss D. claims that yellow-red can be worn with orange, both hot colors. The average woman is incapable of matching two so "difficult" colors, and if she tries to follow the rule will most likely emerge as a caricature. If the same woman were to choose the standard royal or navy blue to go with her red, instead of attempting the difficult orange, she would be on safe guard.

The same objection applies to Miss D.'s idea that yellow can be matched with red in dress, and even more strongly to her concession of even one accessory in either color.

Comment by Mrs. W., characterized by herself as "a woman of many talents, merely the wife of a gifted man."

I cannot take too tragically the statement by Miss D. The lady's first thought—to say that there are no rules and regulations—was a sensible one, but along came the temptation to set down all her grade-school rules and women's magazine do's and don't's, and the floundering began. These rules sometimes make sense, except for one little thing—they've all been changed at one time or another—and by experts just as expert as the other experts! For example: under one heading she says "don't mix black with brown." Well, there are experts who will tell this lady that black and brown is one of the most subtle and elegant of combinations and that only a really sophisticated woman will wear it! And lo! Under another heading called "deliberate disharmony" or something, the lady herself says it is now permitted to use black and brown! With this same kind of rule-by-decree sort of reasoning I could give endless examples of rules in the history of fashion that were broken. These dicta are being flouted endlessly. For example: blondes must never wear red and suddenly the rule is: "Blondes, stop looking wishy-washy in those blues and greens—try red."

From Mrs. E., prominent interior decorator:

My definition of a well-dressed woman: The first prerequisite is to be soignée. A woman must study herself to ascertain what lines improve her carriage and general look of chic. She must then decide the colors that flatter her skin tones, eyes and hair. She must decide "who" she wants to be, as there is an infinity of styles that fall into the category of being well-dressed: In all cases she must keep her accessories simple and coordinated in color. One can dress in monotone or one can dress using accent colors, as for example: black dress, white gloves, white hat, black bag and shoes. The proper use of accessories can improve chic or can definitely spoil the entire effect of the ensemble. An inner feeling of being well-dressed is essential to the reaction on other people. Proper clothes at the proper time.

As to the typical mistakes: the easiest error that a woman can make because of lack of taste is in her knowledge of line, color and form. Also in mixing of inappropriate items of dress. For example, a dressy suede shoe with high heels, and a country tweed suit. Or vice versa, low-heeled sport shoes with a dressy print. The inappropriateness of one item to the other is the most serious error made. The lack of knowledge of what certain fabrics represent in regard to time, place and suitability. Skirts too long or too short, waistlines too high or too low. The lack of knowledge of the personality will permit a woman with a long narrow face to wear an off-the-face hat. The hair-do that accentuates the wrong features. Mixed-up color combinations, i.e., print dress, red shoes, black bag, and yellow hat. The accent color used with a print dress must be the predominant color of the print. Too much jewelry and too many flowers are another common error of bad taste. Scale is of the most importance both in pattern and size; i.e., big woman with peanut hat, small woman with a cartwheel hat, big woman with a small purse, small woman with a big purse. To summarize, these remarks can be expressed by: too many wrong things at the right time.

As to the choosing of colors in the clothes ensemble, this is the most difficult of all the questions because there are no rock-bound rules. In answering the preceding question, I brought up some of the points, such as, colors must be used that are flattering to the skin tones, eyes, and hair. The next most important point is that one must never wear too many colors. There is a rule-of-thumb saying that three is the maximum that is in good taste. When the dress is a plain color I prefer only one accent color, i.e., black dress, black shoes, black or white hat, black or white gloves, black or white bag. This depends upon the season and the occasion. Yellow could also be used as an accent color in the hat and gloves, or any bright colored hat, providing all other accessories are black, or a flowered hat. If the dress is a multi-colored print material the accessories should be sober, and preferably the dark background color of the print. If the print is on a light background the accessories should pick up the darkest color in the print, i.e., navy, black, or brown. If the print combines two or three colors, then the accessories, depending on the season, should be either the light ground or the dark ground. Under no condition will white shoes be worn in town by the well-dressed woman.

Mrs. E. misunderstood the routine of my questionnaire, and instead of returning her manuscript to me to be passed on for criticism, went ahead on her own and collected half-a-dozen other statements. In the sequence in which they are reproduced, the replies came from two of Mrs. E.'s main co-workers, two of *their* friends, Mrs. E.'s maid, and a friend of her maid's.

(A) A well-dressed woman is one, not necessarily in the latest fashion, whose ensemble and style are coordinated to her figure, her personality, and the occasion. She is never over-dressed nor under-dressed. She is well-groomed.

The typical mistakes prompted by the "lack of taste" are color combinations, size of prints, no restraint in accessories or make-up, and following everything that fashion dictates, regardless of the individual.

The color choice in the dress ensemble should go with the individual's coloring, and should be limited. A tonal quality is best, with small touches of another color.

(B) A well-dressed woman is not a slave to fashion—neither does she ignore it.

She knows the fundamental lines and colors that are best suited to her and adapts fashion to her pattern.

She dresses simply, is never over-adorned. Clothes enhance her rather than overwhelm her.

Women lacking in taste either dress fussily or blatantly. No one ever accuses the baggy Bostonian of lacking taste —it's a matter of over-dressing.

Some women, unsure of their taste, or lacking a style of their own, copy women they admire, ignoring their own figure or personality.

Another mistake is the inability to see the costume as a whole. Each part of a costume may be smart in itself but cancel out or fight when put together.

As to color, the first rule is to know your most flattering colors. After choosing a color for an ensemble it should be decided how and where it is to be used. If the basic costume is to carry the color the accessories should be neutral or vice versa.

Too much color, head to toe, is like over-seasoning.

(C) A well-dressed woman is a well-assembled person whose personality is first noticed, and clothes secondly.

Lack of taste is chiefly shown in an inability to decide on one over-all effect; by bad color combination; by mixing types of clothing that should not be worn at the same time or to the same social event.

Choice of color should first compliment the wearer, and secondly be suitable to the occasion.

(D) The well-dressed woman is the woman whose ensemble is so coordinated as to be secondary to the woman and yet a direct compliment to the woman.

The typical mistakes most often repeated through lack of taste in dress are combined in the lack of ability to coordinate accessories with costumes, the improper timing of an ensemble, and the incorrect correlation or use of colors.

There are no rules to regulate the choice of colors in an ensemble. Since fashion colors vary with the season and the choice of *the* color of the season can be becoming or unbecoming to an individual—it is best to refer to the definition of a well-dressed woman. She chooses color only becoming to her, and if she does not have an eye for color, she had better dress in her basic background color with only one small color accent in her costume. The all-over one-color ensemble is always considered chic.

(E) A woman is well-dressed when her clothes are suitable for the occasion.

Typical mistakes: color unsuitable or not flattering, pattern that doesn't make the best of the figure. Size and height play a most important role in choosing clothes. Large women should never wear horizontal stripes. A very tall girl should stay away from vertical stripes. And so on.

In choosing a dress ensemble, the dress itself should be the dominant color. If a solid color, choose accessories that harmonize with it, and are flattering. If the dress is a print, choose any of the colors from it for accessories.

(F) What makes a well-dressed woman? Simplicity—generally—but character, personality and *posture* have a lot to do with making a woman look well-dressed; therefore, I think there are many types that can be called well-dressed.

Typical mistakes—over-dressing, with gay and gaudy ornaments, too much jewelry and pancake make-up—also wobbly, extremely high-heeled shoes, which aren't a help to a graceful walk.

Best color combinations—neutral shades to blend with almost everything, so that one doesn't spend hours sweating over what goes with what.

From Mr. F., designer (color specialist) and advertising artist:

COLOR: ITS IMPORTANCE TO WOMEN WHO WANT TO DRESS IN GOOD TASTE

To begin with, it is extremely difficult to discuss color with words. One should have the actual color in front of one, since the technical names of colors as used in artists' pigment are not generally known, and such invented names as "desert rose" or "blush red" are advertising copywriters' fantasies that may not mean the same color to two different people.

Another limitation is the confinement of writing about color only in relation to women's clothes. Here too, it must be pointed out that women follow constantly changing dictates of fashion. A perfectly good color scheme may not be "smart," because at any particular season it may not be the fashionable scheme as sponsored by *Vogue* or *Harper's Bazaar*.

Every natural impulse can be exploited and commercialized, and the normal desire for change and creation is here expressed in a constantly changing parade of fashionable color schemes, designed to create sales and interest, and calculated to make any fashion-conscious woman miserable at the prospect of being seen in last year's dress.

There are as many misconceptions, prejudices, distortions and facts about color as on any other subject. It is impossible to deal with all of them in detail, and only the broadest generalizations can be made here.

For example, the misconception that the same color can be worn by any woman; the prejudice that some colors are "bad" for you; the distortion that all one has to do is follow the color wheel, without sometimes disastrous results; and the fact that wearing new and interesting color schemes can become a creative pleasure.

It is to the individuals who do get a specific pleasure from putting together new and becoming color schemes in dressing that this monograph is dedicated, and to whom any suggestions here outlined could be of any value. With these limitations in mind, we may proceed.

It is my opinion that all aesthetic creation has a number of common denominators: It must have UNITY, COMPOSITION, VARIETY, CONSISTENCY and THEME. This is true of a painting, a symphony, a play, a novel, a building or a woman's dress, if we treat dressing as a pleasurable aesthetic value, used by an individual with sensitivity, knowledge and ability to express or create a particular mood.

To avoid misunderstanding, I will clarify the above terms by definition and example.

UNITY is that quality in any aesthetic creation that gathers the various elements that go into the presentation of that particular creation; elements that sometimes are elaborate, conflicting and apparently unrelated, and fuses them together into a single whole; a clarification of intention, as it were, that the creative personality must work out in order to make its presentation simple, directional, impressive, and cohesive.

COMPOSITION is the method by which unity is achieved. This is the job of selection, arrangement, change, exaggeration or sublimation, contrast and harmony which goes into every work of art. It is here that the component parts of a creation must be kept together without too heavy a hand. Composition that flows from one part to the other without obviousness is indeed a creation.

VARIETY is the key element in composition. Without it, the composition can become dull and repetitious. Or barren and uninteresting. Or superficial and boring. These three qualities: UNITY, COMPOSITION and VARIETY make up significant technical elements to be found in each aesthetic creation.

PERSONALITY and IMAGINATION are the emotional elements. Without personality a creation is a mere copy, no matter how perfect the technique. Without imagination, it is not a free expression. It becomes formalized, stultified and a prisoner to technique. Every new situation is resolved in the same old way and repetition and decay follow.

CONSISTENCY and THEME are the ordered, logical elements. They represent the willful and considered placing of limits to any particular expression. A theme is chosen, and everything is made to be consistent with the best possible presentation of that theme, or idea, or feeling. It is here that economy of means is necessary. *How* to arrive at a creation that expresses one's personality with imagination and technical virtuosity with the least effort and in the simplest terms is a question not easily answered, if it can be answered at all. At this point, it would be a good idea to illustrate the definitions given.

Michelangelo's "Last Judgment" is a masterpiece of UNITY, COMPOSITION, VARIETY, IMAGINATION, PERSONALITY and THEME. The powerful theme finds expression in the CONSISTENCY of his technique, powerful beyond words. The fact that he picked the theme "From Creation to Doom" with which he decorated the walls and ceiling of the Sistine Chapel, shows that he picked a monumental theme to express his Herculean personality. The richness of his imagination is expressed in the infinite variety of bodies in all sorts of positions, depicting all forms of emotional and physical human experience, magnificently composed into a unit that is easy to grasp at a glance, yet so rich in subordinate details that one could spend a lifetime enjoying its diverse parts.

A flower is a masterpiece of nature. The graceful rising of the stem, enriched with the repetition of leaf formation in a variety of sizes, decorates and supports the culminating bulb that bursts into a contrasting colorful bloom, again with petals repeated in design for consistency, but offering a variety of size and delicate variation of color for interest. Some add even smell to their aesthetic dimensions, and of course, a constantly changing life-cycle: the time dimension.

These two examples were picked not without reason. Between the consciously picked and organized masterpiece of Michelangelo and the natural growth and beauty of the flower lies a woman's creation of the perfect dress to express her particular mood at a given occasion.

Precisely because a specific occasion limits the range of expression, a woman has to dress CONSISTENTLY with the occasion; the first element of good taste is to evaluate correctly the kind of function one dresses for, and dress accordingly. This parallels THEME in art.

Here begins the emotional part of the creative process. How to express one's personality with imagination . . . and since our specific interest is here further limited to a discussion of COLOR and its importance to women who want to dress in good taste, and get a specific, creative pleasure from that form of aesthetic expression, I would like to present at this point some personal opinions about COLOR and PEOPLE.

I must emphasize an important distinction: PERSONAL PREFERENCE of specific or even vaguely understood but much felt color schemes, and the AESTHETIC REFINEMENT of any color scheme through intelligent application, sincere interest and knowledge of these elements that make a color scheme an aesthetic creation and not just colors that have been thrown together, must be differentiated.

I doubt if anyone really knows why they prefer a particular color scheme. It has been my experience that color scheme preferences constantly change with the individual even to the point of acceptance and liking of schemes once abhorred. One thing is certain: color schemes do have an emotional content, and can either express or create a MOOD.

It is not my purpose here to go into the phase of the discussion which interests itself in the mechanism of the relation between the personality and its emotional expression in terms of specific color schemes. That is a study in itself; my concern here is with the possibilities of REFINING THE CHOICE.

To return, then, to the problem of expressing one's personality with imagination and consistency for a particular occasion, and, accounting for a particular mood, a color scheme is chosen. What should be kept in mind?

Our old friends, the common denominators of all artistic creation: UNITY, COMPOSITION, and VARIETY. I have already defined them, and I have given examples in art and nature. I would like to show how they operate in relation to a chosen color scheme.

The UNITY factor in dressing is the recognition that not only the dress, but the color and texture of one's skin, the color of the hair, and color of the eyes are an integral part of the entire picture. Unity therefore must be achieved with these details in mind. Since all parts must be related, and because no one's skin is absolutely white, no woman should wear a "pure" color. All colors must be muted to go with one's other characteristics.

The COMPOSITION element is represented by the various parts of clothing: hat, shoes, bag, hose, jewelry, etc., that are to be worn with a dress or suit, or skirt, and blouse and perhaps a coat. Make-up should be included as the finishing touch, also to be related to the time of day or night, occasion and mood. The harmonies or contrasts that one may use are endless but here again, the composition of all the elements must achieve unity, or we have disaster. Bright color should be used sparingly and only as an accent.

VARIETY is very easy to obtain in women's clothes since we always have a number of elements that are a relief from a monotonous harmony. The parts of the head, arms and legs that show, the various textures worn, such as material for the dress, leather for the shoes and gloves, some details like a belt, jewelry, a flower . . . even though they can be the same color, they are different enough to create the necessary interesting variety.

This is as much as can be said with words regarding COLOR as an element in a woman's wardrobe. Specific teaching, with visual colors, a lot of experimenting, and the usual pitfalls that attend any creative process can be expected. As an aid for beginners, I might recommend the careful study and copy of color schemes in one's favorite pictures. Remember the artist has spent a lot of time mixing the right colors in the proper amount to achieve his purpose. To the woman who wants to dress in good taste one can only say: "go ye and do likewise."

Comment by Mrs. B., fashion artist and painter.

I fully agree with Mr. F.'s deduction and enjoyed and admired his truly artistic *seeing* of the problem. His opinions coincide to a large degree with my own, as expressed in my contribution. (See page 160.)

Comment by Mr. Z., prominent etcher and poet:

Undoubtedly, the two cardinal requirements stressed by the above specialist—and by Mr. I., whose statement I have also read—are: first a certain degree of conformity to what prevailing fashion has decreed as suitable to a particular occasion, and, second, a sensitive and creative adaption of the current rules of the game to the individual's peculiar style of beauty. Both authorities are at pains to deprecate a too slavish subservience to the dictates of fashion—and what male has not cried out against this tyranny? —but they might have pointed out that such discipline, when intelligently accepted, is but an extension to the group of that principle of unity which Mr. F. so rightly insists upon in speaking of the individual. Observance of the general trend assures a definite aesthetic harmony among the human elements of any occasion while individual modifications guarantee the equally necessary variety.

I have no quarrel with Mr. F.'s detailed aesthetique except to question whether a woman's "Theme" is not rather the enhancement of her particular charm (matched by the minimizing of any defect) rather than the requirements of a given function. If she has gorgeous hair, whether blonde or red, then her real theme is color, and line and cut and texture will inevitably be subordinated in the radiant glow which results from the fusion of color. Such women, above all, should most carefully study the various possibilities of color combination. They can command the most dazzling harmonies, yet at the same time it is they who must exercise the greatest caution. Their coloring calls for spirited support but they must see to it that even the most sumptuous arrangements never transcend the role of an accompaniment.

Black-haired beauties, and the dark-complected generally, have perhaps the greatest freedom in the display and enjoyment of bright colors for their own sake. With them, and only with them, it is possible for the eye to include the brightly colored coat or dress and the striking hat in a single unity. The majority of women, however, should not attempt to imitate their more fortunate sisters, whether blonde or brunette. Perhaps their theme is "line," the revelation of a beautiful figure, in which case bright color may well be subordinated to the limited role which Mr. F. recommends. But in any case, whatever the personal theme, an observer's first reaction should always be, "What an attractive woman!" and only secondarily, "What a stylish outfit!"

Yesterday, a striking color scheme blazed into the subway car where I was riding. All too obviously the "theme" was autumn, and fascinated, my eyes wandered from the maple-red coat to the scarlet lips and finger-nails; from the black-threaded chartreuse skirt to the golden hat; from the neutral hose to the sage greens and russet of gloves and handbag. Who would be wearing such an outfit? Curiously, I sought out the face, a wan pretty face it turned out to be but with no support anywhere save in a half-hidden rope of pearls and two large opalescent buttons.

Even when there is a real harmony between the wearer and her ensemble, I, for one, am repelled by the too striking composition, the too calculated color scheme. In feminine attire, most of all, art should conceal art.

The result should be far closer to a flower than to any painting and surely least of all *The Last Judgment.* How could Mr. F. have passed Renoir and Titian by to make his extraordinary obeisance to the never very colorful and now hopelessly smoked-up masterpiece of Michelangelo?

But now, I come to think of it, I have heard women of an older generation say in a self-critical moment that they looked like the wrath of God.

From Dr. G., a woman of scientific achievement:

I. *Definition of a well-dressed woman:*

A woman is considered well-dressed if her general appearance is harmonious in its color scheme, if the style of the clothes—including hat—correspond to the build and age of the woman, as well as the occasion on which the clothes are worn.

II. *Typical mistakes revealing lack of taste:*

1. Any contradiction in the definition given above. Examples:

2. Accessories and clothes must harmonize with each other. There is a general principle that only two to three out of the four should match. The four are: shoes, gloves, pocketbook and belt. Some include the hat, which I don't. According to my idea, the hat belongs to the dress.

If all the accessories are too closely matched, the woman may look over-dressed, in the sense of "too much of a good thing." She also betrays her insecurity or inexperience in matters of taste (style).

3. Another violation of good taste is the incongruity between the type of clothing and build. A tall athletic type of woman should not wear frilly clothes. The same holds true for a woman who is overweight.

4. Almost everybody has a body image of greater youthfulness than is actually true, and some women have adhered too strictly to the kind of clothes they liked to wear when they were young.

5. The opposite is also often the cause for pitfalls. Some women dress too somberly, hiding the feminine advantages instead of stressing them, and giving the impression of being garbed instead of dressed. They apply no highlights such as jewelry, or some other form of embellishment, as if they were in mourning. This, in turn, gives the observer an uncomfortable feeling. These are called the mousy type.

III. Principles of choosing color and color combinations:

A woman chooses color in order to provide the most favorable frame for her hair, eyes and face. It seems that the eye travels faster than the image of the retina, and color from the "frame" is superimposed on the color of the three items mentioned above, thus creating—at least momentarily—a new blend. This influences, either favorably or unfavorably, the three items mentioned. The woman summarizes: "This color (of the frame) does something for me," or "I can't wear this color, it makes me look terrible." An illustration of this mechanism is: the blue eyes of a woman look bluer if she wears a dress of a light blue color, but much less so if the dress is green.

Some shades of color seem to detract from undesirable components of color of the hair or face. For instance, a red-headed woman looks well in green, but it must be a yellowish green. It seems that this takes away some of the yellow component of the red hair; while a blue-green would accentuate this element and make the woman look less attractive. Strong colors enhance a woman's face if she has a ruddy complexion but give her face a yellowish tint if she is naturally pale, even if these are otherwise becoming to her. A dark complexioned woman does not look well in red because the skin might look yellow unless she wears make-up. Yet, another skin receives glow from a red dress and may be made to appear gray if framed with a green color. A great many women know which color suits them better than another, although they are not aware of the reasons.

All of these ideas are greatly offset by modern cosmetics which can change not only the color of the face but also the color of the hair. This, for most women, leaves the eyes as the determining factor.

In regard to color combinations, the following can be stated. It is not only necessary that the main colors harmonize but that their component colors do, too. For instance, a bright red may look well in combination with a darker red, but if one of them is a blue-red and the other a yellow-red, they would offend good taste.

Some women, I am afraid, do not have the eye for these differences; neither do the very young teen-agers. It seems that a greater discrimination comes with experience and interest, as well as with cultural advancement in the appreciation of the arts.

In reading over these notes, it occurred to me that I omitted one rather important point. It is not only the color of the face and eyes that count, but also the build of the face. Women with marked features will do well to neutralize in their hair style and style of dress markings that might be too pronounced. For instance, a woman with a big nose ought not to wear her hair off the face because it would accentuate the size of the nose, or a woman with a strong nose-mouth line (like mine) must be careful not to repeat the same direction, either in her hairdo or in the style of the upper part of her dress. The reasons are the same as described with the carry-over of color from the blouse to the face.

As far as the general appearance is concerned, women with too thin, or too heavy legs, do better by not wearing short dresses. I am not speaking of such things as bow legs, or knock knees, which obviously need covering up. Also, the proportion between the upper part of the body and the lower part of the body demands attention. Long-waisted women appear to more advantage than short-waisted women in suits that break the line. Short-waisted women look better when the waistline can be adjusted with a belt to create more harmonious proportions.

Wherever these rules are disobeyed, we have a violation of good taste. You mentioned a tall woman who wore pyramid hats to make her appear taller. Other examples are a tall woman who wears dresses longer than the current style, or a very short woman who wears a beret and knee-length dresses. These errors, however, I believe, are connected with the body image of the wearer, mentioned in an earlier paragraph.

Comment by Miss D., poet.

I do not believe that successful dressing is always dependent on following the rules. Dr. G. calls "incongruity between the type of clothing and build" a "violation of good taste," and also states specific cases in which long or short skirts, off-the-face or on-the-face hair styles, bodice lines of one type or another, should or should not be worn. There is a great deal of waste energy involved in the attempt to minimize obvious faults of face and figure. I do not really believe, although I like to believe everything I read, that face and figure deficiencies can be ameliorated through a style of dress. (The obvious exception, of course, is the kind of underclothing which eliminates errors by supplying an artificial understructure.) Most of the time, the best that can be done with deficiencies is to give them up as a bad job, and ignore them as much as possible. One of the most effectively dressed women I know has a fat, badly-proportioned body, beautiful feet, and a beautiful head. She emphasizes her head with flowers, earrings, etc., her feet with unusual, brightly colored shoes. She habitually wears black dresses, loosely fitting, and of meaningless shape. If she were to try to minimize her figure, through careful corseting and discreet lines, people would still be aware of its ungainliness. As it is, she acknowledges its existence and ignores its importance; and consequently, so does everyone else.

Otherwise, I agree with the general lines laid down in Dr. G.'s comment.

Comment by Mrs. H., acclaimed novelist.

In her definition of the well-dressed woman, the doctor stresses appropriateness. While this leaves out many of the fine points and the possibility of imagination, it is as good a simple standard as I can think of.

In her description of lapses of taste, I would say the doctor was speaking by too strict a rule, and definitely in terms of current fashions in and around New York City. She has tried to break down her rule of appropriateness, and inner consistency, into detailed recommendations, which must necessarily be incomplete.

From Mrs. H., novelist:

De gustibus non est disputandum. You cannot dispute about tastes because you cannot define them. You can circle around a definition of taste in clothes as you can about style in art by telling the things that it is not, but that still leaves the essence of the thing undefined.

1. A well-dressed woman would have to be described in a series of paradoxes. She would have to dress within the

framework of the fashion of her time and society in order to avoid the error of being conspicuous, but she must not be slavish to fashion because that would make her conspicuously fashionable, and it would also detract from her individuality, and taste must certainly be individual.

Her clothes should be appropriate to the occasion but not overly specialized. Since there must be a principle of organization of color and of texture and of style, her clothes cannot be carelessly assembled, but if they are too careful, they will reveal a preoccupation with clothing which is certainly an unattractive accessory to any costume.

In a society in which clothing is more than utilitarian, and not uniform, the choice of clothing is an art, of which the most important component is the art of concealing art.

2. Mistakes that indicate lack of taste can only be defined in terms of here and now. Excess is, of course, a lapse of taste, but an outfit that would be excessive in one era and in one place might be quite appropriate in another.

A consistency of atmosphere is a mark of taste, but inconsistency in the form of contrast of color and of texture and of attitude can be a costume's great charm and most important ornament; although this contrast must always be within the framework of design which has its own internal rules.

3. Color choice depends on what is fashionable and on what a woman considers becoming to her own coloring. Some temperaments seem to find pleasure in shocking contrast of sharp colors and others like only blends and muted colors. Sometimes the sharp colors are used by strong personalities and the muted colors by people who are timid in their choices, but this is by no means a safe generalization, as the strong colors are sometimes used by pale personalities to bolster their spirits or to attract attention, and the muted colors by those who are afraid that perhaps the strong colors will not be considered ladylike.

Sometimes colors are chosen just for a change. Moreover, in a ready-to-wear society like ours, choice is limited by the colors available in the shops.

Comment by Mrs. B., fashion artist and painter.

A brilliant dissertation, too general to be of practical use. There is no basis for objections, since all specific points are avoided. Definitions, even if correct and excellent, are no guide for the well-dressed woman.

Comment by Mrs. K., fashion consultant.

I admire novelists, especially female novelists. They have the ability of mastering literary style and manipulating psychological situations. But they also have the habit of circumlocution, perhaps a necessary prerequisite for filling the three hundred printed pages which make a novel. Unfortunately, Mrs. H. took too extensive advantage of that privilege when answering the three *specific* questions you asked on fashion. *Specific* answers were requested; the upshot is a *generality*—"choice of clothing is an art." Quite true, but what yardstick is this when confronted with a specific problem? As a fashion consultant, I would starve if I dealt in generalities like this. But, after all, Mrs. H. can afford it—she is in the "business" of art.

From Mr. I, stylist and textile converter:

A well-dressed woman is a woman who never overdresses, who is always aware of trends in style, capable of combining the new silhouette pattern and color to conform to her particular type of person, taking into consideration her figure, height, personality and coloring, and is always aware of the environment, function and occasion.

As to the typical mistakes of lack of taste in dress, one of the outstanding errors a badly dressed woman will make is to wear a wrong type of shoe with her costume, such as ankle-strapped shoes with a suit. The next worst mistake is wearing the wrong hat. For some unknown reason, women sometimes make themselves look idiotic by wearing a freakish looking hat just because some magazine or newspaper promotes it as the newest and latest creation from Paris. The third mistake many women make is to wear too much color or colors that are not too complimentary to their complexions, hair, or eyes. Another very bad mistake is to wear the wrong clothes in the wrong place at the wrong time.

The average woman is influenced by the magazine and newspaper advertisements when she chooses color combinations in a dress ensemble. This woman usually pictures herself as one of the beautiful models of sylph-like descriptions of models in the advertisements she reads, but then there is the instinctive woman who looks and reacts to color the same as she would to music, knowing instinctively that certain colors harmonize, and flatter her personality, while other colors clash and make her unhappy. This woman will picture herself as the focal point in a painting and use clothes and colors as a frame. She will always consider color in the same relationship to a small spotlight on a masterpiece rather than a great big glaring light. Color acts as a highlight to her, just as a spotlight does on a painting, bringing out the highlights and the important details of the picture. Color does the same for this woman.

Of course, environment and occasion play an important part in the influence of color. For instance, the primitive woman living in the jungle instinctively resorts to gay bright colors. If you look at the different periods of civilization, you find that musicians, master painters and architects had great influence on the cultural background of the people, and directly influenced style, and naturally, color. Beginning with the Romans and going right on to the Renaissance, including the Spanish influence, we find that woman became particularly aware of these influences, and her sense of being instinctively selected color to conform.

Even today, if a woman were to visit a bull-fight in Mexico, she would instinctively wear a red handkerchief or something very bright to conform with the surroundings and the emotional excitement, while on the other hand, if that same woman were to attend the opera, she would instinctively wear something formal in keeping with the surroundings. Sense of color becomes part of all our senses, part of touch, sight, taste, hearing, and smell. We've heard the expressions: "Boy, that's hot!"—"I feel blue"—"She's in the pink"—"That yellow makes me nauseous"—"Cool as a cucumber"—"Heavenly blue"—"That looks smart"—"That looks somber or weird."

Every one of these expressions, and many more old and many more new ones that are coined, are coordinated reactions of people whose senses are pleased or displeased with colors.

Comment by Mr. Z., etcher and poet.

To me, the most interesting part of the above comment is Mr. I.'s observation of the subtle and inevitable harmony existing between styles of costume and contemporary arts and decor. The relation was especially remarkable in the Gothic and Rococo periods, but is also apparent in our own time where our "Well-Dressed Woman" tends to have a hard, sleek, machine-made and chromium-plated type of beauty, in marked contrast, say, to the soft, romantic, impressionistic Belle of the last century. The latter, although somewhat too prone to the fussiness of double blooms, was presented as the fairest flower of the garden, while our contemporary ideal is nowhere so well set off as in her automobile, the final, perfectly appropriate adornment of the streamlined vehicle in which she rides.

At the same time, we may note in the contemporary make-up of the mouth a tendency at variance with the simple, functional design of the machine, and which may perhaps be ascribed to modern painting. Here, the eyes are dethroned and the unity of the face destroyed by the undue emphasis of this single feature, apparently in an effort to restore, by a palpably symbolic and expressionistic exaggeration, that dynamic of femininity which in other times radiated from the whole figure.

Otherwise, Mr. I.'s remarks do not add much to what has already been said. He, too, is cynical about the fair sex's tendency to make monkeys of themselves in the name of Fashion, but, in his case, the cynicism is redeemed by a chivalrous faith that, left to their own devices, they will intuitively strike the style note appropriate to any occasion.

Comment by Mrs. E., interior decorator.

This is a smart guy, aware of life, and who has coped even with women. His answer to the first question is fine; his answer to the second, fine, with the exception: hats are like male plumage. Women wear "freakish hats" to attract attention, and men do look at women who are "different." Once the woman gets the man's attention, she can—if she's smart—begin to sell him on her good points. But she has to get herself looked at first.

As to the third question, I think he is dreaming. Few of us are paintings, with face the focal point and clothes the frame. We have to excite by means of our clothes, figures, extras like exciting jewelry. We design thrills and sell thrills, for the sake of the man who can be sold . . . I assume his "blurb" on color means a woman should be "hep" (a point!) in her timing . . .

As far as my feelings, professionally (regarding design and decoration), I think my job is to study my client objectively, find out who she wants to be, and why, and then see to it that she is presented, in that way, to her friends—of course in a way that will also be satisfactory to my ego and my standards of proficiency. My only failures have been when I thought very little of the person to begin with, and was aware that they had pretty dim views of themselves, too.

9 Are There Sartorial Anti-Talents among Women?

Aldous Huxley once wrote a novel called *Two or Three Graces*. There was nothing figurative about this title; it meant, literally, that his heroine, Grace, showed different facets of her personality in different situations. Using Huxley's analogy, one could speak of two or three *hundred* Marys, Annies, Lisbeths, and Harriets, using as testimony the outfits accumulated or discarded through the years. The story is not new: Madame de Preizeux expressed the identical thought, "Women cherish fashion because it rejuvenates them, or at least renews them."

These few hundred outfits which a woman buys in her lifetime can be "tastefully" or tastelessly chosen. Women "with taste" simply shrug their shoulders at their less tasteful, "untalented" sisters, and let it go at that. Invisibly, they pat themselves on their own backs, pluming themselves on their own possession of that undefined, undefinable asset, exquisite "taste."

The material I have collected (partly subsumed into the previous chapter on reputation) has convinced me that there are fewer "tasteless" women than would seem to be indicated by sartorial exteriors. Paradigmatic are changes achieved in successful analysis. I had learned, long ago, this rule-of-thumb: *conspicuous tastelessness in dress is mostly an unconscious pseudo-aggressive and defensive attack on the enshrined mother image.* If, through the use of analytic procedure, one removes the masochistic substructure, the "tasteless" woman emerges as a sartorial "talent."

Nobody denies that some women are dressed in a manner which reminds one of Horace's epigram, "Difficile est satiram non scribere." Nevertheless, there is an unconscious reason for this error in the majority of cases—a *neurotic inhibition.*

The most grotesque as well as the most revealing errors of taste occur in the sphere of colors. These errors can be classed under two heads. 1. Psychology of colors, and neurotic mistakes in choosing colors, and 2. Neurotic mistakes in self-evaluation.

1. *Psychology of colors, and neurotic mistakes in choosing colors.*

Over one hundred and forty years ago, Goethe complained in his *Theory of Colors:* "If you hold a red cloth up to a *bull,* he becomes furious; but the *philosopher* changes into a raving maniac if one even mentions colors." Fury—on the part of the philosopher at least—is no longer encountered, but ignorance prevails.

Today the science of colors has, empirically, quite progressed; the *psychology* of colors, however, remains largely unexplored. Color scientists are conscious of this fact. Matthew Luckiesh points out[1] that it is the function of psychology to explore the complex problem of why colors appeal or do not appeal to individuals, but that practical experience with colors has progressed far beyond any scientific base. The response to color is subjective, Luckiesh declares; while color is a conscious sensation, it is the individual who sees the object as colorful and gives the object color. The psychological effects of color are built up by

[1] *Color and Colors,* D. Van Nostrand Co., New York, 1938.

experience, and we are conscious of their existence, but we tend to attribute the effect to the color itself, instead of acknowledging its actual origin. But the process of identifying subjective reactions as objective facts is, as Luckiesh says, "convenient and practicable."

Opie, as quoted by Luckiesh, added some sentimental flourishes to what is at bottom the identical thought. In his opinion, there is a suitable shading to match every human emotion, and the use of appropriate colors is helpful both in dissecting and in expressing emotions. Color, he declares, can strengthen joy, intensify love, heighten anger, increase sadness, etc.

Colors are "subjective," one can agree; this does not explain the individual's varying and contradictory reactions to one and the same color. Luckiesh points out that *blue*, the favorite color of adult males in Western countries, and close runner-up to red in the opinion of all persons, plays not one role but many. It represents coolness, serenity, pleasantness; it is also the traditional synonym for Weltschmerz and depression. Among Occidentals it is rarely, if ever, repulsive, but in China dark blue is associated with death. Luckiesh cites the case of a manufacturer, unaware of this fact, who exported to China a shipment of pins fastened to dark blue cards. The pins sold below his expectations.

Yellow, too, is either pleasant or repulsive, Luckiesh declares. It represents cheerfulness, brightness, cleanliness; at the same time, it is the color of the flag of quarantine. Dirty journalism is "yellow" journalism. In Christian ecclesiasticism it is the color of Judas' garments. In China, however, yellow is the regal color, appreciated by all.

Interestingly enough, Goethe in his *Farbenlehre*[2] (1808) tried to solve the contradiction of yellow by enumerating its various shades:

[2] Goethe's *Collected Works*, Vol. XX, pp. 337-8 (Ullstein edition).

Yellow, in its maximum purity, always has the connotation of brightness, and has a cheerful character . . . When yellow is transmitted to unclean or unrefined surfaces . . . a disagreeable impression results. Through a small and imperceptible shift the beautiful impression of fire and gold is changed into the feeling of dirt,[3] and the color of honor and enjoyment is transformed into the color of shame, repugnance and displeasure. Thus perhaps the yellow hats of bankrupts, the yellow rings on the coats of (mediaeval) Jews were inaugurated, even the so-called cuckold-color is but a dirty yellow.

Analytic experiences with colors, sparse as they are, confirm Goethe's suspicion: the borderline between the "beautiful" and the "detestable" in colors rests on the *near-by-nearness* and *too-much-nearness* to fantasies and connotations of the infantile. Therefore yellow can produce the connotation of sun, or that of "dirt," depending on slight differences in shading.

The fact of *subjectivity* in color predilections and color-reactions is acknowledged. That subjectivity has *unconscious* reasons, which are not consciously known or under conscious control. Thus the same color will have completely different connotations for different people.[4]

[3] Goethe uses the words "*Empfindung des Kotigen.*" *Kot* has, in German, not only the connotation of dirt, but simultaneously that of fecal matter, to a much greater extent than is suggested when the word is translated into English.

[4] Dr. Felix Deutsch, one of the distinguished workers on psychosomatic medicine, states: "Color brings about a reflex action upon the vascular system, if only through the feelings and emotions. The effect achieved is *not specific for any one or any certain hues.* Warm colors may calm one person and excite another. Cool colors may likewise be stimulating to one person and passive to another.—Irradiation with red or green light may produce an elevation of blood pressure and a quickening of pulse rate. Or the opposite may take place, *depending on the particular psychic make-up of the individual.* An organic, non-optical color sense has not been proved so far." (See "Psycho-Physical Reactions of the Vascular System to Influence of Light and to Impressions Gained through Light," *Folia Clinica Orientalia,* Vol. 1, fasc. 3/4, 1937.

Especially stressed should be Dr. Kurt Goldstein's work on colors. Dr. Goldstein believes that "it is probably not a false statement if we say that a specific color stimulation is accompanied by a specific response pattern

One can put forward another argument in proof of this contention: the use of color by poets in poetic imagery.[5] The contradictions are no less outspoken than those encountered in experimental research. To quote some examples:

RED

He is come to ope
The purple testament of *bleeding war.*
Shakespeare, *King Richard II*, Act III, Scene 3.

I am the very *pink of courtesy.*
Shakespeare, *Romeo and Juliet*, Act II, Scene 4, line 63.

And let's be *red with mirth.*
Shakespeare, A *Winter's Tale*, Act IV, Scene 3.

'Tis beauty truly blent, whose *red* and white
Nature's own sweet and cunning hand laid on:
Lady, you are the *cruell'st she alive,*
If you will lead these graces to the grave
And leave the world no copy.
Shakespeare, *Twelfth Night*, Act I, Scene V, line 259.

When it is evening, ye say it will be *fair weather,*
for the *sky is red.*
Matthew, XVI, 2.

There is no *red* outside the *arteries of archangel* which
can compare with it. (Scarlet *Doctor's gown* from Oxford).
Mark Twain, Lotos Club speech, Jan. 11, 1908.

Beaufort's *red sparkling eyes* blab his *heart's malice.*
Shakespeare, *King Henry VI*, Part II, Act III, Scene 1.

---

of the entire organism." (*The Organism*, Am. Book Co., New York, 1939.)

For a compilation of the extensive literature, see Faber Birren's *Color Psychology and Color Therapy*, McGraw-Hill Co., New York, 1950.

[5] Luckiesh was the first to suggest this approach; in his book *Color and Colors* there is an "Appendix" containing a few examples. Although his collection is incomplete, and needs enlargement and reworking, his idea is feasible.

Flushed with a purple grace
the *scarlet* honor of your peaceful gown.
John Dryden

Celestial rosy *red, Love's* proper hue.
John Milton

If the *red slayer* thinks he slays,
Or if the slain thinks he is slain,
They know not well the subtle ways
I keep, and pass, and turn again.
Ralph Waldo Emerson, "Brahma."

A, black; E, white; *I, red;* O, blue; U, green.
Rimbaud, Sonnets, "Vowels."

The king sits in Dunfermline town
Drinking the *blude-red wine.*
"Ballad of Sir Patrick Spens."

In Clementina's artless mien
Lucilla asks me what I see,
And are the *roses of sixteen*
Enough for me?
Walter Savage Landor, "Of Clementina."

O Rose, thou art sick;
The invisible worm
That walks in the night,
In the howling storm,
Has found out thy bed
Of *crimson joy,*
And his dark secret love
Does thy life destroy.
William Blake, "The Sick Rose."

And in the midst of this wide quietness
A *rosy sanctuary* will I dress . . .
John Keats, "Ode to Psyche."

Oh! wherefore come ye forth in triumph from the north,
With your *hand* and your *feet* and your *raiment all red?*

Thomas Babington Macaulay, "The Battle of Naseby," Stanza I.

Yellow, and black, and pale, and *hectic red,*
Pestilence-stricken multitudes.

Percy B. Shelley, "Ode to the West Wind."

GREEN

Duke: And what's her history?
Viola: A blank, my lord. She never told her love,
But let concealment, like a worm i' the bud
Feed on her damask cheek: she pined in thought,
And with a *green* and yellow *melancholy,*
She sat like patience on a monument,
Smiling at grief.

Shakespeare, *Twelfth Night,* Act II, Scene 4, line 112.

To what *green altar,* O mysterious priest,
Leads't thou that heifer lowing at the skies.

John Keats, "Ode to a Grecian Urn."

My *salad days*
When I was *green in judgment,* cold in blood.
Shakespeare, *Antony and Cleopatra,* Act V, Scene 5, line 73.

The *memory* be *green.*[6]

Shakespeare, *Hamlet,* Act I, Scene 2, line 2.

Our *bed* was *green.*

The Song of Songs.

Jealousy's eyes are *green.*

Shelley, "Swellfoot the Tyrant," Act II, Scene 1.

O! beware, my lord, of *jealousy:*
It is the *green-eyed monster* which doth mock
The meat it feeds on.

Shakespeare, *Othello,* Act III, Scene 3, line 165.

[6] "Keep his memory green"—Thomas Moore, "Oh Breathe Not His Name."—"Lord, keep my memory green."—Charles Dickens, "The Haunted Man" (last line).

Oh *green* is the color of *faith* and *truth*
And rose the color of love and youth,
And brown of the fruitful day.

Charles Kingsley, "Dartside."

But to her fears to cease
Sent down the meek-eyed *Peace;*
She, crown'd with *olive green,* came softly sliding
Down through the burning sphere.

John Milton.

And *ice,* mast-high, came floating by,
As *green* as emerald.

Samuel T. Coleridge, "Rime of the Ancient Mariner."

In a moment a delicate fire has overrun my flesh, my eyes grow dim
and my ears sing, the sweat runs down me and a trembling takes me
altogether, till *I* am as *green* and pale as the grass . . .

Sappho, Wharton's translation.

No white or red was ever seen
So *amorous* as this lovely *green.*

Andrew Marvell, "The Garden."

BLUE

Where's the eye, however blue
Doth not weary?

John Keats, "Fancy."

All in the *blue unclouded* weather.

Alfred Tennyson, "The Lady of Shalott."

Eyes of unholy blue.

Thomas Moore, "By That Lake Whose Gloomy Shore," Stanza 2.

Blue colour is everlastingly *appointed by the Deity*
to be a *source of delight.*

John Ruskin, Lectures on Architecture and Painting, at Edinburgh, November 1853.

It's true I've got no shirt to wear;
It's true my butcher's bill is due;
It's true my *prospects all look blue,*
But don't let that unsettle you!
Never you mind!
Roll on!

W. S. Gilbert, "To the Terrestrial Globe," Stanza 2.

Is the *blue* in eyes
As awful as in *stockings?*

Elizabeth Barrett Browning, "Aurora Leigh," Book I, line 379.

Some *ladies* were very *blue* and well informed.

W. M. Thackeray.

Oh, coward Conscience! how dost thou afflict me!
The light burns *blue.*

Shakespeare, *Richard III,* Act V, Scene 2, line 180.

Something old, something new,
Something borrowed, something *blue.*

Wedding Rhyme.

Hobbs hints *blue,*—straight he turtle eats:
Nobbs prints *blue,*—claret crowns his cup:
Nokes outdares Stokes in azure feats,—
Both gorge. Who fished the *murex* up?
What porridge had *John Keats?*

Robert Browning, "Popularity."

YELLOW

All seems infected that th'infected spy,
As *all looks yellow* to the jaundic'd eye.

Alexander Pope, "Essays on Criticism," Part II, line 358.

My humour shall not cool: I will incense Page
to deal with poison; I will possess him with *yellowness,*
for this revolt of mine is dangerous.

Shakespeare, *The Merry Wives of Windsor,* Act I, Scene 3.

His very *hair* is of the dissembling colour
Something browner than *Judas's.*

Shakespeare, *As You Like It,* Act III, Scene 4.

In winter I get up at night
And dress by *yellow candle light.*
In summer, quite the other way,
I have to go to bed by day.

Robert Louis Stevenson, "Bed in Summer."

And *Fame,* with *golden wings* aloft, doth fly.

Spenser

O *jealousy,*
Thou ugliest fiend of hell! Thy deadly renown
Preys on my vitals, turns the healthful hue
Of my fresh cheek to *haggard sallowness,*
And drinks my spirit up.

Hannah More.

A primrose by a river's brim
A *yellow primrose* was to him,
And it was nothing more.

William Wordsworth, "Peter Bell," Part I, Stanza 12.

Golden lads and *girls* all must
As chimney-sweepers, come to dust.

Shakespeare, "Fidele."

The *world's great age* begins anew,
The *golden years* return.

Shelley, "Hellas."

Much have I travelled in the *realms* of *gold* . . .

Keats, "On First Looking Into Chapman's Homer."

Fashion experts and women who believe themselves to be well-dressed (see Chapter Eight) are quick to point out the ridiculous mistakes which arise when women mix their colors "without taste." Except for exceptional cases of color-blindness,[7] and more frequent cases of downright inexperience, my experience has been that it is not lack of taste, but *neurotic inhibition* which is responsible for the wrongly mixed palette. The real trouble seems to be that specific colors carry very personalized, entirely unconscious, meanings. Thus, *colors express emotional-symbolic innuendoes.* This leads to one of three possibilities: *incorrect combination of colors; avoidance of specific colors, or predilections in disguise.*

This must be strongly stressed: *only specific* neurotic elaborations of the *specific* personality are to blame. A color-wheel for neurotic mistakes of this kind cannot and does not exist. One color may have two completely different neurotic implications for two different people.

Psychologically speaking, our knowledge of these "unconscious color-hints" is still in its infancy. Still, what has been learned to date permits of a preliminary conclusion. Psychoanalysis of the neurotic is quite capable of clarifying and changing these neurotic inhibitions. A humorist might ask whether there is an implied invitation here, suggesting that "tasteless" women embark on costly and prolonged treatment for the specific purpose of changing this alleged symptom. There is not; my observations were made incidentally, when analyzing women who came into treatment because of completely unrelated severe inner conflicts. On the other hand, if one is familiar with the terrified helplessness with which some women face the task of choosing a new outfit, and if one is aware of the amount of ironical

[7] Allegedly four per cent of males are affected with one of the many types (18) of color-blindness, and only one tenth of this proportion is found in females. This is especially claimed of dichromatism.

scorn the tastelessly dressed woman meets with, it is not hard to believe that female analytic patients and analysands will in the future draw their analyst's attention to this point, and request that this specific symptom be included in the scientific scrutiny of their "total personality."

The usual objection could be adduced here; it could be claimed that conclusions drawn from experiences with neurotic women cannot apply to "normal" people. This argument is easily refuted. Analysis has conclusively proved that the gap between "normal" and "neurotic" is by no means as great as the gratuitous assumption has been in the past. The difference is merely quantitative: One can define a normal person as one who "isn't *too* neurotic." What we learn from those whose "percentage" is "high" teaches us a great deal about the people who are stabilized—frequently only temporarily—on a lower or only slightly lower level of neuroticism. Emotional health and neurosis are "sisters under the skin." [8]

With one exception, the following examples are taken from clinical analysis. The "cases" are selected from an extensive material. They were chosen because they satisfy two essential requirements: an obvious interpretation, based on the patients' associations and the analyst's knowledge of the patient's life-history, both internal and external; a situation sufficiently clear-cut to eliminate the need for long, detailed, pre-histories.

Some "color-allergies" and "color-sympathies" are so complicated that the necessary backgrounds would cover many pages. Such examples are omitted. The order of presentation is determined by the specific color involved.[9]

[8] I have devoted a book to this topic, *The Lower and the Higher Neurotic Brackets* (in preparation).

[9] The rule, "everything is allowed which is pleasing and restful to the eye," seems to concede to that organ only a limited amount of work capacity and some kind of static attitude. In any case, color charts have been worked out for the use of designers. These are little known to the general public. Still less known is the fact that a complete, scientific sys-

RED

1. A painter, in analysis because of extensive personality difficulties, mainly of psychic-masochistic nature, included among his grievances the "silliness of the critics," who repeatedly disapproved of his partiality for—red. The painter admitted that he had a "strange pull" towards this color, and that he frequently painted women in red dresses. "That's my business," he went on. "What right have the art critics and their idiotic parrots to tell me that I'm bloodthirsty? And they're all wrong—red has a strange *reassuring* effect on me. I'm not responsible for other people's associations. Red doesn't mean blood and revolution to me. It has an entirely different meaning for me." When asked for his associations with the color red, the patient said: "I don't think that colors can be explained by associations. If you insist, I can tell you my association, silly as it is—a bathtub." Since no other associations were forthcoming, we relinquished further search for the time being, putting the material in the "psychic icebox" to wait for a more propitious moment.

This moment came a few weeks later, when the patient was describing his puritanical upbringing, in connection with some details of his tenth year. He blamed his mother for his restrictions. Even movies were forbidden: "I was allowed to go to the movies only once, when I was five or six. Even then it was only because a part of the biblical

---

tem of color notation and terminology, applying to any given color, was perfected by Albert M. Munsel in 1912. For details, see *The Art of Color and Design*, by Maitland Graves (McGraw-Hill, New York, 1941). The terminology is complicated, and includes the division in *hue* (quality by which one color is distinguished from another); *value* (degree of luminosity of a color); and *chroma* (strength, intensity or purity of color). Every color, therefore, may be precisely described and its relation to any other color be stated thus:

$$\text{Hue}\,\frac{\text{Value}}{\text{Chroma}}.$$

history was dramatized. I believe the film was called the *Ten Commandments*, one of the early mass-scenes of Cecil de Mille. I admit that the crossing of the Red Sea made quite an impression on me. I was naive enough to think that the Red Sea was really red, like red ink. And besides, the fact that God helped His chosen people, and rescued them from a hopeless situation, had a *reassuring* effect on me."

I asked the patient whether the "reassuring effect" of the color red, mentioned by him a few weeks before, could not have some connection, pointing out that he had used the very same words each time. The patient laughed. He considered the connection far-fetched. "May I remind you," he said, "that you are choosing eclectically from the contents of the 'psychic icebox'? If my memory serves me correctly, my association with the color red was 'white bathtub.' " After a moment of silence, the patient had to eat his own ironic words. He had suddenly remembered something completely repressed. In his infantile fight against the mother's puritanism, he constantly searched for additional arguments to use against her. He found such an argument when he read (or was told of) the technique used in creating some special effects produced in the film. The grand scene of the crossing of the Red Sea, the parting of the water, had all been a studio trick, done in a bathtub, and later enlarged from the bathtub photograph.

The "reassuring effect" of the color red was thus explained, as was his original "silly" association. For this man, RED unconsciously meant: "God can deliver you from all dangers"; this consoling thought accounted for the feeling that red is "reassuring." The repressed counterthought, centering around the mysterious bathtub, alluded not only to his own reproaches ("Mother is good, she took care of you when you were a baby and a child"), but also to his fight with his mother, and constituted another reproach, this time for his acceptance of reassurance from her when otherwise he rejected her and her precepts so completely. And at bottom, in spite of his denial of any aggressive connotation, red was also reassuring because it maintained his fiction that he was fighting aggressively against the mother to whom he was, unconsciously, masochistically attached.

2. A schizoid woman made herself conspicuous by wearing dyed red hair of the most "burning" variety, with a kind of Empire dress. Her whole appearance had a touch of the caricature. In spite of protests from husband, children, relatives and friends, she refused to make any change in the color of the dye she used to disguise her prematurely white hair. She lived in a world of fantasy. She was a "reclusoid." [9] The fairyland she inhabited was ruled by a cruel and beautiful queen, whom she imitated in her dress.

Her predilection for the redder-than-red dye she used was easily clarified. During a walk which she took, at the age of six, with her hyper-puritanical mother, she saw a woman with red hair, conspicuous in dress and behavior, obviously a prostitute. The child asked her mother who the woman could be. The mother's answer to this was intimidating: "Don't talk about such people, Baby."

The "baby," when grown up, did not talk about "such people"; she simply played the role of one of them by imitating their external appearance, as she believed she had seen it as a child. This recollection, leading to clarification of the reason why red was her favorite color, was, of course, repressed. Consciously, she merely claimed: "I just adore—red."

In inner reality, the ostentatious use of this loud color became one of the weapons in the patient's unending fight to disprove her masochistic attachment to her mother. It

[9] For psychological description of this type, see *Money and Emotional Conflicts,* Chapter IX (l.c.).

was a defensive weapon; since her mother had violently objected to the color, didn't the patient's constant use of it prove her cruel aggression towards the person who so disliked it?

GREEN

A woman in her early thirties, a librarian, habitually wore grass-green dresses, with gold belt and accessories. This was her costume, regardless of the occasion, except for a rare appearance in a gold dress, with grass-green accessories.

Her conflicts were centered around the eternal triangle: she was chronically in love with one or another married man who "exploited her as a prostitute," as she dramatically claimed. What she meant, obviously, was that she inevitably attached herself to a "hopelessly" married man, who had no intention at all of marrying her. Otherwise, behind this Oedipal palimpsest, she constantly lived out the infantile masochistic attachment to mother which she had failed to overcome; there was always an "unjust wife" in the background to serve as mother substitute. She was, of course, entirely oblivious to the fact that she constantly provoked these conflicts herself, by choosing the wrong man.

The reasons for her obsession with grass-green and gold became clear after some time. The girl was the "revolutionary" member of a conservative Catholic family in Vienna.[10] She proclaimed the doctrine of sexual equality, to which her mother responded with raging fury, and her "unimportant" father with pious statements. The mother, as the child suspected at a rather early age, was less moralistic in her private actions than in her public protestations. She had cultural and intellectual pretensions, she was rather well read and something of an inhibited but aspiring writer. In these ways, she was the leader of the family. My patient

[10] The patient was analyzed twenty years ago; at that time I practiced in Vienna.

and her mother had only one common interest, literature. The patient often consulted her mother on her own literary endeavors during puberty.

Her sexual activity more than fulfilled her proclaimed doctrine; for a long time she was practically a nymphomaniac, "out of principle." That principle consisted of being a "garçonne"—"aren't men polygamous?" In her external behavior she played the prostitute: the episode of her defloration proved it. She was picked up in the street (she was eighteen) by a man who mistook her for a prostitute; he took as "comedy" even the difficulties of defloration, and considered the few drops of blood as part of the trappings of her profession, used for the sake of extracting higher pay . . .

On the other hand, this woman's cynical attitude, consciously so outspoken, was counteracted by hidden guilt. This was revealed in a peculiar way. I had asked the patient her first name, and her reply was a barrage of fury; never, never would she divulge that "secret." Her name was Mary. The patient's education had been that of a devout Catholic, and evidently she believed that she defamed the very name of the Holy Virgin,[11] therefore her determination not to speak of blasphemy.

Her fidelity to gold and grass-green had a rather strange, "literary" explanation, although one which was built into the whole conflict with the patient's mother. The patient hated drab colors, which were predominant at home. In prepuberty while studying Goethe's *Faust*, she came across the following lines: "Gray, dear friend, is all theory; and green, life's golden tree." ("Grau, teurer Freund, ist alle Theorie,—Und grün des Leben's goldner Baum.") The poet's lines seemed contradictory to the girl, and she consulted her mother, the literary expert. The mother explained poetic license, but the girl was not satisfied. To get

[11] See a similar situation, differently elaborated, page 213.

rid of her, the mother said ironically, "Perhaps the tree was in sunshine, and the green means the surrounding grass." The girl took the irony badly, and exclaimed, "How can you call yourself a poet, when you are so prosaic!"

Years later, when the girl was able to decide on her own wardrobe, she selected exclusively grass-green and gold. This inner irony at her mother's expense was also expressed in her profession, where she handled books other people had written. This, in her opinion, was all her mother could do. In an unconscious, ironic, identification, the patient chose to become a librarian, although other possibilities were open to her.

It is superfluous to add that the patient had no idea why she just "loved" these two colors; the lines of poetry were repressed, and the whole scene had to be analytically deciphered.

BLUE

1. A woman in the early forties, in analysis because of neurotic depression which had allegedly been caused by "constant disappointments with men," dressed expensively and in good taste. What made her attire conspicuous was that she always wore one color, a mixture of blue and violet. A superficial observer would assume that she had only one dress; closer inspection would prove that she had dozens. Their uniformity of color blotted out the differences in style.

She had no answers to inquiries about her preference for this color, although she volunteered additional information: she was so obsessed with the color of her choice that, when she looked at a white wall, she frequently imagined a thick blue-violet line. Analysis of her personality revealed a banal "penis envy" type of the hysterical variety. She "hated" men, using her numerous disappointments as excuses. All men were impotent, she said. Naturally, she did not suspect that she herself unconsciously engineered her disappointments by choosing all her men from one conveyor belt—that is, of the one type already found unsatisfactory.

Her total emphasis on blue-violet could be clarified after a previously repressed recollection from her fourth year came to the surface. At that time she had inspected the penis of a boy much older than herself; she was startled by the sight of the thick vein at the "bottom" of the organ. This sight-seeing expedition stabilized, in her mind, the old (pre-Oedipal) feeling of being deprived by mother; she rescued herself to the Oedipal level, using two defenses. These were: "First, man's penis is non-existent—an impotent man can be identified as a castrated one. And, second, I have a bigger penis—my whole body is a penis." Exhibitionistically, therefore, she displayed the organ—in her dresses.[12]

2. A colleague, Dr. Olga Knopf, told me of a promiscuous woman with a Catholic background, who dressed well; the analyst observed, however, that the patient seemed to avoid blue, although she could not give any reasons. Analysis revealed that guilt feeling, in connection with her promiscuity, was involved. Recollections—previously repressed—reached far back into childhood: the Madonna of the little church, in her home town, was painted in blue, with some admixture of gold. Blue thus became the "moral" color; as inner penance, the color was avoided.

3. The following incident is the only example not drawn

[12] See *Basic Neurosis,* p. 16. It would be fallacious to assume that this woman's dresses represented a *direct* symbolic innuendo of *direct* unconscious wishes. They were but defenses, directed against more deeply repressed masochistic tendencies, visible also in her chronic "disappointments."

from analytical records. The incident was found in an article by Clifford B. Hicks;[13] it was described to Hicks by Louis Cheskin, whom Hicks identifies as a top color expert.

A man consulted Cheskin because of his antipathy for dark blue, and his near-speechlessness when in the vicinity of any man who wore a dark blue suit. Cheskin inquired about childhood experiences, and was told of a childhood incident involving a policeman, stolen apples, several hours in the local jail, and the family's subsequent embarrassment. As the questioning continued, the man became aware of the source of his discomfort—the color of the policeman's uniform. According to the article, his aversion for deep blue then disappeared.

I am citing this example, despite the optimistic deduction, because it corresponds tangentially to some of my experiences with patients. In real analysis, of course, discovery of unconscious reasons is a more involved process, the cases per se are more complicated, and the results are neither so prompt nor so dramatic. For reasons of discretion and necessary protection of my patients, I prefer to quote Mr. Cheskin's case, rather than one drawn from my own clinical experience.

WHITE

A man of means, in his middle forties, perpetually searched for a woman with a "perfect white skin." He was very precise in differentiating between shades of white. He deserted a few girl friends—and wives—because he found that, "after all," their skin tones were "disappointing." He was in the habit of ordering expensive white dresses for his current women; the material for these dresses was always chosen after what amounted to a fierce battle with the sales-person involved. He would go into veritable tantrums

[13] "Your Color Type and How To Live With It," Popular Mechanics Magazine, Vol. 93, No. 2, Los Angeles, February, 1950.

when there was an attempt to make him purchase an "unbecoming" white.

The man came into analysis because he lived above his emotional means; everything excited him out of proportion to its importance. Since he was a self-made "success-hunter,"[14] who had found success, he treated everybody with contempt and superciliousness. Finally, one of his many physicians told him: "You are intolerable. I don't want to see you again. Before getting rid of you, I'll give you one last piece of advice: if you don't want to kill yourself with overwork and overtension, consult a psychiatrist. Let him take the beating—these people seem to be accustomed to it. I prefer civilized people as patients."

In analysis, as can be imagined, the patient lived up to his reputation. He was intolerable. Still, his constant tension diminished during treatment. One day this "perfect white skin" half-fetishism was brought up.

"There is nothing to discuss," the man objected. "I can afford to have some preferences."

"You can afford it financially, not psychologically. Look at the troubles your so-called preference has brought you: a few divorces, dozens of discarded girl-friends. Prove to me that you can afford *that* from the 'tension-viewpoint,' as you called it."

"How can I be blamed for the fact that women have poor skins?"

"How about analyzing the reasons for your predilection for the whitest white?"

"I have nothing to say—I'm just the customer."

"Your business-like approach will not solve the riddle. Any associations?"

"Don't bother me with this nonsense."

The discussion ended at this point—temporarily. It was

[14] For the psychology of this type, see *Money and Emotional Conflicts* (l.c.) Section: "The Success Hunter."

later resumed, in connection with a dream in which a nurse appeared. I asked him whether he had had any hospital experiences as a child. At first, the patient denied that there had been any, but later remembered that as a child of four he had spent a few days in a hospital because of a tonsil operation. The memory of his terror, both before and after the operation, gradually returned. The first thing he had seen after awakening from narcosis had been an enormous black spot—the black habit of the nun who was his nurse. (It was a Catholic hospital.) Later his eyes had caught her stiff white coif, and he had continued to stare at the coif, fascinated—perhaps to counteract his fear of black. To the child, black had the connotation of death, since he recollected the mourning clothes worn by his family after the death of his grandfather. Whenever the nun approached his bed, he had shivered and trembled.

I asked the patient: "Is there any connection between your predilection for white, and the nun-nurse's coif?"

"Nonsense! I love white, and I was mortally afraid of the nun's white coif!"

"This is less of a contradiction than you believe. Didn't we establish the fact that by skillful unconscious maneuvering you push every woman into the position of being unjust towards you? Haven't we discussed, time and again, your masochistic attachment to your fantasy of woman?"

"Don't use the word 'we.' You mean you said it time and again, and I contradicted you time and again."

"Still, on the basis of working through exactly this feeling you have of being constantly overwhelmed, which means being pushed into the masochistic corner, your tension has diminished."

"Don't capitalize on that. I accepted the interpretation of being overwhelmed by situations, not by women."

"Your distinction is fallacious. Situations don't float around in a vacuum; they are represented by people. Your unconscious fantasy of being overwhelmed became so generalized that even men could arouse it—weren't you overtense, even with business associates? Have you forgotten that you suspected yourself of homosexuality, until I was able to dispel this suspicion? And have you forgotten our running discussion about your jealousy of the girls you paid for and supported? You can conveniently forget the links in the chain, or separate them, but it still adds up to the unconscious wish to be mistreated."

"What has all this got to do with my fondness for white?"

"Only this: why not assume that you singled out—as pars pro toto—the white of the cap worn by the nun—a woman—as fear object? You had a masochistic attachment stemming, of course, from much earlier sources—from your mother. To counteract it, you became attached to a different shade of white. And later this was shifted to the skin of women, where it came from originally."

"Sounds fantastic."

"Not more fantastic than your hunt for perfect white, or the tantrums you have about it. By the way, what kind of white do you dislike so intensely? Has it some similarity to the white of a nurse's cap?"

After some minutes of silence, the great man signed off, slightly deflated.

"Let's forget the white," he said.

"I take this as confirmation of my deduction."

The great man did not answer. This was his way of confirming.

By the next day, however, he had got his second wind, and continued the "argument."

"Your deduction is full of holes. If I'm afraid of white, how can I love it?"

"Ever heard the term 'psychic masochism'?"

"But you don't understand. I hate a specific white, I

love another. I can understand my hatred, or even fear, of the cold white originally seen in the nun's coif. Why don't I detest *all* white?"

"Because, like a moth attracted to the light which will kill it, you were capable of shifting the type of white without dissociating yourself from it. For you, white means: cruel woman."

"But the nurse was rather helpful. That washes out the argument."

"On the contrary. That clinches the argument. It means that you did not work with a reality factor when you were afraid, in the hospital. You were working with a preconceived notion, left over from your infancy."

"Do you seriously claim that my mental development simply progressed from one shade of white to another? Don't you underestimate my mental capacities?"

"How frequently do you have to be told that emotional and intellectual capacities are not identical? Emotionally, nobody is as old as his birth certificate says—and especially not a neurotic!"

"Very consoling to hear the formula for my emotional immaturity is from 'white to white.' "

"Irony does not solve problems. Did you believe that the baby in you, unlike the baby in everybody else, would be grown up? Did you expect that analysis would just confirm the greatness of the great man, in short, add a new achievement to your exploits, glorified in *Who's Who?*"

"But *Who's Who* does not register 'neurotic' after my name!"

"That is your good luck. Neurosis is painful, but at least it's private."

GRAY

A woman in the middle thirties, in analysis because of marital conflicts, habitually wore gray. She was known in her circles as "the lady in gray." At first, one had the impression that she merely wanted a good foil for her blond hair, although black would have underscored it more effectively. Asked why she wore only gray, she answered, "I like it."

"Does gray correspond to your gloomy mood?" [15]

"I liked and wore gray in happy times, too."

"When did the predilection for gray start?"

"As long as I can remember, I've had it; or at least since I've been choosing my dresses myself."

It developed that this exquisitely masochistic woman went through a period (between the ages of eighteen and twenty-four) in which she tried to compose music, and wrote ballets. Her great disappointment began when one particular ballet, upon which she had pinned great hopes, was rejected.

"You never mentioned your artistic ambitions before."

"They are water over the dam: puerile follies."

"What was the last ballet about?"

"It represented moths attracted by light. It was beautiful, although, of course, all the moths were burned to death."

[15] The problem of moods as related to color is still unknown territory. The reasons are twofold: first, the psychological term "mood" has so far not been investigated; a first attempt has been made by the author in *The Superego* (Chapter X). Second, the connection between *transitory* moods, and colors, has never been studied either. The ironic question posed to the patient, "Does gray correspond to your gloomy mood?" was on the popular level, and I was more concerned with its possibilities as an invitation to talk than with a serious answer.—It is interesting, by the way, that Birren in his *Color Psychology* mentions that "Buddha's color was yellow or gold; however, he wore red when he pondered on the vicissitudes of man; and the Blessed One, putting on a tunic of double red cloth, and binding on his girdle, and throwing his upper robe over his right shoulder, would go thither and sit down, and for a while remain solitary, plunged into meditation." (Quoted from Hindu Upanishads). To complicate any deductions, Confucius hated purple: "I hate the purple color, because it confuses us with the red color; I hate the goody-goodies because they confuse us with the virtuous people." (Quoted from the book *Heang Tango*).

"Did it occur to you that you identified yourself, unconsciously, with one of the burned moths?"

"That's preposterous. My symbolic idea was exactly the opposite: life's short, enjoy it."

"By being burned to death?"

"Do you want to say that I identify myself with the Maid of Orleans? I may have had such glorious ideas as a child."

"No. I wish to inform you that the artist represents, in his work, secondary defenses against his real, though repressed, inner wishes.[16] In your case, masochism was warded off with joie de vivre. Hence the idea for the moth-ballet."

"But according to you, I identified with the victim."

"You are confusing the conscious with the unconscious."

"And my love for gray?"

"Aren't moths—gray?"

The patient did not answer.[17]

[16] For elaboration, see *The Writer and Psychoanalysis* (l.c.).

[17] Some color specialists, in empirical subdivision, claim that they "know" what color the average person will choose in his home. All these statements, emanating from an empirical science in its infancy, must be subject to a great many reservations. In any case, these claims are put forward: there is no reason why they should not be registered, as long as their tentative nature is stressed. In the paper by Clifford B. Hicks already referred to previously, there is a summary of some of the findings of Louis Cheskin. Cheskin declares that the "emotionally normal" male will prefer a certain shade of blue to any other color; his wife's favorite color will be magenta red. The average reaction is to be depressed in a room that is strongly blue, to get a headache from bright yellow, to get nervous when surrounded by bright red, and bored in a room decorated in leaf-green. Cheskin's research has shown him that colors have individual personalities. He cites an experiment: a living room was painted in two colors, two adjacent walls green-blue, the other corner warm peach. The two corners were then furnished exactly alike. A married couple with suitably diverse temperaments were invited to enter the room. The husband, an anti-social person, sat down in the warmly-painted corner; the wife, a lively and fun-loving woman, walked to the blue-green, cool, corner. According to Cheskin, they had chosen the colors that "complemented their personalities." Similar results were reached in further experiments.

In the light of the subjective complications present in individual personalities, I am rather skeptical of this deduction. The terms which Cheskin

BLACK

Marital quarrels frequently begin with conflicts centering around colors. The wife's favorite color in dress may infuriate the husband, who—for reasons unknown to him—"hates" that particular shade. If his wife, also for unconscious reasons, refuses to give up her favorite color, conflict is inevitable, and unending.

One could, of course, protest that this is a "trifle," of no importance, and should be disregarded. And so it is, under not too neurotic conditions. Under neurotic stress the story reads differently. In a previous book, *Conflict in Marriage*,[18] I devoted a long chapter to these chronic irritants, using seven detailed case histories,[19] to show the complicated substructure of the attitude, "Malevolence in Trifles."

Marriage partners do not pick their "trifling" complaints at random, nor maintain them at random. The trifles are "hitching posts," and in the following example the hitching post is the color black.

A successful business man in the forties, who had only recently become rich, had this to say about his wife:

"I can safely say that I love my wife, though I am sometimes filled with irrational anger towards her. What starts me off, most of the time, is an insignificant thing, sometimes a really silly thing. There are three sure starters. One

---

uses to describe opposing types, "nervous" and "quiet," are not scientific. Moreover, the test itself fails to take unconscious determinants into account. What if the two test colors have some subjective-unconscious connotations, independent of the "nervous" or "quiet" personalities of the people tested? In short, color science still has a long way to go.

[18] Part I, "The Inexpressible Reproach."

[19] The "infuriating details" in these case histories were: the phrase "if you know what I mean"; the gesture, "half-open mouth, head slightly deflected to the left, indicating impatience to talk"; "governess-like tone"; the gesture of smoothing the hair; the husband's facial expression when writing checks; a handkerchief in the husband's breast pocket. Ridiculous as these trifles were, they contained the symbolic sum total of these people's inner conflicts.

is the way my wife dresses, in nothing but black. I insisted that she buy some new clothes, and she finally bought a few—all black. Left to herself, she would have gone on wearing that same old black outfit. I told her, time and again, how I detest the color, but it did no good.

"Then there's her habit of letting the water in the bathroom run for a long time before she washes her hands. She claims she has to, so that the water will be warm enough. And besides, she never closes the bathroom door—unfortunately, my room is next to the bathroom.

"The third thing is the way she insists on using left-overs when she plans a meal. This, too, infuriates me beyond rhyme and reason. I detest that type of economy in food. And in our circumstances, it isn't necessary."

The patient was unable to explain the "murderous irritation" he felt when he saw his wife in black, or when his wife let the water flow from the faucets in the bathroom. All he could offer was the information that the sound of the water seemed to be the interfering factor, and that he would shift his anger so that it was concentrated on his wife's "forgetting" to close the bathroom door. In such situations, he would run from his room and slam the bathroom door, shouting, "Why don't you close the door, damn it!" His irritation was so intense that he anticipated his anger every time his wife even approached the bathroom.

"What are you thinking about during these scenes?" I wanted to know.

"I am furious with my wife, and heap abuse on her."

"For instance?"

"Oh, silly things."

"Name a few."

"It's so idiotic I'm really ashamed to."

"How much coaxing do you need? What are the words?"

"Well, there's one particular word I use that makes me

think something irrational is involved in all this. The word I mutter furiously to myself is the infantile term for urination. I use the word as a noun, as if my wife were committing a crime. The strange thing is that it's so illogical—there's no connection with what is really irritating me, which is the sound of running water."

"Could you find some connecting link between the sound of running water and urination?"

"Perhaps this—I've heard of a trick mothers use to induce stubborn children to void the bladder. They open the faucets. The idea—if it makes sense at all—is obviously to invite the child to imitate the sound of running water."

"Who told you the story?"

"Don't remember."

"And what about your irritation concerning left-overs?"

"My wife is an excellent cook, but she has a mania for using every bit of food that's left over. She concocts ingenious dishes out of these left-overs. This habit of hers infuriated me, and I put a stop to it. She doesn't make these dishes for me any more, but she still makes them for herself. That infuriates me even more. She doesn't see my point. She insists that what she eats is none of my business."

"Why do you object?"

"It reflects on me, that's why. It makes me look cheap. I am very generous in all my financial dealings with her, as she herself admits."

"How does her mania for left-overs reflect on you?"

"It gives the impression that I want to save money on food, or that there isn't enough money. I insist on her eating the same food that she serves me. And when I am presented with a steak,, and she eats something left over from last week, I go into a rage."

"What are your wife's arguments?"

"She says she hates waste. And she has a new rationalization—all the starving children in Europe."

"Did it ever occur to you that there might be neurotic reasons for your wife's insistence on 100% utilization of food?"

"I did. Nothing helps; even if her mania is neurotic, it still infuriates me."

This patient had entered analysis because of irrational conflicts with his business partner. This partner happened to be his brother-in-law, the husband of his sister. The patient felt irritated with his partner, contradicted him at every turn, and at the same time understood that this conduct was endangering his business. His official reason for consulting me was "nervous irritation," a self-made diagnosis.

His childhood situation could be reconstructed as follows: He had been confronted with a weak father and a rather domineering mother. "She was very proud and self-centered. Whether she had any feelings at all I don't know; if she had emotions, she didn't show them. I remember my feeling of being alone, of having nobody to turn to. Strangely enough, my mother showed a certain, though superficial, affection for my sister, perhaps because she was born so late—we are seven years apart. I remember two instances of real hatred for my mother. One came at the age of six, when my parents took a trip to Europe and left me in the care of my grandmother. I felt excluded and rejected. They brought me a present: a watch. I hated that watch; I had the feeling that they gave it to me to buy me off. The second instance was rather amusing, really, but at the time the story wasn't funny at all. I was five or six. My mother and I were taking a walk in the park. I told her to help me to urinate. I insisted that I couldn't do it alone. She was furious, told me that a big boy like me should be ashamed of asking for help, but finally helped me. A *short time later*, my sister was born. I felt some tenderness for her, but at the time I was furiously jealous of all the attention she got. I also remember a feeling of self-pity and hot fury later on, when my sister was being trained to use the bathroom for urination. My mother was with her, and I wanted to be there, too. But I got a scolding and strict orders to stay outside. I stood outside listening, with tears streaming down my cheeks. Isn't it funny, how silly children are?"

"Not only children. Don't you see that you still haven't digested that specific disappointment?"

"Are you serious?"

"Don't you see that your fury with your wife in connection with the bathroom has its emotional basis in exactly the incident you described?"

"Impossible."

"Let's see. What makes you irrationally furious with your wife? The sound of water running in the bathroom. You call her names—four-letter-word names. You make disparaging remarks connected with micturition. Don't you see how you are unconsciously repeating, with her, the fury you felt when your mother cared for your sister in the bathroom?"

The patient exclaimed with great excitement, "Sounds plausible but must be wrong."

"Why?"

"That was a long time ago."

"True enough. But neurosis means exactly that: unconscious repetition of bygone conflicts, projected upon innocent people."

"That sounds just fantastic. If my fury with my wife goes back to this specific incident, then it has nothing to do with my wife at all."

"All of these emotionally enlarged trifles which irritate you, pertain to *you* exclusively."

"Strange . . ."

"But true . . . We would get an even better picture if we could connect what we had already clarified with some additional material. What about your distaste for black? Do you have any idea of where this aversion comes from?"

"I don't think that aversions to colors have to be explained."

"You are mistaken. Any associations with black?"

"Sorry, I can't oblige. No associations. No superstitions, so black doesn't remind me of death. I didn't even lose money on the ill-famed "Black Friday"—or was it "Black Thursday"—in 1929. I had no connection with the Black Tom explosion. I don't mean to be facetious, I just hate black, that's all."

"That's not all."

"By the way, you must have had something in mind when you said that one could somehow connect my aversion to black with the bathroom scene. I don't see any connection."

"Meaning that the material is repressed? I could imagine at least two connecting links. First, your infantile peeping. How do you know that you didn't do exactly that? To a child unfamiliar with female anatomy and with the existence of pubic hair, the whole region frequently seems—black. Second, you told me of a scene in a park when you tried to force your mother to help you with voiding. Do you by any chance remember the color of the dress or blouse your mother wore on that occasion? You also told me that your sister was born shortly after the scene in the park. Therefore your mother must have been pregnant, and maternity dresses are frequently black, so that the woman will look less voluminous."

At this point occurred one of the few dramatic moments

experienced in every analysis, when the suddenly recollected "basic" material coincides with an analytic assumption previously rejected as senseless by the patient. The patient had to confirm both guesses, to his amazement; his mother's maternity dress had been black; his repressed Peeping Tom experiences had been of the type described.

After recovering from the shock of analytic "crystal-gazing" into the past, the patient asked a reasonable question:

"But why my distaste for black? If I am repeating so many infantile experiences with my innocent wife, why not this one, too?"

"You overlook the guilt connected with it. In this instance and in many others, you work on the basis of defense, allegedly proving to your conscience that you did not harbor these forbidden wishes connected with peeping centering around your mother's pregnancy, and fantasies derived from that."

The third trifle—the "left-over" trifle, as the patient called it, had a more complicated structure. As can be seen from the childhood incidents described above, the patient's relationship with his mother had been a demand for 100%, exclusive attention. This was far from possible, partly because of the mother's personality, but mostly because the child's demands were quantitatively irrational. Every "refusal" provoked fury in the child. That fury was in turn counteracted by guilt, based on the realization, "Mother is in general good to you." This set-up is common; in cases leading to eventual normality, the child gives up, or more precisely, shifts the aggressiveness to people less "holy" than the parent. In a masochistic child this stage is not achieved. The vicious circle of anger and guilt can be endured only if a libidinous remedy is found, and the third link in the chain is the libidinization of guilt, or psychic masochism. Thus a glutton for punishment is produced. The sequence—aggression, guilt, and finally transformation of guilt into unconscious pleasure—is later generalized, and projected upon innocent bystanders (Freud's "*genetic picture*").

Gluttony for punishment, after it is definitely established, is still counteracted by *secondary* guilt, and leads to the "*clinical picture*" described by myself. For the inner conscience, the superego, cannot be fooled completely; it discovers that an *unconscious* pleasure has been fabricated from a consciously experienced punishment. No educator likes to be cheated out of the punishment he imposes. As one of its essential elements, the masochistic "solution" includes an ironic inner attitude towards the punishment, an attitude which reduces it to absurdity. The neurotic superego is basically interested in cashing in on punishment. It is "bribed," for a period, with the constant self-damage which is inevitable for the psychic masochist. To some extent also, it is mollified by the efforts of the ego, which attempts to "prove" that the poor glutton for punishment does not enjoy his beatings and defeats, but is the helpless victim of the bad, cruel, outer world which forces him to retaliate (with pseudo-aggression!). But these are temporary palliatives; sooner or later the superego demands additional ransom.

There is no more tragic situation for a psychic masochist than an encounter with someone too naive—or too malicious—to conform to his inner expectations. There is a continuous performance, in this neurotic's private theatre, of a scene with two protagonists: the innocent victim (himself, the psychic masochist), and the "cruel" tormenter. This makes it possible for him to go in for outrageous provocations, to remain unaware that he was the provocateur, to feel only the injustice of being rebuffed, and finally to revel in hatred and self-pity.

This patient's wife had committed the unpardonable

crime of failing to conform to her husband's inner expectations. When she presented him with a steak, and ate left-overs herself, she was constructing a situation which could not possibly be construed as injustice. The patient was confronted with the exact opposite: a sacrifice. No hitching post for his expected and familiar feeling of injustice presented itself, and his unconscious disappointment manifested itself in anger.

On the other hand, when his wife fed him with left-overs, she was "unjust," she was "refusing" him choice food. He "collected" the expected "injustice," and consequently exhibited defensive fury.

How could the poor wife win that hopeless battle? When dealing with a neurotic, there is no chance of winning. Her husband's neurosis would automatically counteract any expedient.

If the wife fed her husband with left-overs, the menu was classified as an injustice, according to the patient's masochistic code. Result: fury.

If the wife fed her husband steaks, and ate the left-overs herself, the menu was classified as an unpardonable offense against the patient's "basic fallacy," in which the wife was assigned the role of injustice-provider. Result: fury.

The third possibility was serving freshly prepared food to both husband and wife. But the patient had an ace in the hole: "On the rare occasions when that happened I was angry, too, because I knew that she was secretly thinking of the left-overs in the refrigerator, and regretting that I had made her waste them by not serving them for dinner."

Neurotic repetitiveness always wins.[20]

[20] I remember a patient who told me that the "food outlook" on life, which is inherent in oral regression and becomes prominent when orality is stressed, seemed ridiculous to him, and that quarrels about food are below the level of intelligence, since "we eat to live, but don't live to eat." Those who agree with him should be reminded that the psychic life of

The patient's wife entered analysis, too. She had peculiar grounds for finally consenting to take this hated step: she was caught in the net of her "left-over" mania. Her husband was frequently absent on trips. When she discovered that analysis was a month to month business, and that appointments, if reserved, must be paid for, she suggested that she substitute for her frequently absent husband in order to prevent "intolerable waste." Substitutions of this kind are typically rejected; in this case substitution was accepted, because she needed analytic therapy, and her husband had specifically asked that she be treated. Her "left-over" compulsion had at least one hidden asset—it impelled her to undertake analysis.

The wife, a thirtyish, energetic person, had "duty" and "serious-mindedness" written all over her face, and accentuated this air by wearing badly fitted mourning clothes. She considered herself a "thrifty, therefore normal" person. It took quite a time before she could be made to understand that her exaggerated hatred of waste objectively constituted a neurotic sign, in spite of her subjective opinion that it was not a neurotic symptom. Strangely enough, her husband had not told me that her "hatred of waste" extended to the quality of her clothing, too. She was the wife of a wealthy man—his wealth had, it is true, been acquired only recently—but she was shabbily dressed. Her husband accepted this "peculiarity" (which compromised him in the

---

neurotics is not regulated by elevated standards. It expresses, on a more naive level, impulses present in everyone. The following news story is an illustration:

SOUP-LOVING MATE DUNKED BY WIFE
By the Associated Press

Los Angeles, Dec. 7, 1949—Mrs. Violet S., 27, won a divorce decree yesterday after testifying that her husband loved soup more than he did her.

"It might sound silly," Mrs. S. told the court, "but my husband's chief complaint against me was that I didn't make soup often enough. Sometimes he would burst out crying and that was the only explanation he would give me."

eyes of his snobbish friends) with equanimity. At the same time, he complained that her "left-over" mania, which was in evidence only when they were alone, would lower him in his friends' estimation. The husband's application of a double standard to his wife's food mania and her clothing mania was proof of the degree to which he had irrationally evaluated the entire situation.

"Why do you always wear black?" I asked the wife.

"I hate waste. Black dresses wear longer."

"But your husband objects. Does this count so little?"

"My husband has fancy ideas. He's supposed to accept my taste. After all, they are *my* clothes."

"Do you have any other reasons for your mourning colors?"

"Stop wasting time."

I asked her what irritated her most in her husband. According to her, he was a trouble-maker in many ways. Pressed for a more specific answer, she described—not his protests about left-overs, but the following habit: "He makes a particular sound with his lips when eating, which is repulsive to me. I never told him how angry this makes me; as far as I'm concerned, trifles like these are a personal matter." She offered no explanation for her irritation, except for a general remark to the effect that, in her opinion, her husband "emphasized eating too much."

Her life history was banal and uneventful. She was the oldest of five daughters, the youngest six years her junior. She described her parents' marriage as "neither good nor bad," and denied having had any conflicts at all. As she expressed it, she stood firmly on her right to deny guilt "till proven guilty." Very soon a stalemate ensued, and she remarked, ironically: "I hate waste, do something. I want something for my money." The only way we could make progress, I told her, called for her to give me analytic "material." Under that pressure, she remembered some dreams, although previously she had protested that she never had any. These dreams were repetitious. Typically, they centered around a restaurant scene, where the waitress would serve food to everybody except her. She felt excluded and furious; all her complaints were futile; the waitress continued to ignore her.

After relating her dreams, the patient shut up "like a clam," to quote her. A few subsequent appointments were spent by the patient in sullen silence. Her resistance was stronger than her constantly publicized hatred of wasting time and money.

"I have a complete blank in my head, what do you want me to do?"

I explained that dreams represent symbolic expressions of repressed wishes and equally repressed reproaches, both stemming from early childhood.

"Nonsense."

"You will admit that 'for the same money,' so to speak, you could also have dreamed that the waitress in the restaurant served you delicious food."

"Correct, provided that dreams make any sense at all."

"I suggest that in the meantime you take, as a working hypothesis, the analytic theory of dreams, which has been tested by hundreds of analysts all over the world for fifty years. Please assume, for the sake of the argument, that dreams do represent a nightly communique, written in symbols that have to be decoded, reporting on what is going on in your unconscious. By the way, could you describe the waitress?"

"An elderly, insignificant woman."

"Do you recognize her?"

"I do not."

"Imagine that your dream is a picture in an art gallery. You are standing in front of that picture. Register every thought."

"That's a waste of time."

"Just do what you are asked to. What comes into your mind?"

"Only nonsense."

"For instance?"

"An old maid in our house."

"Who was she?"

The patient jumped off the couch and left the office, with an energetic "To hell with you!" Amazingly, she was willing to sacrifice the twenty remaining minutes to her resistance. What a waste! She did not go far; two minutes later, she rang the bell once more and announced, "I changed my mind." She gave me some information about the maid. With some discomfort, she admitted that the maid, a distant relative of her mother's, had been shamelessly exploited by the family. She was an "honorary member" of the family, a dubious honor for which she paid with hard work, near-starvation, and of course absence of wages. The patient had great pity for this woman and seemingly identified with her, frequently remonstrating with the mother on the maid's account. These complaints were passed over by the mother with an impatient "keep out of it."

"Are you any wiser now?" the patient asked ironically.

"I am."

"How come?"

"I know, for instance, that in your dream the maid stands for your mother."

"Nonsense."

"Don't overwork that poor word. I can prove to you that the maid symbolizes your 'refusing' mother."

"How?"

"The maid would never have refused you food. You were good friends. Wasn't it so?"

"That's true. But I still don't see where it leads you."

"Simply to the conclusion that you accused your mother of being 'refusing,' and of starving others, including yourself."

"Nonsense."

"What would you do without that handy word? Whenever you use it, you find yourself taking it back, and admitting you were too hasty. Why not simplify the procedure? Reserve judgment, instead of making snap judgments? Your whole psychic situation is inexplicable without the assumption of the reproach directed against your mother."

"Stop that. My mother did not starve me."

"Of course, she didn't, not directly. The reproach of 'refusal' has different connotations. I suspect that you were jealous of the food given to your younger sisters, of the breast or bottle. Do you have any recollections?"

The patient denied everything. However, during the next few appointments we were able to piece together the following picture. The child had been deeply attached to her mother, wanting her exclusive love. Periodically, her mother would feel "sick," the regular result being a new baby upon whom the mother concentrated her attention and care. The patient was born abroad, and all the children were breast-fed. She had a very precise memory of her youngest sister being fed; she hated, and bitterly resented, her mother's giving the breast to the baby. Once her mother made a joke, as she claimed, spilling a few drops of milk on the floor before giving the breast to the baby. The "joke" infuriated the child; she started to cry, and ran for a mop to clean the floor. At that point I asked the patient: "Is that situation the prototype for your waste mania?"

"Never thought of that."

"Of course not. But to see superabundance wasted made your mother's crime—'refusing' you—even greater in your eyes. In this recollection, milk is a symbol, just as the food in your dreams is a symbol. Milk represents the first maternal kindness shown to the child, not only real food, but also love, care, attention, exclusiveness."

"Nonsense."

"Here we go again. How do you explain the fact that in your recurring dreams you are refused food, even though everybody else gets it?"

"You have to explain that. You are being paid to."

"The trouble is that whatever I tell you, you just say 'nonsense,' like a parrot."

"Don't mind me, just do your work."

"Say it more aggressively, if possible. How do you explain this: In your distorting fantasy you are confronted with an allegedly 'refusing' mother. Why, then, are you yourself so stingy?"

"I'm not stingy!" the patient shouted.

"That's what you believe. Don't you see that, unconsciously, you identify with the 'refusing' mother of your fantasy?"

"How?"

"Why aren't you giving, lavishly giving, when you complained so bitterly about your mother's 'refusing' attitude?"

There was no response, not even a "nonsense," to this. A few days later, the patient "figured out" an objection.

"Assuming that your silly reconstructions are correct, how do you explain my utilizing left-overs? You told me that I'm identifying with my refusing mother unconsciously in my fantasy. I don't starve my husband."

"Your triumph is premature. I told you, yes, that you are unconsciously identifying with your 'refusing' mother. That accounts for the way you treat yourself as a sort of caloric outcast. But at the same time, you are caricaturing your mother and improving on her, the idea being to show her that with proper management there would have been food enough for all."

"Tricks, nothing but tricks."

"Is 'tricks' your substitute for 'nonsense?' "

"I have another objection, too. You said that I am masochistically attached to the fantasy of rejection. But if I identify with the refusing mother, as you claim, then I'm not masochistic, I'm aggressive. That's plain common sense, isn't it?"

"Hunting for contradictions is the favorite sport of every analytic patient. There are a few decisive facts your objection does not cover. Here they are. Your inner conscience objects to your masochistic pleasure. Therefore you must produce an inner defense mechanism. There is only one effective defense against masochistic submission, and this is pseudo-aggression. And even when you use your defense, you smuggle in your masochistic wish, in three ways. First, by acting your mother's part, you again demonstrate to yourself her alleged meanness. Second, you conveniently shift the roles: you also identify with your husband, and his helpless complaints become your own complaints against your mother. And third, by your stubbornness, and your refusal to agree to your husband's wishes—for example, in your clothes—your create the usual masochistic situation, in which you can feel that you are being unjustly treated."

The patient found no answer, only an ironic comment: "Do you ever have an explanation in less than three parts?"

By the next day she had found a new "contradiction" to attack. "How does my aversion to the way my husband smacks his lips when he eats fit into this pretty picture?"

"Very precisely; it reminds you of your baby sister smacking her lips and enjoying her food, while you were 'starving.' Didn't you tell me, too, that you think your husband puts too much emphasis on food, and on the pleasure of eating?"

After these few dramatic highpoints, the rest of the patient's analysis consisted of working through, in the transference, the material sketched above. Her mule-like stubbornness came to the fore again only once, and that was when we finally got around to discussing her predilection for black. I told her:

"Shouting and anger don't solve problems. You had better tell me the color of the dress your relative-servant generally wore."

After going through the usual scene, the patient had to admit a sudden recollection: her mother had been in the habit of providing her poor relative with black dresses, claiming that dresses in other colors would be soiled and worn out too quickly.

"There you are—one more proof that you masochistically identified with that poor relative. She was exploited; that was your hitching post to prove that you were as badly off as she was."

"But I told you that I hate waste . . ."

"Do you have to start that again? You see what resistance means: seemingly discarded arguments are brought to life again."

"Stop. Do you really think I'm just rationalizing when I say that I hate waste in clothes, too?"

"I do. I also believe that when you dress shabbily, you are nullifying your husband's financial success. This gives you an additional inner pleasure: you are standing on your masochistic stage again, playing your role of Cinderella and outcast, but this time on the sartorial level. And at bottom, of course, it is a posthumous, neurotic, pseudo-revenge on your mother. It's like the story of the little boy who froze *his* fingers, and thought: 'Serves my *mother* right—why didn't she buy me gloves?' In your case the story is even worse: your husband wants to buy you expensive clothes."

This time the patient had no reply. Some time later, she paid me the highest compliment she had to bestow, when she told me one day she did not consider her appointment "wasted."

In the long run, this "caloric outcast," sartorial Cinderella in black, and specialist in rejections of the deepest masochistic variety, developed into a human and feeling being.

In her case and her husband's, there were completely different reasons governing their respective predilection and hatred for black. And in both cases, the reasons were deeply repressed.

2. *Neurotic Mistakes in Self-Evaluation*

These mistakes are either conscious or unconscious; but even the "conscious" misjudgments are merely reverberations of deeper conflicts. "Absolute honesty with oneself" is repeatedly declared a prerequisite for the well-dressed woman in the symposium quoted in the previous chapter. This is easier said than done.

Every person carries, within himself, an unconscious mental self-portrait. The picture has no connection with reality; nevertheless, it determines the person's type of behavior—and choice of clothes. In general, this invisible picture is a *beautified, rejuvenated and idealized* edition of oneself. As an instance: Time stands still in the unconscious. A woman may be middle-aged, and see herself, inwardly, as still young. As a result, a mature woman may make herself ridiculous by dressing like a girl of twenty.

Or: There is something wrong with a woman's inner identification. Without knowing it, she imitates a person whose exterior does not match her own. As a result, she will choose the kind of clothing which, in the period of her initial identification, suited her ideal. These clothes will of course not suit the woman herself. This is how the "athletic" type of woman happens to choose "soft" dresses, or vice versa.

Or: Even the clothes which one might expect will suit a particular woman look "wrong" and do not seem to fit, because the habitual awkwardness of her movements (caused perhaps by neurotic shyness) testifies to her inner desire to be a failure.

Or: Salespeople, couturiers, milliners, classify this woman as a "stubborn" customer, the kind "who doesn't know what's good for her." This "stubbornness," again, is due to the presence of an incorrect mental picture, masochistically tinged.

Or: This woman is what the informants in the previous chapter called a "fashion-ape," incapable of choosing selectively from the current fashion, swallowing it all, whether it becomes her or not.

Or: Because another woman is still, unconsciously, reducing her mother to absurdity, she wears the wrong clothes on the wrong occasion, or combines colors ineptly, adopts exaggerated or silly make-ups or hair-dos, or makes any one of the innumerable sartorial "mistakes." [21]

Psychic masochism is a storehouse containing many rooms. But just as "all roads lead to Rome," all hallways in this storehouse lead back to the entrance. And over that entrance—invisible to the trapped wanderer, but nevertheless there—is a large sign reading, "I want to make a fool of myself." In fashion, that desire is easy to attain.

I quote from a letter written by a clever woman, a former patient:

"I believe that women, in dress, present to the world their ideal of themselves. All quite unconsciously, of course. But what woman can admit to such a thing—even if she is aware of it, and most are not? No, the whole thing must be put on a superficially convincing 'fashion' and 'good taste' level, because the real truth must never come out.

[21] See examples in Chapter Eight.

'Dress according to personality' is the cry. The truth of the matter is that, unfortunately, everyone does.

"Take the fat woman who wears large prints, reds, and stuffs herself into a tight girdle. Ignorance of the rules? Not at all. I learned about psychic masochism from you, and I believe that it applies here. The woman unconsciously wants the world's laughter and contempt. But this same woman will have five or six acceptable 'rules' by any number of experts to justify her taste.

"In other words, if people are masochists, they will use every means that is at their disposal to be kicked—but they'll never admit it."

There is little to add to the lady's apt summary.

10 *In Defense of Men*

By the end of the eighteenth century color and adornment had virtually disappeared from masculine dress in Western Europe. In its stead had come the drab attire which is still called the "correct" suit of clothes. Flugel calls this process "the great masculine renunciation." The results are visible in every part of the world which conducts its sartorial business according to European standards of taste. Masculine fashions, since that time, have been in their essence stabilized; there are only minor differences between the masculine attire of one generation and the next, whereas women's clothes change—sometimes radically—every season.

Psychological literature seems to be in agreement on the causes of this upheaval. It is traced to the French Revolution: with the overthrow of the aristocracy, the elaborate trappings of aristocracy disappeared, to be supplanted by the "equalizing," tripartite costume of the middle class now economically preponderant. Popular ideals changed accordingly; the concept of "work as a duty," foreign to the land-owning aristocracy, became fashionable.

Flugel points out that before the French revolution there was a rigid division between work that was acceptable to an aristocrat, and an activity that was "degrading." Either the production or distribution of useful commodities was "degrading." The professions open to an aristocrat were those of courtier, soldier or politician. What really mattered, according to this classification, was what happened on the battlefield or in the drawing room, not what was done in the workshop or the counting-house. This evaluation was reversed as the ideals of the Revolution spread, and the approved manner of dressing became the simple costume associated with the newly approved centers of activity.

I do not believe that pure utility, plus the "equalizing" ideas which grew out of the high-sounding declarations of the French Revolution, can be accepted as a full explanation of the change. There is a simple psychological factor to be considered: the impulse, on the part of any new order, to "clear the deck" by discarding whatever external vestiges of the old order remain. Since the surface is easier to alter than the essence, change of dress was a logical first step after the French Revolution. And so it was; the new middle-class symbolized its victory over the aristocracy by sweeping away the "enemy's" characteristic attire.[1]

In my opinion, a psychological problem cannot be explained if one adduces social and economic factors exclusively. Not that these factors are to be disregarded, but first priority in matters of psychology belongs to the unconscious, or there is danger of maneuvering into a dead end.

The drab "duty" clothes prevalent at this time, for instance, serve to stress man's last refuge, which is his business or occupation. They are a reminder to the man's wife that in one province, at least, he is still the He-Man. At home, woman is the stronger sex and He-Man does not exactly cut a heroic figure. Austerity in man's dress, therefore, can

[1] There is an exception to this rule: the victor can accept the fashion of the vanquished. This is reported of Alexander the Great, who imitated Persian dress for himself and his entourage after his conquest of Persia. Why did the nineteenth century merchant reject aristocratic attire after his economic victory instead of accepting it? The most probable reason is fear: when aristocrats were being hunted down, during the Revolution, they were recognizable by their elaborate dress. To counteract this external fear, the "equalizing" costume was favored, later.

be used as an inner argument. Nobody can deny that man's role in the home, whether that of weakling or not, constitutes a psychological problem.

Here is another instance: There is such widespread acceptance of simplicity and inconspicuousness in men's clothing that any man who shows "too much" interest in dress is likely to be suspected of homosexuality. The suspicion is unjustified; contrary to the popular misconception, the homosexual is *not* "inwardly" a girl.[2] Unfortunately, even an incorrect theory has strong propelling results when it is widely believed. The fear of being misjudged as homosexual is an undeniable psychological factor.

The only part of their attire in which *some* men still find color-pride is the necktie. The reasons may be symbolic-sexual or purely social. They are illustrated in an early scene in Frederic Wakeman's *The Hucksters*,[3] where a young man, on his way to be interviewed for an extremely important and well-paying job, walks across Park Avenue towards Radio City, dressed in the most effective and "sincere" items of his very expensive wardrobe. He is wearing a black knitted tie; his other ties, he had decided, were too loud to suit the occasion. He is caught by a splash of color in a shop window; it is a hand-painted, rich-looking and "very sincere" tie. He pays thirty-five dollars for the tie, even though all that leaves him is fifteen dollars to face the future with, and walks on to his interview full of confidence.

A woman's observations on the recent history of men's fashions should be illuminating. The following survey was written by one of the participants in Chapter Eight's symposium on female clothing.

"In the last three decades, many attempts have been

[2] The obvious fallacy in this line of reasoning has already been pointed out: for every "feminine" homosexual, a "masculine" partner is needed—a fact which cannot be explained by the theory quoted.

[3] Rinehart & Co., New York, 1946.

made to introduce some innovations into men's clothing; the more radical of these have all failed ignominiously. This does not mean that minor aberrations do not appear on the scene and seemingly become entrenched for a season or two, nor is it meant to imply that changes do not occur. The starched collar and the stiff straw hat *have* disappeared; the legendary pink shirt every tourist of twenty years ago was expected to bring home from Paris and hide in his bottom bureau drawer is now worn as a matter of course; there have been really noticeable changes in summer and leisure wear. It is true that no appreciable headway has been made in the direction of lightening the actual weight of men's clothing, in spite of persistent popular appeals. The rebellion against the old traditions may be gaining headway, but its participants remove their coats with an air of uneasiness and bravado, and always seem on the verge of calling a retreat, especially in the presence of the 'weaker sex.'

"There is ample evidence to prove that men 'follow the styles' as obediently, if not as assiduously, as women. The difference seems to lie in their willingness to adopt what might be called accessory variations, and their reluctance to accept a basic change. Thus the cut of a collar, a lapel, a shoulder line is frequently changed, gravely noted in *Esquire* and in New York City's theatre programs, and worn without further demur or remark.

"Basic changes, however, seem to be almost automatically limited in their scope. The flapping pants of the twenties, like the flaunting raccoon coat, were worn by the youth. The recent Edwardian revival reported from London, with its exaggeratedly slim trousers and tight cutaway, has so far made not even a tentative appearance on this side of the Atlantic; in view of its delayed introduction, its acceptance seems very doubtful.

"One basic change, however, has been universally

adopted. This is in the bathing-suit, which, twenty-five years ago, was a modestly scoop-necked, shoulder-strapped woollen union suit. The first relaxation of the rule that men's chests were to be covered on the beach called for an involved criss-cross of suspenders to substitute for the actual layer of cloth. Only after this intermediate stage was passed did the present custom of wearing bathing shorts meet with acceptance. One immediately thinks of the parallel in women's wear, the Bikini bathing suit, in which, again, what you call the 'intervening magic layer' of cloth is being supplanted by an 'intervening magic criss-cross.' It is interesting, though not fruitful, to speculate on whether this, too, may become transitional, and lead to the eventual disappearance of the 'criss-cross.' In my opinion, the odds are against it; it should be remembered that nude bathing is an escapade that traditionally takes place in the dark."

After these discussions of men's fears, his frantic countermeasures—which culminate in the establishment of the dubious He-Man attitude—his sartorial and other renunciations, even a not-too-biased reader might lose patience and claim that the picture is "unfair." His argument might run: "After all, the institutions of this world are man-made—man cannot be such a nonentity! And in one way he rules supreme: he invented romantic love. Can you deny that?"

Man's activity is admittedly remarkable: in all ways except in his inner relation to women. Man may or may not have invented romantic love as an avenue to woman. There is no intention of deprecating man; the conclusions in this book are the result of clinical observations, and as such are impartial. If some of the results of these observations are unpleasant to man's narcissism, it cannot be helped.

A short scrutiny of romantic and sensual love, and of

jealousy, is called for in connection with our study of fashion, if only because clothes are—as many people believe—assembled and worn by women to arouse these passions. Many a married man, both in and out of fiction, deduces the presence of a rival from his wife's suddenly increased attention to her wardrobe. And appropriately, the greatest tragedy of jealousy, *Othello*, uses as prop—a handkerchief.

This scrutiny is also in order for more searching reasons. A psychological investigation of fashion, as already shown, must also be a psychological investigation of all pertinent sectors of the unconscious. This study is a cross-section of the inner mind, with the cut made at the point on the outside marked "Fashion." The line of reasoning, as it proceeds, may be only secondarily linked with the original starting point; the insuperable argument against stopping short is the advantage of a complete picture over a partial one. Clothes are a clue to the man—at least, in relation to women.

The problem of romantic love, to begin with, needs some qualification. Romantic love does not, like Pallas Athene, spring full-blown from Zeus' head, at once beautiful and complete. Romantic love has an unconscious prehistory, which begins in the *inner conscience.* Psychologically speaking, no human reactions can be taken for granted, and no human phenomena are self-explanatory. Romantic love, common as it is, is no exception. It cannot be understood without a rather lengthy description of the development of conscience.

The importance of the inner conscience is still underestimated, even in analytic literature.[4] For a long period of time it was overshadowed by the unconscious libidinous wishes, which had been an earlier discovery of the new sci-

[4] For elaboration, see *The Superego* (l.c.).

ence. At first, the role ascribed to the superego was a purely inhibitory one. It had been viewed as "censor," and the emphasis placed exclusively on unconscious wishes. It was decades before the inner conscience was finally revealed as the *real master of the inner personality*.

The riddle of the Sphinx was child's play, compared with the enigma of conscience. Humanity's best minds have been working to solve that conundrum for thousands of years, with results that have been, on the whole, unimpressive. Modern psychiatry, when confronted with the problem, found a confusing jungle of contradictory interpretations. God was invoked; so were biology and environment and morality. The existence of conscience was denied, affirmed, queried. But conscience was not explained.[5] Nor was there any acknowledgment of the existence of both conscious and unconscious conscience.

The beginnings of conscience are quite humble; its basis is the discrepancy between the child's biological endowment of aggression—which is quantitatively different in each individual—and the child's inability to express that very aggression. With "too much aggression" on the one hand, and "too little power" on the other, the result is inevitably frustration. And from this frustration is developed the first corner-stone of the *inner conscience*, which is later called the *superego*.

The sequence of events is invariably the same. For a long time, the child lives on the basis of a fantastic misconception of reality. He does not acknowledge his complete dependence on his mother. On the contrary, he be-

[5] The presentation given above corresponds to the author's personal opinion, originally worked out in collaboration with Dr. L. Jekels (Freud's oldest living pupil, and one of the most distinguished of the old guard), and had been first published in *Imago*, 1934. It contains enlargement and modification of Freudian principles on that topic. Later these opinions were enlarged in *The Battle of the Conscience* and *The Superego* (l.c.).

lieves that he is a master of omnipotence, creating *for* himself, *out of* himself, everything that he wants and needs.

The understanding of reality is a very gradual process. As reality impinges on his fantasy, every disappointment is an offense to his infantile megalomania (omnipotence), and leads to fury.

That fury and aggression is ineffectual, of course. All the infant can do is cry, spit, vomit, and later make uncoordinated muscular attempts at hitting. All of this is to no avail; the "cruel" outer world has its way. Aggression is curbed, inhibited, punished, and later on subjected to a moral embargo. The result is stasis, and the accumulation of undischarged aggression.

The educational routine dams the flow of aggression, but only at its visible outlet. The child's show must go on; when outward expression of fury becomes impossible, the inner route is taken. The aggressive drive detours to the child's own personality, thus preparing for the later channeling of his aggression *against the child himself.*

At the time, the child frantically tries to maintain at least vestiges of omnipotence—as hopeless a task as maintaining a "big shot" attitude while prisoner in a concentration camp. For, despite the external atmosphere of love, care and attention with which the mother surrounds her child, the child's internal situation is that of a prisoner unceasingly subjected to oppression and humiliation. To the child, still living—unaware of reality—on the principle of alleged omnipotence, even minute and necessary delays and refusals are highly offensive.

More than that, care and attention are taken for granted. All that is "good," meaning all that is desirable, is perceived by the child as something he has provided for himself. In the child's distorted psychic bookkeeping, all the "bad" is blamed on the mother, and all gratitude for the "good"—since he believes it is self-given—is blotted out.

To get an adequate notion of the extent of infantile megalomania, one need only listen to and *take seriously* the average child's bragging. "I can lift the Empire State Building with my thumbnail," a typical utterance, is an actual quotation. The adult reaction is generally a condescending smile. But the child is in earnest; his braggadocio is the external manifestation of an inner crisis which will have tragic consequences.

In the course of his desperate attempts to hang on to fragments of the first and most cherished infantile fantasy—that of alleged omnipotence, megalomania, autarchy—the child finds an ingenious expedient. This "brilliant idea," which comes at about the age of two, or two and a half, consists of identification with the prohibitions handed down by the parents. Instead of constantly hearing from his parents, "Don't do this," the inner conscience, meaning the child himself, pronounces: "I myself, of my own volition, abstain from the forbidden." Since birth, the child has been the constant target of a barrage of *external* prohibitions. Now he institutes an *internal* prohibition, covering exactly the same ground. Only the official source of the prohibition has been changed; the content remains identical. The tactic is an immediate success; the child becomes a "good" boy or girl of his own volition, saves face, avoids punishment, and even saves a few remnants of omnipotence.

Freud called this clever inner device the *ego-ideal.* In it are combined the child's original, indestructible, megalomania ("narcissism," self-love), and the image of parental prohibitions. Quantitatively, megalomania is the more important ingredient. This mixture, unhomogeneous as it may seem, holds firm even under stress.

In establishing the ego-ideal, the child has solved an external conflict. Ignorant of the reasons for their spectacular success in educating their child, parents happily congratulate each other—and their equally happy and ignorant child.

Internally, however, the child's conflicts continue, because of the accumulation of undischarged aggression dating back to his infancy. By this time the child has greater control of his muscular apparatus, and can aim his aggression outward in games, activities, sports. Unfortunately, his muscular control has come too late. His inner usurer is already firmly in position, and will not be dislodged.

The inner usurer, the accumulation of cruelty and aggression directed against oneself, is called by the forbidding term "*Daimonion.*"

Jekels and I owe this term to Socrates, who used it when, at the age of seventy, he stood accused before his ignorant judges in Athens. He was defending himself against the charge that he had corrupted the younger generation. The accusation, as Plato quotes it, ran: "Socrates is an evildoer; he offends by prying into things under the earth and in the heavens; he makes the weaker thing appear the stronger; and he teaches these doctrines to others." [6] In essence, he was accused of disbelieving in the gods venerated by the populace.

In Socrates' famous speech (Apologia) before his judges —who *were* the populace—the defendant uses one specific argument which *he* found convincing. In explaining why he was willing to give advice to individuals, except in matters concerning politics, Socrates said:

> But the reason for this, as you have heard me say at many times and places, is that something divine, as I might call it—something spirit-like and as it were heaven-sent—comes to me (*moi theion ti kai daimonion gignetai*), the very thing which Meletus ridiculed in his indictment. I have had this from my

[6] Except where otherwise indicated, the translations from "Apologia" and "Criton" are by Benjamin Jowett.

childhood; it is *a sort of voice* that comes to me (*emoi da tout' estin ek paidos arxomenon phonetis gignomene*), and when it comes it always *holds me back* from anything I may be considering doing, but never instigates me to do something, or urges me forward (*he hotan genetai aei apotrepei me touto ho an mellottrattein protrepei de onpote*). This it is which opposes my engaging in politics.[7] (My italics.)

It is this very voice ("Daimonion") that—by its silence—convinces the condemned man that death is not evil. After his judges, by a majority of sixty, have found him guilty, but before sentence has been pronounced, Socrates declares:

For, judges, . . . a wonderful thing has happened to me. For hitherto the customary prophetic and in-dwelling, genius-like monitor (*he gar eiothyia moi mantike e tou daimonion*) always spoke to me extremely frequently and opposed me in even very small matters, if I was going to do anything I should not. But now, as you yourselves see, this thing which might be thought, and is generally considered, the greatest of evils has come upon me; but the divine sign (*to tou theou semeion*) did not oppose me either when I left my home in the morning, or when I came here to the court, or at any point of my speech, when I was going to say anything; and yet on other occasions it stopped me at many points in the midst of a speech; but now, in this affair, it has not opposed me in anything I was doing or saying. What then do I suppose is the reason? I will tell you. This which has happened to me is doubtless a good thing, and those of us who think death is an evil must be mistaken. A convincing proof of this has been given me; for the accustomed sign would surely have opposed me if I had not been going to meet with something good.[8]

In short, as Plato reports it, Socrates concluded that death was desirable. For this reason, he provoked his judges

[7] Because this passage, and the one following, are more illuminating in a translation that is closer to the original than Jowett's, they have been especially translated for this book by Dr. Henry A. Bunker. I am indebted to him for his kindness.

[8] Translation by Dr. Henry A. Bunker.

mercilessly by presenting his defense in exactly the form of ironic, reducing-to-absurdity deduction that had brought him before the tribunal in the first place. With dignity, and apparently without fear, he told his judges that, since he himself had achieved the wisdom of understanding his own ignorance, he had made it his life work to show other people theirs.

Socrates describes his "Daimonion" as invariably intervening in *unimportant* matters, invariably remaining silent when the situation was *decisive.* The typical conclusion would have been that the "inner voice" was not much use; Socrates, however, interpreted the absence of the "voice" as approval. Since the voice was not heard at any point in the trial, he reasoned that death was desirable. One can easily imagine how ruthlessly Socrates would have demolished this line of argument if it had been presented to him by one of his more ignorant opponents in a discussion, providing the argument had centered about a subject less charged with personal emotions.

As Socrates explains in his final speech to the judges, he has had no illusions about the outcome of the trial. He expected a verdict of death:

> There are many reasons why I am not grieved, O men of Athens, at the vote of condemnation. I expected it, and am only surprised that the votes are so nearly equal; for I had thought that the majority against me would have been far larger; but now, had thirty votes gone over to the other side, I should have been acquitted.

No warning sign came from the "Daimonion," and Socrates proceeded in his usual provocative fashion. The rest of his speech is a dispassionate, though ironic, lecture on truth, appropriate if the purpose is to recall the tribulations suffered in an otherwise peaceful period, but entirely out of place as the final philippic of a defendant fighting for his life.

Socrates' wish to die is further clarified in his apotheosis of death, and in the dialogue with Criton. In the former, he declares to his judges:

. . . there is great reason to hope that death is a good; for one of two things—either death is a state of nothingness and utter unconsciousness, or, as men say, there is a change and migration of the soul from this world to another. Now, if you suppose that there is no consciousness, but a sleep like the sleep of him who is undisturbed even by dreams, death will be an unspeakable gain. For if a person were to select the night in which his sleep was undisturbed even by dreams, and were to compare with this the other days and nights of his life, and then were to tell us how many days and nights he had passed in the course of his life better and more pleasantly than this one, I think that any man, I will not say a private man, but even the great king will not find many such days or nights, when compared with the others. Now, if death be of such a nature, I say that to die is gain; for eternity is then only a single night. But if death is the journey to another place, and there, as men say, all the dead abide, what good, O my friends and judges, can be greater than this? If, indeed, when the pilgrim arrives in the world below, he is delivered from the professors of justice in this world, and finds the true judges who are said to give judgment there, Minos and Rhadamanthus and Aeacus and Triptolemus, and other sons of God who were righteous in their own life, that pilgrimage will be worth making. What would not a man give if he might converse with Orpheus and Musaeus and Hesiod and Homer? Nay, if this be true, let me die again and again . . . What would not a man give, O judges, to be able to examine the leader of the great Trojan expedition . . . or numberless others . . . What infinite delight would there be in conversing with them and asking them questions! In another world they do not put a man to death for asking questions . . .

The dialogue with Criton took place the day before the date set for carrying out the sentence of execution. In it, Criton informs Socrates that he can escape and save his life; money has been provided, friends have been informed, and the guards have already been bribed. Socrates' refusal to take advantage of his friend's offer is couched in his usual form; the lofty but ambiguous arguments serve to make a fool of his would-be rescuer. Of importance is Criton's remark: "My whole wealth is at your disposal . . . You had not reason to stand trial." (Meaning, "You could have escaped beforehand.") Socrates and death were on good terms; Socrates wanted to die.

Socrates' recognition of his "inner voice" was astute; there does exist a still, small, vetoing voice within the psyche of every individual. But the philosopher was tragically wrong, as the above excerpts indicate, in classifying the Daimonion as a benevolent institution.

The Daimonion and the ego-ideal are the two constituents which make up the unconscious conscience (superego). These two impersonal departments work in this way: Daimonion uses the ego-ideal for its campaign of torture. By constantly reminding the ego of its self-created ego-ideal, Daimonion in effect incessantly asks: "Have you achieved what you promised to achieve when you were a child?" The question never varies, and never loses its sting. If the answer is in the negative, the reaction is a feeling of guilt.

Clearly, this arrangement is a defeat for the ego. The ingenious expedient of identifying with the parents' prohibitions, which paved the way for the establishment of the ego-ideal, was designed to *protect* the ego from blows to its self-esteem. Now, the ego's weapon is turned against the ego itself.

The child's idea had really been an excellent one. Its flaw lay in its limitations. It had been planned to cope with external conflicts, arising from the commands of the stronger educators. But human beings must fight on two fronts—external *and* internal. The external conflict was neutralized, but the "second front," Daimonion, was left unprotected. The child's narcissism, seemingly rescued and protected by means of the ego-ideal, is seized on by Daimonion, which then proceeds to use it for unsavory purposes.

The inner departments of the personality, once they have been established, cannot be given up, remade or modernized—by the individual himself. The child cannot call it quits, threw in the towel. Once begun, the battle continues throughout life.

Helplessly caught in its own devices, struggling to pay off on the promissory notes innocently signed by the child, the ego suffers pain and humiliation. There is no escape. "You promised yourself you would be the greatest writer in the world—look at you now, you third-rate hack." The discrepancy between "the world's greatest writer" and the "third-rate hack" precisely corresponds to the extent of the punishment meted out by Daimonion.

Or: "You promised youself you would be the Admiral of the fleet. Look at you now—second mate on a tramp steamer. Admit your failure, and pay the fine of depression and dissatisfaction."

Or: "You were going to be a tycoon—look at your income! Even your income tax is too small to complain about. You were going to live in luxury—look at the way you live! Pay penance!"

Extenuating circumstances—hard times, restricted opportunities, cut-throat competition, one's own intellectual limitations—are no excuse. Daimonion rejects all alibis, and dictates punishment. Punishment is the first, second and last word, and punishment it is. For Daimonion has the power to enforce its own laws.

The situation is not entirely hopeless. Some defenses exist, the strongest of which is aggression. Since Daimonion is composed of aggression, maliciously used, this is the only argument the inner jailer really understands and respects. But it is a weapon available only to a *normal* ego. In normality, the ego has at its disposal a good stock of aggression. It is used to fight, and sometimes even to win, the battles of reality. But part of the stockpile is unproductively used, to counteract Daimonion. Even under the most favorable circumstances, therefore, the psychic apparatus is only 50% efficient—half its energy must always be concentrated on the job of keeping the inner conscience in check.

The process of silencing merely the *unjustified* reproaches of conscience can best be described by the formula "put up and shut up." The "put up" can take the form of work,[9] where the individual takes in his stride the thousand and one annoyances which crop up every day, and in which he weathers occasional "lousy moods," and accepts all varieties of disappointments, sickness, thoughts of inevitable death, worries, regrets. All of this is payment to conscience. If, after this, there is an attempt on the part of conscience to exact additional payment, the second form of defense is used. There is an energetic "Shut up!" uttered angrily by the ego, and here the matter rests. This defense works, in the normal person, because normality has been achieved at the cost of renouncing many infantile pleasures, and consequently the individual has reduced the number of his possible conflicts with conscience. Having sacrificed a good deal, he attains a kind of "peace of mind," to make up for his renunciations.

In neurosis, on the other hand, the ego is in a much worse bargaining position vis-a-vis the superego. The amount of aggression at its disposal is insufficient for

[9] It may sound paradoxical to consider that in this connection, work is punishment, a ransom paid to the inner conscience. The connection between work and punishment has been intuitively known to mankind since time immemorial. Adam and Eve, expelled from Eden, had to work—as punishment. The great majority of people find work unpleasant. In the psychic economy, work as punishment plays an important role.

the necessary war on two fronts: the battle of reality and the battle of conscience. The neurotic is a loser in both; he has an outside chance of success on the reality level, but no chance at all in his fight with conscience. The tremendous allure of neurosis rests on this fact: unconsciously the neurotic can continue to enjoy innuendoes of infantile repressed wishes. The innuendoes take the form of double defenses, which substitute for the original wishes. These pleasures are not small, and the price paid for them is accordingly high. Not only that: Daimonion calls for ever-increasing ransom payments, and therefore neurosis grows and deepens as years go by.[10]

The neurotic's way out, since the aggressive defense is closed to him, is a fantastic one. He accepts the punishment dictated by conscience, and makes of it an unconscious pleasure. This "exchange," which is the neurotic's main defense, is psychic masochism.

Every neurotic is a living repetition machine: fantasies enshrined in the unconscious personality are repeated over and over again. Unless the process is stopped by psychoanalytic cure, it ends only with natural death.

These repetitions are not uniform; they vary from individual to individual, growing out of the stencils which are cut in early childhood, and which preserve the *specific* solution of the *specific* individual conflict.

It is clear that the infantile conflict is repeated, not simply because it happened, but because specific situations were neurotically elaborated on. This fact is of prime importance in understanding neurotic reactions. If not for

[10] It is interesting that Socrates' description of the working of his "warning voice"—prompt with its veto when minutiae are involved, silent in a major crisis—really corresponds to one of the observable techniques of the superego in some neurotics. In this way, an artificial pseudo-security is achieved in the victim. This is one of the "rules of torture" of the superego. There are a round dozen of these "rules"; they are expounded at length in *The Superego* (l.c.).

this, every neurosis would merely represent a photographic copy of reality, which is not the case.

Let us assume that two children have been confronted with a *cold and rejecting mother*. There are such mothers —not as frequently, however, as neurotics claim. The children have an identical conflict, which, in our example, is elaborated in two variations. In later life, the first boy attaches himself to a *loving and kind woman,* with whom he lives in relative contentment. The second boy, in later life, marries a *cold and rejecting* wife, with whom he constantly quarrels. Obviously, the first boy has *overcome* his childhood disappointment, and the second has *perpetuated* it. Obviously too, the reality situation, which was the same in each case, can have had very little influence; the difference in outcome can only be accounted for by the difference in psychic elaboration.

Reality is only the raw material of neurosis; to it the child adds other ingredients, in the form of infantile fantasies and defenses. Not that unfavorable family circumstances can be discounted; they do have results, but realistic circumstances are only one of the determining factors in neurosis. The use, or misuse, of reality by the individual is the decisive point.

It should be remembered that the child is far from being an objective or unbiased observer. The child frequently colors "reality" to suit his own inner purposes. The most typical falsification of reality is based on projection. If the child's aggression towards the mother or father becomes too strongly counteracted by inner guilt, the child shifts his *own* aggression on to the educator. As a result, the educator, now endowed with the child's own aggression, is perceived as "cruel" and "malicious," although objectively he may be kind and benevolent.

From the scientific point of view, the child exists, not in a "reality situation," but in a situation of *reality as the child perceives it;* a world like the world Alice found when she went through the looking-glass, where objects and events have the appearance of reality, but are at the same time distorted or fantastic.

Neurosis, the illness of the unconscious, is made up of three constituents: biology, environment as perceived by the child, and psychic elaboration of both biology and subjectively colored environment. If any one of these three is overstressed, the conclusions reached must be erroneous.

As an added complication, neurosis is not a direct reflection of the child's fantasies and wishes. These fantasies and wishes are covered by a screen of defense mechanisms. An unconscious wish *never* enters consciousness undisguised, and in direct form. Only the *secondary defense against the wish* becomes visible, and even then it is clothed in a rationalization. The inner conscience is responsible for that camouflage. (For elaboration, see *The Superego,* l.c.)

Among the antidotes for inner guilt, the most powerful, in my opinion, is tender love.

Tender love is an *episode* in the great *battle of the conscience.* Since this theory was first co-promoted by myself, I am familiar with all the possible irony, disbelief, and even more serious objections advanced against it.[11] Though I am of course biased, I can only state that none of the objections have changed my convictions. I fully maintain my opinion, as expressed more than seventeen years ago.

As has been said, the unconscious conscience is made up of two opposing forces: the ego-ideal, and Daimonion. Daimonion's typical technique of intrapsychic torture consists of constantly reminding the intimidated ego that it

[11] First presented, in collaboration with Dr. L. Jekels, at the Vienna Psychoanalytic Society, on November 8, 1933. First published under the title "Transference and Love," *Imago,* XX; pp. 5-32, 1934. Further elaboration in *Unhappy Marriage and Divorce* (l.c.), *Divorce Won't Help* (l.c.), and *The Battle of the Conscience* (l.c.).

has failed to come up to its self-created ego-ideal. The expectation of achievement is contrasted with the real achievement, and the inevitable discrepancy is paid for with depression, guilt, dissatisfaction.

The ego is caught in its own net. It cannot deny that the bill of particulars is exact; there was grandiose ambition, and there is relatively minor achievement. It can plead only ignorance and extenuating circumstances; and these pleas do not affect the outcome. Daimonion insists on its pound of flesh. The payment is in the form of guilt.

Up to this point, the ego has been hopelessly outmaneuvered. Its own weapon, the ego-ideal, has been seized and turned against it by the hidden enemy, the Daimonion. Again, in its desperation, the ego comes up with an ingenious tactic. Daimonion is a formalist; when torturing its victim, there is always an ironic request that the ego produce a witness who will attest to the ego's promised greatness. The ego resolves to find a witness, one who will be fully convinced that "greatness" will be achieved in the future. What a defense against Daimonion that would be: a testimonial from a person who has complete faith that the "wonderful" victim will more than fulfill his childhood ambitions, who is convinced that only the malice of the evil outer world has prevented the hero from getting his chance, who actually conceives of the victim as the most desirable, lovable, admirable, successful human being in the whole world!

And this is precisely the unconscious preamble to the emotional hurricane of love. *The lover projects his own ego-ideal on to the beloved,* and in so doing deprives Daimonion of its instrument of torture. Since the object of love approves of everything done by the lover, there is no longer a visible discrepancy between the ego and the ego-ideal, and the feeling of guilt disappears. The ego-ideal is restored to its original state of benevolence, and as long as love lasts cannot be used for Daimonion's anti-libidinous purposes. That projection of the person's own ego-ideal on to the beloved explains the ridiculous over-valuation lovers place upon one another, when the process of projection is mutual. It also explains the strange dependence on the opinions of the beloved: *every* discrepancy between ego and ego-ideal must be eliminated.[12]

Tender love, viewed genetically, is not just a "romantic" admixture to sensual satisfaction, which can be taken or left at will, but a *powerful weapon against inner guilt;* in fact the most potent weapon available.

This also explains why it is only the not-too-neurotic (so-called healthy) person who is capable of "love." The neurotic is incapable of feeling tender love; he finds his substitute in endless repetitions of infantile patterns; in other words, in transference.

In neurosis, real people do not exist as protagonists. On the contrary, real people are misused; they are objects upon which an unconscious conflict can be reeled off. Still, real people are needed, which enlarges the gallery of reasons for man's "gregarious nature."

Tender love and transference, respectively, are in my opinion pathognomonic for health and neurosis. They indicate the extent of the individual's success in his fight against the chronic inner enemy, the superego.

The key to the normal person's ability to experience tender love lies in his unconscious attitude toward guilt. The normal person avoids guilt, using different devices, of which tender love is the most powerful. Because he is a

[12] The shift of the lover's fantasies on to the beloved was intuitively understood by Stendhal, whose opinions were quoted on page 37 f. In more modern terminology, we would say that Stendhal understood the narcissistic basis of tender love and the projection mechanism—a great and admirable feat in the beginning of the nineteenth century. What distinguishes the Jekels-Bergler theory on love from that of Stendhal is the linking of love with inner guilt, and consequently with the problem of fighting the superego.

psychic masochist to a much lesser degree than is the neurotic, his reaction to unconscious guilt and punishment is one of pain unmixed with pleasure, and he can therefore be single-minded in his search for antidotes.

The neurotic, on the other hand, does not want to free himself of guilt. The Oedipal and pre-Oedipal fantasies to which he clings are bound up with guilt, which thus becomes their accepted companion. Since he refuses to renounce the fantasies, the "companion," like a Spanish duenna, must accompany them. And in his secret deals with his superego, the neurotic uses his guilt as a bargaining point: "See how unhappy I am!" The whole structure of the neurosis rests on this "bribe."

Psychoanalytic psychiatry has to contend with an initial disadvantage: it is forced to contradict many a homely and cherished precept based on so-called "common sense." Common sense is unfortunately not the yardstick of the unconscious personality. But instead of grasping the "facts behind the facts," as translated by psychiatrists, people concentrate on a feeling of anger towards the translator.

A case in point is the almost universal reaction to the reasons why people search for objects upon whom they can project their inner conflicts. It sounds so "unlikely" that one human being should use another for this exclusive purpose. Worse: it doesn't sound "nice," and it isn't consoling.

The concept of "the other person as movie-screen" is repugnant enough to the average layman when it is applied to neurotics. It becomes totally indigestible when it is shown to be one of the unconscious processes in normal love.

After I had told one witty patient of the part played by projection in the choice of the love-object, he exclaimed, in a shocked voice:

"That means dethroning the real object."

I reassured him: nobody disputes the external reality of the love-object. The patient regained his poise and his sense of humor and said:

"As a matter of fact you ought to stop calling it the love-object. Call it the projectate."

"How did you arrive at that strange neologism?" I wanted to know.

"Well, if the love-object is only the bearer of the lover's projection, then it's no more than a projectate."

"Isn't your term slightly clumsy?"

"No more than your whole theory."

"Thanks for hitting below the belt. Why the ending 'ate' in projectate?"

The patient defended his joke. "Why not? What about potent*ate*, mand*ate*, protector*ate*?"

"Isn't there danger of confusion with 'project' in the sense of plan, design, scheme? The term projection is scientific, and not exactly colloquial."

"What of it? Don't overlook the salient fact that your silly theory is only a scheme to confound people, anyway."

"How deeply a 'silly theory' hurts you!"

"Nonsense. As far as your terminological scruples go, I can reassure you in my capacity as professor of English literature. Even if there is confusion, the terminological confusion will be infinitesimal compared with the emotional confusion resulting from the theory itself."

"How about analyzing your emotionalism?" I suggested.

"No comment," was the patient's reply. "Better tell me your reaction to my newest addition to the million and a half words already in the English language."

"If it makes you any happier, and at least helps you to digest an indigestible theory, as you called it, go ahead and offend the King's English. Say 'projectate.' "

The learned and touchy professor offered these comments as ironic repartee, but they can be used for purposes of clarification.

What was important here was not the terminological designation, but the patient's emotional reaction to the "dethroning" of the object, in the theory propounded to him. This very reaction has been so frequent and so typical that a common reason for it had to be found. In this situation, people behave as if the solid earth upon which they are walking has suddenly been withdrawn from under their feet.

In the two decades which have passed since publication of this theory, I have never met with a detached evaluation. The listeners and readers (if they communicated their reactions) were shocked, angry, indignant, or enthusiastic. In the rarest of cases, the theory was accepted or rejected without accompanying emotional response. What is so explosive about it?

Nietzsche once said that not the smallest charm of a theory is that it can be refuted. This does not imply that refutation must be accompanied by deep indignation, or acceptance by enthusiasm.

As far as I can make out, there are four reasons for the emotionalism that was encountered.

First: people don't want an explanation of the phenomenon of "tender love." This wish not to be bothered, which covers fear, is not restricted to laymen. "Les savants ne sont pas curieux," mocked Anatole France. At the bottom of that unexpressed fear lies the insecurity which, for the average person, surrounds everything connected with the problem of love. In that defensive attitude, people behave like schoolboys, plagued by guilty conscience. Their approach, too, is reminiscent of the schoolboy: they are afraid of a bad mark in love, as they once were in Latin. Remnants of that attitude are responsible for the feeling that they had "better let well enough alone." This unconscious reasoning makes it possible for even an intelligent critic to declare: "Love is a natural phenomenon, there is nothing to explain."

Second: emotional critics—like the professor of English literature quoted above—behave as if the love object were "dethroned" by the theory. What they really mean is that they fear they will lose their "sense of reality." Unconsciously, people do perceive that the object is used as a hitching post for projections. It is for precisely this reason that they cling with desperate determination to the "reality" of the object.

Third: defensive fear, the narcissistic basis of love, tends to be understood as "egotism" or "selfishness." Attempts at consolation on this point are futile; every genetic argument is counteracted by emotional resistance.

Is the light less real when looked at through the spectroscope? There are obviously people who dislike the spectroscope, and are at a loss for a method of "putting together" the colors of the spectrum. What has this emotionalism in common with science? It is obviously nothing but an emotional stumbling-block to knowledge, apparent even in scientists. Science, one will admit, is not a deep freeze for preserving illusions.

Finally, there is a fourth emotional objection which one person rationalized to read as follows: the proposed theory is far too complicated to be generally accepted. When I replied that the inherent truth of an explanation is totally independent of its prospects of popularity, I was reminded of the ironic saying of a critic (H. Bahr), to the effect that "a clever writer should pretend to be as stupid as his readers really are, so that the readers can imagine themselves to be as clever as the writer." I admit that the business-like approach had not been godfather or godmother at the formulation of the theory.

If one assumes that the narcissistic basis in every love-relation does correspond to unconscious facts, and that tender love is the classical antidote against inner guilt, three points emerge:

Proof must be found that *prior* to "falling in love" a pre-stage is discernible, in which the prospective lover is tortured by *guilt.*

It must be shown that *narcissistic elements* are predominant in tender love.

Conclusive evidence must be brought forward that *fantasy* is of far greater importance in love than the reality of the object. All three prerequisites can be established clinically. To bypass the familiar argument that clinical material is "inconclusive"—("How am I to know what's admitted, and what's being omitted?")—literary material will be used as examples.

A. *Pre-stage of feeling of guilt.*

Tender love is preceded by a period of heightened inner guilt. It would be naïve to assume that the guilt—or its actual content—is conscious. The candidate for future love cannot be spotted by the way he beats his breast or tears his hair, crying, "Mea culpa, mea maxima culpa, why am I not in love?" There are, of course, no such manifestations. What does rise to the psychic surface, in consciousness, is dissatisfaction, boredom, self-derision, and the type of complaint and doubt expressed in such familiar clichés as, "life has no meaning," "life has no purpose," "life isn't worth living," etc. In some cases, there is a feeling that one is living a "vegetable" existence, which indicates a mechanization of activity, coupled with depression.

Psychologically, all these feelings are surface reverberations of a typical conflict, in which the exaggerated ego-ideal is compared with the ego's real achievement. The difference between the two is balanced by guilt. In this quandary, the *normal* person tries the "slave revolt" of tender love, by which he can wrest the instrument of torture from his inner Frankenstein. The normal person projects his ego-ideal upon the beloved, receives credit—before the event—for the achievement of all his ambitions, and thus eradicates the discrepancy between fantasy and reality. In consequence, guilt is eliminated.

Without consciousness of the real connection, intuitive writers have described these facts correctly. True writers have that strange ability. "Poets utter great and wise things which they do not themselves understand." (Plato, *The Republic*)

In Anatole France's *The Red Lily,* Therese says:[13]

If you knew my life, if you had seen how empty it was without you, you would know what you mean to me, and you would no longer think of leaving me.

In another passage, Therese repeats the same thought:

As for my past, if you knew how empty it was you would be content. I don't believe any other woman made for love, as I am, could have come to you as untouched by love as I did. That I swear to you. *In the years I passed without you, I did not live.*

In his *Letters to Elisa,* Charles de Coster writes:

1851/52. Before I met you I did not know what love was . . . *Only now (do) I realize the meaning of life* . . . In emotional matters my judgment has become correct and certain, I should say unfailing. And what caused this change? My loving you . . . . . . Nothing can hurt me, nothing offend me. If I gambled today I would win millions, if I had to take an examination I would surely pass . . . *I have thrown off a cursed burden and from now on I shall be myself,* because I love you as you deserve and because I want to make you happy . . .

1852/53. . . . What I feel now I have never felt before . . .

[13] Calmann-Levy, Paris, 1896; pp. 205 and 275.

I was blind and now I see . . . You have taught me the meaning of living, of thinking. I owe you everything.

Elizabeth Barrett[14] makes an admission in a letter to Robert Browning dated February 24, 1846:

. . . you are all to me, all the light, all the life; I am living for you now. And *before I knew you, what was I and where? What was the world to me, . . . and the meaning of life?*

B. *Excessive growth of "narcissistic elements" in the acute frenzy of love.*

At bottom, what the lover loves in the beloved is himself; the beloved is the depository of a part of his own personality, the ego-ideal.

Beethoven,[15] for instance, wrote in an undated letter to his "immortal beloved":

My angel! my all! my second self! . . . I weep in thinking that you will receive no intelligence from me till probably Saturday. However dearly you may love me, I love you more fondly still . . . Oh, heavens! what a life without you!! . . . I must live either wholly with you, or not at all . . . Never can another possess my heart—never, never! . . . Continue to love me . . . Oh! love me for ever . . .

And Charles de Coster writes to Elisa (1851):

. . . *I know a heart belongs to me that is almost my own,* that loves me more than I could love myself . . . Each of us is incomplete without the other . . . Now I have two hearts in my bosom, yours and mine. Your blood is my blood . . . you know my thoughts, . . . you love what I love, and hate what I hate.

It is characteristic that "I and you" should be equated; additional evidence of this feeling is seen in the tender

[14] Quoted from *Robert Browning and Elizabeth Barrett Browning,* Vol. I.

[15] *Beethoven's Letters* (1790-1826), by Dr. L. Nohl, translated by Lady Wallace. 1866. Vol. I, pp. 26, 28, 29.

lover's emphasis on his complete absorption by the beloved object.

John Keats to Fanny Brawne (October 13, 1819):[16]

. . . *My love has made me selfish. I cannot exist without you.* I am forgetful of everything but seeing you again—my life seems to stop there . . . *You have absorb'd me* . . . I could die for you. My Creed is Love and you are its only tenet.

And Keats again, in May, 1820:[17]

I am greedy of you. Do not think of anything but me . . . I see *life* in nothing but the certaintly of your love . . . If I am not somehow convinced I shall die of agony.

Natalie Sacharin wrote to Alexander Herzen in 1835:

. . . I remember the day we . . . said adieu . . . My heart was so heavy at the time that I could not possibly express myself in words, and yet, I felt as if I had said everything, *as if my soul had joined yours, secretly*. Then I forgot the whole world . . .

Elizabeth Barrett wrote to Browning, Feb. 24, 1846:[18]

. . . *I am a great hero-worshipper* . . . by two or three half-words you made me see you, and other people had delivered orations on the same subject quite without effect . . . Then, when you came, you never went away. *I mean I had a sense of your presence constantly* . . . Your love has been to me like God's own love, which makes the receivers of it kneelers.

Gustave Flaubert expressed his profoundest wish in "Novembre":[19]

Oh, if I could hug something, smother it with my warmth or *become two myself,* love this other being and *become one with it* . . .

[16] From *Letters of John Keats to Fanny Brawne,* pp. 35-37.
[17] Ibid., pp. 117-120.
[18] Ibid., pp. 501-503.
[19] *Oeuvres de Jeunesse,* II.

C. *An unconscious fantasy of the lover is secondarily amalgamated with the love object.*

The narcissistic basis of tender love explains why lovers so frequently claim that they have known each other all their lives.

Elizabeth Barrett to Robert Browning, February 24, 1846:[20]

. . . *I had loved you all my life unawares, that is, the idea of you.* . . . Women . . . love such and such an ideal, seen sometimes in a dream and sometimes in a book . . . One's ideal must be above one . . . it is as far as one can reach with one's eyes (soul-eyes), not reach to touch. And here is mine . . . even to the visible outward sign of the black hair and the complexion . . . if it had been red hair quite, it had been the same thing . . .

Since one's ego-ideal—a part of one's self—is loved in the beloved, the latter is idealized.

Sir Richard Steele to Mary Scurlock, August 14, 1707:[21]

The Vainest Woman upon Earth never saw in her Glasse half the attractions which I view in you. Your Air, Y^{r}. Shape, Your every Glance, Motion and Gesture have such peculiar Graces that you possesse my whole Soul, and I know no life but in the hope of Your approbation.

Claire Clairmont to Lord Byron in 1816:[22]

If a woman, whose reputation has yet remained unstained, if without either guardian or husband to control she should throw herself upon your mercy, if with beating heart she should confess the love she has borne you many years, if she should secure to you secresy and safety, if she should return your kind-

[20] Ibid., pp. 500, 501.
[21] *The Epistolary Correspondence of Sir Richard Steele;* John Nichols and Son, London, 1809; Vol. I, p. 95.
[22] *Claire Clairmont, Mother of Byron's Allegra,* by R. Glynn Grylls, pp. 55, 59.

ness with fond affection and unbounded devotion, could you betray her, or would you be as silent as the grave?

You bid me write short to you and I have much to say. You also bade me believe that it was a fancy which made me cherish an attachment for you. It cannot be a fancy since you have been for the last year the object upon which every solitary moment led me to muse.

And Henrik Ibsen, aged sixty-two, wrote to eighteen-year-old Emilie Bardach in 1889:

. . . Well, for the time being I must do without your photograph. But I prefer it this way, I wait rather than have an unsatisfactory picture. And besides—how vivid is my memory of your charming, most serene appearance! I still believe there is a *mysterious princess* behind it. How about the mystery? Well —*one is free to dream about it and adorn it poetically*—and that I do. Anyway, it compensates somewhat for the unattainable and—unfathomable reality.

Ibsen put the lover's motto very well: "one is free to dream (about the mystery), and adorn it poetically."

The narcissistic character of tender love is brought out in a unique but little known satiric novel, *The Future Eve,* written in 1887 by the French poet Villiers de l'Isle Adam. It does not seem that this is by accident a novel of satire: apparently satire and irony were the only forms in which the writer's "shocking" thought, "Love is self-love," could become even indirectly conscious.

In the book, the inventor, Edison, constructs an artificial woman who works by electricity. This "Future Eve" is designed as consolation for a young lord, who has had an unhappy love-affair. The mechanical woman is supposed to have in her bosom a collection of phonograph records, perfectly reproducing her predecessor's voice and language. In appearance, she is an exact replica. When the young man objects, pointing out that there is a difference between a real woman, and this electrically driven machine-Eve, Edison replies:

You said: that which you love in the living person and which alone you consider real is not what you actually see in this woman, but is merely alive in your thoughts. Therefore you love that which is not alive in her—that which, as we are sure, cannot possibly live in her.—Neither this woman nor yourself were able to deceive you. Voluntarily you close your eyes, your mind's eyes—voluntarily you subdue the denial of your inner feelings in order to see in this beloved one only the phantom so ardently longed for. Therefore her true personality is for you nothing but the illusion aroused in you by her beauty.

It is only this phantom you love, for it you want to die! This alone you recognize as true! In short, you address, you see a vision born in your own mind. You created it in the living person and in fact it is nothing but a duplication of your own soul! Thus is your love.

Again there was a silence between the two men.

"Well," concluded Edison, "since I have proved to you that it is nothing but a phantom to which you so ardently and inventively wish to attribute reality, I suggest you make the same experiment with another phantom—that is all. Illusion for illusion: the consciousness of this dual being called Hadaly depends upon the free will of the one who dares to create it. Imbue it with her being. Breathe life into this ideal forehead! You will see to what high degree the Alicia of your desires will be realized in it, will animate this phantom! And thereafter you will weigh deep down in your conscience whether the phantom of your own making which is to fulfill the highest wish of your life, isn't really more entitled to be called a human being than the living ghost whose wretched so-called "reality" never inspired you with other than suicidal ideas . . .

The French poet's intuitive satire was more firmly founded on psychological fact than he could have suspected. There is an actual, as well as an intuitive example to illustrate how far-reaching is this unreal projection, and how minor is the role of the actual object in the inner process of love. This is from the life history of Honore de Balzac: the great novelist fell in love with Mme. Hanska (who later became his wife)—before ever having seen her at all!

Tender love, the highest and most poetic emotion possible for the human being, reduces itself to a desperate attempt to rescue the individual from unconscious guilt, and an equally desperate attempt to regain narcissistic bliss. The irony of the situation is unparalleled: double mental indemnity, and double mistaken identity, are both involved.

First, what the *beloved* really represents is unknown to the lover;

Second, who *he himself* is, to start with, is unknown.

Small wonder that love is considered the descriptive domain of the poet. For poets add to the confusion which surrounds the problem, and express it in "beautiful words."

This tragi-comedy is not yet complete. It is further complicated by the phenomenon of jealousy, which—like conscience—has been food for speculation by poets, writers and philosophers throughout the ages. The psychological value of this accumulation, one finds with some surprise, is virtually nil, once three exceptions have been noted. These are: Shakespeare's words in *Othello* (Act III, Scene 4) to the effect that jealously is created for its own sake, a senseless monster "born on itself";[23] La Rochefoucauld's opinion—there is more self-love than love in jealousy;

[23] Desdemona: Alas the day! I never gave him cause.
Emilia: But jealous souls will not be answer'd so;
They are not even jealous for a cause,
But jealous for they are jealous; 'tis a monster
Begot upon itself.

finally Schleiermacher's dictum: "Jealousy is an emotional hurricane, on a thorough search for self-torture." [24]

Psychoanalytically, we know a great deal more about this emotion. Freud's subdivision of jealousy into three types has been repeatedly tested and confirmed.

Type I, on the surface, seems to accord with the popular notion that jealousy is a matter of outraged pride and wounded self-esteem. On the less superficial level, this type of jealousy is a revival of the Oedipal triangle; the interloper is identified with the father of the nursery, or—if it is a two-woman, one-man triangle,—with the mother of the nursery.

Type II is a projection of the jealous person's own unconscious wishes. In reality, the jealous person wants to be unfaithful to his wife; what reaches conscious awareness is his "feeling" that his wife is being unfaithful to him. Since there is no objective basis for his suspicions, it is not at all surprising that objective proof of his wife's innocence should be rejected as unconvincing.

Type III refers to the *negative* Oedipus; it is the jealousy felt by a man who is unconsciously passive-feminine, and identifies with his wife in her relationship with her purported or real lover. The unconscious wish to be seduced by the other man is warded off with jealousy.

Aside from these broad subdivisions, jealousy presents many other psychological problems. For example:

Why is the amount of subjective pain arising from jealousy so out of proportion to the extent of the narcissistic injury?

Why do so many cases of jealousy disclose the presence of a "visual imperative" in which the jealous person is

[24] This statement of the pastor and philosopher is untranslatable. In the German (its original authorship is unknown) it reads: "Eifersucht ist eine Leidenschaft, die mit Eifer sucht, was Leiden schafft." Since the original is a play on words, the many shades of meaning cannot be reproduced in another language.

obsessed with visions of the partner in a love scene with the rival?

What factor determines whether the fantasies and actions of revenge are directed against the rival or the unfaithful object?

Is the purpose of jealousy that of winning back the beloved, or of healing the wound dealt to self-esteem, or of enjoying the emotion itself?

Is the type of jealousy shown an accurate indication of the type of underlying love?

Does the jealous person wish to conceal or to parade his jealousy?

How many unconscious layers are involved in jealousy? Is it a reaction to an unconscious wish, or an inner defense mechanism, or a defense against a defense?

Do people really commit suicide because of jealousy?

Why is the case against the unfaithful object always based on such flimsy grounds?

The jealous person himself, if queried, would claim that jealousy is merely a reaction to tender love. Psychologically, this cannot be entirely excluded; jealousy is a possible postscript to the inner process of tender love, which—as already defined—is an emotion based on projection of *one's own* ego-ideal on to the beloved. The beloved must satisfy two emotional requirements. One is to fit into the lover's "type," and in this way fulfill the lover's infantile wishes. The other is to disarm the torturing Daimonion; this is accomplished by the acceptance of the lover's self-created ego-ideal as fact. The discrepancy between ego and ego-ideal, between aim and achievement, which had enabled Daimonion to exact payment in the form of guilt and depression, is thus wiped out. An Eden of guiltlessness and megalomania follows.

This type—the *submissive* type—of love is characterized by psychic dependence upon the beloved object. The results include the temporary inability to exercise the critical function, and the extravagant over-valuation of the beloved's charms and abilities. Over-valuation seems to be a method of increasing the effectiveness of this antidote to guilt and depression.

Less commonly, one encounters the *protective type* of love, in which the lover plays the part of the grand seigneur, guarding, tending and championing his entirely dependent "baby." The psychic origin of this type of love is again the mechanism of projection, but here the lover projects his *ego*, not his ego-ideal, on to the beloved, unconsciously playing the role of his own ego-ideal. Although the roles seem to have been reversed, there has been no change in either aim or result.

The rarer, protective form of love, curiously enough, tends to appear in highly narcissistic, but at the same time essentially passive, individuals. For in defeating Daimonion by means of submissive love, the lover has placed himself in the position of meek and passive dependence upon the beloved object. Inevitably, the inner conscience reproaches him for that passivity. If the ensuing guilt feeling is strong, and the individual is sufficiently narcissistic, the defense against the accusation of passivity may be a revolt against submissive love and an assumption of the grand seigneur role in subsequent love episodes. An example of this shift in type may be found in the life of the poet Heinrich Heine.

When very young, Heine fell in love with the daughter of his well-to-do uncle; her utter indifference to his feelings was, as he put it, "a stab in the heart." Considerably later, Heine married a primitive and uneducated Parisian grisette. She was Heine's "creation" in every way: he sent her to school in order to make a lady of her, and even changed her name from Crescentia to Mathilde. In Heine's unhappy youthful love affair he had been the poor boy, disdained by the "queen"; here he reversed the roles, and smiled down from his eminence at the presumably grateful grisette. This was clearly a "magic gesture"; on the surface he was demonstrating how he wanted to be treated—kindly. On a deeper level, he really wanted exactly the opposite—mistreatment. The surface demonstration was a defense to conceal the inner masochistic wish. The masochistic wish supposedly routed by this move sprang to the fore soon enough: Mathilde tortured him soundly.[25]

Only the self-assured man can experience submissive love without subjecting himself to reproaches of passivity from the superego. The inner choice of the weak man is necessarily the protective type of love; he must play the super He-Man in all his relationships to counterbalance his inner passivity and serve as a defense against it.

What happens when the lover of either type is faced with the beloved object's infidelity or lessening affection?

Jealousy can become conscious only after the groundwork for its appearance has been laid. The beloved's behavior is not the signal for jealousy; the progress of the battle being fought within the lover's unconscious is what matters.

The lover's unconscious ruse of projecting either ego or ego-ideal on to the beloved object deprived Daimonion of its main weapon. But Daimonion is not totally disarmed. Shifting its point of attack but not its technique, Daimonion continues to contrast fantasy and reality, pointing out the big and little defects of the beloved in an attempt to regain control.

The lover is handicapped in his defense. Unconsciously, he has never been certain that he succeeded in cheating Daimonion. The human psyche is capable of a slave revolt against its inner torturer, but it is so lacking in the ability to win that even successful revolt is viewed with suspicion.

[25] From an unpublished book by the author, *The Misunderstanding of Heinrich Heine.*

This is the atmosphere in which jealousy thrives: the lover's lack of confidence in his own weapon, and Daimonion's renewal of attack.

Jealousy is the conscious expression of the unconscious battle between Daimonion, desperate to wipe out its defeat, and the unconscious ego, already doubtful of its ability to maintain its freedom. And as soon as the ego's doubts become serious, the battle is as good as lost. For the ego swallows the enemy's propaganda whole. This explains why

> Trifles light as air
> Are to the jealous confirmation strong
> As proofs of holy writ.
>
> *Othello*, III, 323.

One gets the impression that Daimonion's tactics at this point are both ironic and revengeful. In jealousy, Daimonion is in the ascendant though not yet restored to power; the slave revolt, though not yet a failure, is no longer a success. Daimonion's attack on the beloved is a barrage of trifles and flimsy complaints, sardonically echoing the "flimsy grounds" on which the beloved was chosen in the first place. And it is on this note of poetic justice that the episode ends.

Jealousy is subjectively so painful because it is a byproduct of the greatest of intrapsychic defeats; the lover's own narcissism, deposited in the ego-ideal, has failed him. The lover has been his own executioner, but he is not aware of that. Neither does he realize that his real purpose was to maintain his freedom from inner guilt, and not to regain the beloved object. In all this, he has been Daimonion's dupe as well as aide; when he swallowed whole all the "trifles" and "little signs" which "proved" his beloved to be untrustworthy, he was trapping himself into jealousy and eventually into renewed servitude to Daimonion. And all this is under the surface; consciously, he merely suffers.

The ego's revolt against Daimonion by means of tender love begins with a brilliant victory, and then goes on from defeat to defeat. Jealousy is the final, and therefore the most painful, defeat in this hopeless contest. There is a "fifth column" within the lover himself, to complicate matters; it drives some lovers as far as suicide.

The last convulsions of freedom from Daimonion, the stage of jealousy, assume different forms, depending on whether the lover is of the submissive, or the protective type. In either case, there is a violent attack, but the submissive lover will invariably attack the beloved, who is the representative of his own ego-ideal, while the protective lover will attack his rival. Neither will rebel against the real torturer, the Daimonion. The submissive lover turns on his own ego-ideal, accusing it of conspiring with Daimonion to achieve his defeat; the protective lover's target is the third party, and the beloved is exonerated as the innocent victim of the competitor's seduction.

Both men and women of the submissive type will direct their aggression against the person of the *opposite* sex; men and women of the protective type will direct their aggression against the person of the *same* sex. The underlying love-type, therefore, can be deduced from the type of jealousy shown.

Regardless of type, two elements are strongly marked in jealousy. These are heightened voyeurism and heightened psychic masochism.

The voyeuristic component is so salient that literature's virtual failure to stress its presence is amazing. One of the rare acknowledgments of this deep-seated impulse is found in Anatole France's *The Red Lily,* where the hero is so jealous of a rival of the past that he breaks off an affair with a woman he still "loves." He is incapable of seeing her "alone"; to his jealous eye "the other" is always with her.

To the jealous man and the jealous woman alike, the

most painful element in jealousy is the *visualization* of love-scenes between the beloved and the presumable rival. Consciously, the "visual imperative" is not accompanied by pleasure—clear proof that it is forbidden. Fantasies of this type are possible only when two safeguards are used: defensive fury, and self-torture.

The forbidden element in voyeurism is a combination of the infantile unconscious connotation of sexual peeping and the unconscious identification with the unfaithful beloved. In men, this identification leads to the enjoyment of feminine repressed tendencies; in women, it leads to the enjoyment of masculine repressed tendencies. The whole procedure is thoroughly masochistic.

There is a famous example of the combination of all three factors in a scene from the life-history of the French writer Stendhal. His great love, Angiola Pietragrua, had an affair with another man; through the indiscretion of her maid, Stendhal surreptitiously witnessed a love-scene between them. The poet's first reaction was an outburst of laughter. His friend Mérimée states:

> Stendhal told me that the peculiarity and ridiculousness of the situation provoked convulsive laughter in him at first. He went to great pains to smother his laughter so that he would not alarm the sinners. Only after some time did he become aware of his unhappiness.

Through Freud's work on the psychology of wit and laughter, we are familiar with the fact that laughter is produced when a certain amount of psychic energy, otherwise used for holding down repressed material, becomes free. The conserved psychic energy must have represented something infantile-forbidden: e.g., observation of parental intimacies.[26]

Another characteristic manifestation in jealousy can

[26] For details, see the author's essay on Stendhal in *Talleyrand-Napoleon-Stendhal-Grabbe,* (l.c.).

also be traced to the voyeuristic component. This is the initial tendency to conceal the feeling, and the subsequent willingness to parade it in an appeal for commiseration. Byron's observation in *Don Juan*—

> Yet he was jealous, though he did not show it.
> For jealousy dislikes the world to know it—

is accurate only for the early stages of jealousy, where voyeurism is unconsciously put into operation and enjoyed in the "visual imperative." Later on, when guilt is present, the guilt feeling itself transforms voyeurism into its opposite, exhibitionism. This self-display takes various forms, such as confiding in friends, asking for their sympathy, making a show of one's affairs in sensational divorce proceedings, etc.

Jealousy is an intrapsychic conflict, in which the beloved is not the cause but merely the vehicle of expression. Jealousy can exist only when the individual possesses marked, though repressed, masochistic and voyeuristic tendencies. It is proof that the individual is lacking in normally functioning narcissism. Contrary to the claims of minor poets and minor prophets, jealousy is *not* a universal emotion.

So far, this description has been limited to the manifestations of jealousy in relatively "normal" persons, meaning individuals in whom neurotic tendencies are comparatively limited. The problem changes as soon as one enters the area of considerable neurosis. The "slave revolt" of love is beyond the capability of the neurotic; his vehicle is transference. Every emotional episode in his life is the reenactment of an infantile conflict. The neurotic is more heavily imbued with masochism than the so-called normal individual, and his sufferings are accordingly greater.[27]

[27] For details of the whole problem, see the author's "Contributions to the Psychology of Jealousy," *Internationale Zeitschrift fuer Psychoanalyse und Imago*, XXIV, 4, 1939 (London). The paper contains a cross-section and critical evaluation of the rather extensive literature on the subject.

Neurotic jealousy is met with on every level of regression. It is therefore possible in *every* neurosis. Psychic masochism is an inherent part of every neurotic conflict, and jealousy is one of its common manifestations. As previously pointed out, every neurotic is essentially an injustice-collector; his booty is imaginary and often unconsciously self-created wrongs. Jealousy is one of the richer sources of possible "injustice." Of course, injustice-collecting as a *general* tendency does not explain the *specific* choice of jealousy as an outlet. Individual determinants must be sought.

In any case, whether it is a pre-Oedipal or an Oedipal situation that is unconsciously repeated in a jealousy-conflict, the fact remains that shifting the blame on to the partner alone is not sufficient to clarify the picture. It is true that there are psychotic cases of jealousy-paranoia, which sometimes lead to murder and suicide. Where *neurotic* jealousy is involved, however, the decisive—though monotonous and never-answered—question has to be posed to the partner: Why did your instinct not warn you to avoid that person? The answer, "I didn't know," is correct as far as consciousness is concerned. But it makes a large detour around a vital sector: the neurosis of the innocent party which frequently makes her or him unconsciously collaborate with the partner's neurosis.

Jealousy, therefore, is merely another attempt to provide an unconscious counter-measure against man's inner fears, defeated—like the others—by inner conscience. One possible hope remains: man's biologically based sex life. The next chapter proposes to show the pitfalls of that argument.

11 "Inactivity-Sex" and the Future of Clothes

THE NOUN "SEX" is the most misused word in the dictionary. Its connotations are too great a burden to be carried by a single word; "sex" may be normal, neurotic or perverse. The confusion is so pronounced that I have suggested the neologism "*counterfeit-sex*," for the purpose of differentiating between neurotic and normal sex.[1]

Under normal conditions, man's tender ("romantic") feelings towards a specific woman are combined with sensual components. Only the combination of *both* comprises the emotion called love. As a result, a relatively normal adult man will not desire sex proper except with a woman whom he also loves tenderly. And vice versa, to a normal and cultured woman sex without love is inacceptable. The attitudes involved in these conclusions are far less moralistic than they may appear at first glance; actually the attitude grows out of experience. Pleasure is increased by the presence of both components: "sex tastes better when combined with tender love." [2]

[1] *Neurotic Counterfeit-Sex*, l.c.

[2] For a discussion of the problem, see *Divorce Won't Help*, Chapter XIV, "The Case for Monogamy." The very simple fact is clinically observable: there exists in every human being an emotional affinity to marriage; every child went through the Oedipal period and identified with the parent of the same sex. This implies, also, usurping the place and prerogatives of the person with whom the identification took place. One of these prerogatives is "sexual" possession of the parent of the opposite

When neurotics of both sexes are consulted, exactly the opposite is heard. By word of mouth or in print, they declare that anyone who proclaims monogamy to be very much alive is a fool, a hypocrite, or a paid hireling of an institution for moral uplift. If they are to be believed, romantic love does not exist, and sex is no more than "release of sexual tension."

What these people fail to mention is that they have made a virtue out of necessity, or, to quote an amateur wit, found a credo to fit their libido. In reality, they are incapable of tender love, and for them the advocated "release of tension" is only too frequently impeded by such minor obstacles as various forms of impotency, frigidity, homosexuality. At best, they are capable of "mechanical" intercourse, another travesty of normal sex.

The term "counterfeit-sex" is applicable to exactly these neurotics. The concept behind the term was borrowed from Samuel Johnson, who stated in another connection that "the world, in its best state, is nothing more than a large assembly of beings, combining to counterfeit happiness which they do not feel." As far as clinical purposes are concerned, one can safely claim that neurotics have produced a complete caricature of sex; that theirs is but counterfeit-sex, with the accent on the part of the word preceding the hyphen; and that this is the full extent of the resemblance between the neurotic notion of sex and normal sex.

---

sex. The elimination of the "rival" ties up with the previously built up fantasy of omnipotence. Hence, the basic inclination towards marriage and monogamy is built up in the child long before any *rational* evaluation of the advantages and disadvantages of marriage can be made. This implies, of course, later de-sexualization of the original oedipal figures. With only slight exaggeration, one could say that this *emotional* affinity to marriage, exclusiveness, and monogamy (there was only *one* father, only *one* mother), was instilled in the child not exactly with his mother's milk, but with the baby cereals given from the age of one and one half to three.

In counterfeit-sex, neurotics—both male and female—misuse the genital apparatus for the purpose of repeating unconscious infantile conflicts which are wholly unrelated to mature sex. This is done with the cooperation of a "partner," who must—although he or she need not even suspect it—be tuned to the other's specific neurosis. The neurosis of the one partner must complement the neurosis of the other.

Why do neurotics insist that romantic love is non-existent or nonsensical? In the preceding chapter tender love was defined as the most powerful intrapsychic weapon against guilt and psychic masochism. Inwardly, neurotics are on good terms with both these plagues, and even cherish them. They are therefore incapable of the pre-requisite to tender love, which is the heroic disclaimer of guilt and psychic masochism. For neurotics, love is but the mechanism of transference: repetition of bygone conflicts with an ever-changing cast of characters.

Neurotic counterfeit-sex illustrates the fact that some people are glued to *transitory* phases of development. Whereas, in sex, not-too-neurotic contemporaries (sometimes euphemistically called "normal") inwardly *progress* to a synthesis, neurotics *regress* to one of the possible intermediary phases in the psycho-sexual development.

From the adult's conscious viewpoint, the results are incredible. All the fantasies of the "septet of baby fears" (see p. 28 et seq.) are encountered, in a noisy miscellany of unconscious fears and misconceptions. There is a resemblance here to the characteristic primitive taboo, in which a particular tree is shunned because it is the seat of a demon, and touching it would mean death. This warning becomes a practical necessity to anyone confronted with a specific example of such misconceptions in a specific neurotic clinical entity.

To state the unconsoling facts succinctly: *approximately*

40% of all men suffer from some kind of potency disturbance, and 90% of all women from some kind of frigidity. The words, "some kind," refer to the enormous variety of possible sex disturbances. To concentrate on those of men:

The vascular apparatus rebels—an erection cannot be achieved. Or an erection is achieved, but the ejaculation comes too soon. Or the ejaculation does not come at all, despite prolonged thrusts. Or "everything goes well," but the after-effects are disturbing—sleeplessness, guilt, distaste and dreary expectations dominate. Or the organ does not respond at the proper time—the man is tortured by sexual ideas with corresponding erections, but when he gets into bed with a woman of his choice "nothing happens." Or the man is potent with casual acquaintances, and impotent with the woman he "loves." Or the prerequisite for potency is derived from the arsenal of fantasies—the man must imagine he is with a woman other than his actual partner. This may be complicated in some cases by various perverse fantasies; for instance, the man may imagine that he is being beaten by another woman. Or perverse actions are essential as the preliminary that will make the organ "behave." Or there is a "preference" for the prostitute-type of woman; here a conscious preference has been made out of a necessity, for men of this type have discovered through bitter experience that they function only with "degraded" women. Or there is alleged bisexuality; the man is at times capable of lustless intercourse with a woman, while his real passion is reserved for a concomitant homosexual affair. Or the man is impotent with his wife, potent with "girl-friends." This type is tragically frequent. Or the man is an adult masturbationist living a double sex life, on one side with an ever-changing fantasy girl, and on the other side a bed companionship, half- or three-quarters impotent, with a real woman. Or the man has "whimsical" potency, sometimes working on record-breaking levels, but more often collapsing for "inexplicable reasons." Or the man has "specific" conditions for sex, conditions which are so stringent or impossible to put into operation that for all practical purposes he is impotent. Or the approach to sex is that of a schoolboy with "examination fright," and if the act is attempted, it is attempted with defeatism. Or the man is an aesthetic rejector of sex who claims that he is "not interested" at all. And so on, ad infinitum.[3]

There are literally hundreds of variations of potency disturbances, although the naive outer world acknowledges but one type: erective impotence. As long as the sexual act can be performed at all, the alibi of normality can be confirmed. "Mechanical potency," however, is not enough.

With or without biological and statistical blessing, with or without whitewash and denial of observable facts, neurosis manifesting itself in sexual (as well as other) disturbances *does* exist. Neurotic counterfeit-sex, and normal sex, have in common only the organs used—or rather misused. In order to get even an approximate idea of what neurotic sex is like, one would have to take the fantastic misconceptions unconsciously harbored by (as an example) prematurists, and multiply them—on different levels of development—by as high a figure as one can choose.

[3] The problem of sex disturbances in women is so complicated that a monograph must be consulted. In *Neurotic Counterfeit-Sex*, half the volume is devoted to it. In frigidity, a propaganda campaign, consisting of denial of painful facts, has recently been undertaken by biologists. Kinsey, e.g., denies that absence of vaginal orgasm is a situation that needs remedying, or indeed exists as a situation at all. He promises to prove his point in Vol. II of his series. Since Kinsey works on purely statistical principles, and—without being aware of it—confuses widespread neurosis with normality after the principle "the majority decides," he will undoubtedly be able to prove that vaginal orgasm is only a rumor. Unfortunately for Kinsey, two distinguished gynecologists, Drs. Kroger and Freed, recently published a paper on the psychogeneity of frigidity in the *official* organ of the American Medical Association (Issue June 10, 1950), in which they accept nearly verbatim practically everything I have been stating on this topic for twenty years. The only change suggested by these gynecologists is a compromise on percentage: they assume 75% vaginal frigidity.

The distortions of sex in neurotics are so strange that I would like to report the reaction of a famous writer, a former patient. He entered analysis sexually and artistically impotent, suffering both from premature ejaculation and writer's block. Before leaving treatment, cured of both plagues, he remarked to me: "If what you call counterfeit-sex corresponds to the facts—and I must admit that you've converted me—then what sex really needs is not more moralists but efficient press agents, who will make people understand how that unhappy word 'sex' is being misused."

Freud once made the ironic observation that modern sex impresses him as representing a dying function. For all we know, this joke may contain more truth than one would generally credit to a casual remark.

George Bernard Shaw, in the last act of "Back to Methuselah," takes as his theme the identical ironic prediction; whether or not he had heard of Freud's statement is unclear. The author's attitude towards this possible change seems to be one of approval; there is evident delight in his description of a future in which sex is relegated to a minor role in the lives of men and women. Placing his scene, in time, "as far as the mind can reach," Shaw describes a civilization in which sex is an activity confined to the "nursery," the nurseries being populated with children who emerge from the egg (not the mother) at the physical and mental age of seventeen. Three years are spent in the nursery, three years devoted to such infantile recreations as dancing, painting, sculpture, literature, conversation—and sex. After which, having become adults, the humans of the future go off to spend the remainder of their natural span of a thousand years of life in the solitary pursuit of abstract thought.

It is to Shaw's credit that, knowingly or unknowingly (the play was written in 1921), he echoed the inferences as well as the outline of Freud's observation. For Freud's witticism obviously referred only to adult sex; the infantile precursors of sex cannot be eliminated. There is a limit to the tricks which can be played on the unconscious, and on biology.

The very existence of clothing has a psychological implication, so far never stressed in the entire literature on the subject: clothing reflects a *peculiar distortion of sex based on a progressive, psychologically conditioned, diminution of the biological drive proper.* Fundamentally, sex seems to be a biological drive demanding satisfaction, as does any other drive, and in some animals it is confined to specific seasons. In higher stages of development, in the higher primates and in homo sapiens, the periodic nature of the drive is seen to have changed. Humans, at least, have paid for that *apparent* biological increase in sex-readiness with psychologically based decrease of function, visible in taboos, fears, neurotic inhibitions.

The idea that "nudity excites sex" is clearly a late invention which can be credited to the moralists. It supplies a stamp of moral approval to an inhibition stemming from other sources. The customs of primitive peoples in warm or humid climates all over the world are proof that nudity does *not* automatically provoke sex desires. Interestingly enough, not even the European observer reacts to universal nudity with sex excitement—after the initial surprise wears off. The typical reaction is expressed in Zimmerman's statement on the naked women of New Ireland:

> I have to state that after a short time of getting accustomed to this thing, one does not find anything indecent ("anstössiges") in this complete lack of clothing . . . I have frequently observed that the dress of a lady not cut after the general fashion drew from me more attention than complete lack of clothing in the natives of tropical islands; add to this that these people don't give the observer any occasion to think of something indecent.

Nakedness in natives of many parts of the world is scotomized [4] by them, as far as sexual excitement goes:

(The Sudanese) pay no attention to their own nudity.
(C. B. Kloss, *In the Andamans and Nicobars*, London 1903, p. 188)

Nakedness by itself causes no sexual excitement in a native (of New Ireland).
(R. Parkinson, *Thirty Years in the South Sea*, Stuttgart, 1907, p. 271)

This fact was also observed by earlier explorers. De Lery, in describing his voyage to Brazil in the sixteenth century, says:

. . . the stay among naked savages is not a provocation to lust, and the nudity of their women proved to be much less exciting than our women's clothes.
(*Histoire d'un voyage faict en la terre du Brasil*, p. 121)

Other explorers agree:

. . . when the sight becomes accustomed to the absence of raiment, your sense of propriety is far less offended than in England.
(Rowley, *Africa Unveiled*, London, 1876; p. 146)

Winwood W. Reade claims that there is nothing voluptuous in the excessive dishabille of an equatorial African girl, nothing being so unlikely to excite passion as nakedness. (*Savage Africa*, London, 1863; p. 546)

In his famous *History of Human Marriage*,[5] Westermarck refers to the above statements and to similar statements made by other observers (Grose, *Voyage to the East Indies*, p. 244; Johnston, *Kilima-Njaro Expedition*, p. 437;

[4] Some anthropologists report that in some primitive tribes the people are sexually excited only by their dances—the only occasions on which the women are "dressed up." One more hint that sexual excitement is aroused by clothing, not nudity.

[5] Vol. I (fifth edition), The Allerton Book Co., New York, 1922; pp. 555-556.

etc.). He cites the emphasis on dances and festivals in the erotic lives of savage peoples, and the effort made to please members of the opposite sex during these festivities by painting and otherwise adorning the bodies of young men and women. He mentions, too, the fact that tribes which otherwise use no coverings at all do habitually wear some clothing at dances and festivals. Bonwick's *Daily Life and Origin of the Tasmanians* (pp. 27, 38) is his authority for the fact that in Tasmanian dances, performed "with the avowed intention of exciting passions of the men," women wore a covering of leaves and feathers which was removed after the dance.

Many other primitive tribes, according to Westermarck, use clothing exclusively for ceremonial purposes. He quotes Curr's *Australian Race* (Vol. II, p. 472) as reporting that the women of the Australian Pegulloburras abandon their usual nakedness for festivities, and don small fringes which hang from the waist; he quotes Hardenburg (*Putumayo*, pp. 161 et seq.) as reporting that the Huitoto Indians of that region prepared for their dances by painting their bodies and putting on necklaces and feathers—and clothing, if they happened to possess any. Additional evidence is drawn from other observers. The Witoto and Boro tribes of the Amazon region (Whiffen, *The North Amazons*, pp. 75, 79) ordinarily use a minimum of clothing, but dress elaborately for a dance or festival. In these tribes, their adornments are more important than their dress. The Uaupés, also of the Amazon, never see their women clothed except at dances. Their ceremonial dress consists of a small bead apron, which is removed at once when the dance is over. (Wallace, *Travels on the Amazon*, pp. 281, 493). The Tahitian Areois, according to Ellis (*Polynesian Researches*, Vol. I, p. 235), were known for their unhibited sexual customs and suggestive dances; for public occasions they would wear girdles of leaves. And marriageable girls in the South

African Basuto tribe (Casalis, *Basutos*, p. 269), when doing their grotesque dances, would wear a sort of petticoat made of rushes.

To complete the picture, Westermack reports the astonishment of an early explorer on the Orinoco, who discovered tribes who considered clothing indecent, and were ashamed to cover their bodies. The pious father Gumila distributed cloth to these Indians to be made into clothing, and was much distressed when both men and women threw the cloth into the river. (Gumila, *El Orinoco Illustrado*, Vol. I, p. 137) Westermarck concludes that "nakedness of savages is not alluring" (p. 546), and that "facts like these must certainly tend to discredit the popular view that modesty is the mother of clothing" (p. 548).

Nudity is *not*, therefore, automatically exciting sexually, which accounts for the fact that the "pre-sartorial terror" previously described as leading to the introduction of clothing obviously does not exist in many aborigines. All the organized and complicated inner fears must be present before "pre-sartorial terror" can be experienced; one of the many possible pre-stages may be the custom which obtains among the Australian bush-women. According to many observers, these women, who are completely nude, always seat themselves in a manner that conceals the genitalia.

As unconscious fears increased, sex proper diminished. To recapture some of the pleasure thus lost, artificial stimulants had to be found. *One* of these is—clothing.

In short, the element of the forbidden, and therefore the effort to overcome obstacles—which in effect means placement of aggression—became predominant. A statement which Freud made in another connection in 1910 seems to be pertinent here:

The value the mind sets on erotic needs instantly sinks as soon as satisfaction becomes readily obtainable. Some obstacle is necessary to swell the tide of libido to its height: and in all periods of history, wherever natural barriers in the way of satisfaction have not sufficed, mankind has created conventional ones in order to be able to enjoy love. This is true both of individuals and of nations. In times during which no obstacles to sexual satisfaction existed, such as, perhaps, during the decline of the civilizations of antiquity, love became worthless, life became empty . . .[6]

In 1910 Freud had not yet acknowledged the importance of aggression, nor did he ever differentiate between *real* and *pseudo*-aggression. The words "*some obstacle* is necessary to swell the tide of libido to its height" may very well be interpreted today, therefore, as the mixture of libidinous and aggressive (pseudo-aggressive) elements.

Clothes are, perhaps, *the last refuge of diminishing sex:* as neurotic fears pushed man further and further towards the passive-masochistic corner, it became necessary to institute unconscious counter-measures. Fear was conquered, pseudo-aggressively, with "transgression into the forbidden" in the form of peeping and mental undressing.

Man's potency is poor; scientific reports from all *civilized* countries confirm that judgment. It is poor because of the *necessary,* the *unavoidable* imposition of incest taboos, *plus* the also unavoidable factor of the human child's long maturation period. The child learns only gradually to overcome his long dependence; his inborn megalomania inevitably comes into conflict with reality. Many children, indeed, are incapable of coping with the conflicts which arise when *inborn megalomania, and inborn aggression*—at least potentially identical with an adult's, and without adequate means of expression—are confronted with *inflexible reality.* The result is an unconscious "saltomortale"—psychic masochism, with all its tragic consequences.

There is still another factor which contributes to the prevalence of inactivity-sex, which in its turn leads to ex-

[6] *Gesammelte Schriften*—"Contributions to the Psychology of Love."

aggerated attraction to female clothes. Sex in the child starts with fantasies, for which models are chosen from the immediate environment. These fantasies are both forbidden (because the choice is made from members of the family circle) *and* at the same time *unrealizable.* These are the cornerstones of the concept, *sex = forbidden.* Under relatively normal inner conditions, that connotation is later unconsciously abandoned: in neurotics, it is *not.* The tragic results for man's potency have already been mentioned: marital sex, since it is sanctioned, loses its attraction. This explains the typical spectacle of the married man, sexually disinterested in his wife, pursuing the socially dangerous extra-marital escapade.

Thus the impression is fostered that in neurotics sex is an aggressive rather than a libidinous function. The impression is misleading unless it is immediately qualified: the aggression utilized in "overcoming obstacles" is but *pseudo-aggression,* and constitutes only a defense against the masochistic attraction of the uncanny and forbidden.

The neurotic more frequently chooses the route of fantasy than the outlet of reality. This leads to activation of infantile and puberal masturbation with the ever-changing "dream girl." The wife of a neurotic is frequently shocked by the discovery that her sexually inactive husband—masturbates.

In its end effects, the neurotic's sex history too often consists of this cycle: protracted sexual fantasy, short-lived sexual reality, protracted sexual fantasy. The sex cycle of neurotics can be expressed in this formula: *in fantasy it begins, to fantasy it returns.* The parallel is difficult to overlook: "For dust thou art, and shall to dust return."

For all these male neurotics, the game of half-concealment and half-exposure in feminine fashion is an ideal way out. By peeping at women and undressing women in thought, they prove their masculinity to themselves. This is what the over-worked popular phrase—"women dress to attract men"—really means!

Sex starts with fears, and is continued under the condition of the forbidden. Only relatively few adults are capable of disassociating themselves from the unconscious formula "sex = forbidden." Consequently, the very unhealthy connection (unavoidable in childhood, avoidable in maturity) becomes stabilized. Since the primitive unconscious part of the conscience constantly objects to the unconscious masochistic pleasure derived from the formula, defenses must necessarily be installed. These defenses are all of the pseudo-variety. As a result, man's sex life gives the misleading external appearance of aggression. Tenderness and inner reassurance are lacking.

There would be only slight elements of exaggeration in the claim that *woman's clothes are aphrodisiacs for man's vanishing potency.* In childhood, sex was *the* forbidden; feminine clothes—and this accounts for the attraction to them—make it the forbidden once more. In short, feminine clothes serve as a convenient proof of hypersexuality, even to the impotent man.[7]

Predicting the "shape of things to come" is among the silliest of all the silly parlor games. Instead of candidly ad-

[7] It is not denied that secondarily clothes can be used for diversified purposes. Examples are: fright-inspiring uniforms in militaristic states; black or white attire of people posing as ghosts; prison uniforms; etc. Another example is the degradation of *impotent* men in some primitive societies by forcing them to put on feminine attire. Crawley's *The Mystic Rose* (l.c.) has a collection of interesting anthropological material. One of the examples he cites is that of the Yukis of California; they equate impotence with "womanishness" and force impotent men to dress in women's clothing. These "men-women," as they are called, seem to be without either desire or virility. They do women's tasks and avoid those duties performed by men. (p. 255) Comparing the situation of the Yukis with present-day society, one can truly say that impotent men have come up in the world; they are dressed as men, and even pose as He-Men in "kibitzer-sex."

The perversion transvestitism should also be mentioned; space is inadequate for any discussion of its tangential connection with the main theme of this study.

mitting that the shape of things to come is—shapeless and unknown, or that (in plain English) we must be ignorant of it, even the most cautious of us occasionally yields to the temptation, drapes himself in the prophet's robes, and installs himself as self-appointed authority on the future. If the prophet is careful to place his predictions at least a century ahead, he cannot be proven wrong during his lifetime, and his guess will be as good (or more likely as bad) as anyone else's. Scientists have no more business to predict the future than non-scientists. Specialized knowledge neither authorizes nor enables the scientists to deliver prophecies. Still, scientists are asked, again and again, to forecast developments in their specific orbits. The record of these predictions is poorer than poor. Exactly because of his specialized knowledge of the present state of his very limited field, the scientist should politely but firmly refuse to play the game. If he fails to resist the temptation, he all too frequently makes a fool of himself. Instances are numerous. To name one a safe century past: The Medical Faculty of the University of Munich was consulted, over a hundred years ago, on the possible effects of the just-introduced railroads on the health of their passengers. The learned body's conclusions were spectacular. Traveling in trains, it was declared, is to be considered suicidal, and even innocent onlookers are bound to suffer from dangerous vertigo. To save at least the onlookers, the professors advised that high fences be built alongside the tracks . . .

Sticking to these scientific (and reasonable) principles, the last chapter of this manuscript, dealing with the future of clothing, should consist very impressively of ten pages covered with even more impressive question marks. I doubt, however, if my ordinarily reasonable publisher would react with either understanding or appreciation. Provided he cared to say anything at all, I rather suspect that he would consider me a disagreeable pedant, and impatiently tell me, "You've had your fun, now write the last chapter. When can we expect the manuscript?"

And I also suspect that, having filed my protest, I should write the last chapter.

To avoid all this potential unpleasantness, I am quite content to shift the responsibility, state my mental reservations, and then "authoritatively" hand down my "considered" opinion.

Trying to make the best of a senseless situation, I can only attempt to draw routine conclusions (of the guess-type) from the few things we know. We[8] know that clothes are a masculine invention, propelled and maintained by man's inner fear. Have we any reason to assume that this fear is diminishing?

As far as I can see, the opposite is the case. Neuroticism in sex, if it is not increasing, is at least not lessening. Man's potency, as this chapter has already shown, is poor. Because of the enormous number of neurotics, "counterfeit-sex" is prevalent.

Since this is the case, I see no reason why man's attenuated "*kibitzer-sex*," in which woman's clothing is used as a form of expression, should decrease. *The greater the poverty of normal sex, the greater the allure of inactivity-sex becomes.*

Nor am I sufficiently optimistic about the full resurgence of the "reality principle" to concur with Flugel's deduction that the "reality principle," in the form of the spread of nudism and the prophecies of imaginative writers such as H. G. Wells and factual writers such as Professor Knight Dunlap, will eventually lead to the acceptance of public nakedness. It is possible, Flugel asserts, that clothing is

[8] The "we" is not a pluralis majestatis, but corresponds to the naive though unavoidable illusion, common to every author, that he has convinced *a few* of his readers. Hence you—the reader—are included. Since life is more pleasurable when harmless fantasies are harmlessly applied, the "we" may be forgiven.

merely a stage in humanity's gradual advance towards a higher culture.

I believe that Flugel's reasoning is fallacious, because his main thesis is based on rational considerations only. In studying an emotional problem, he has omitted the decisive emotional point: man's unconscious fear of woman's body. This fear is fully irrational; it goes back to the earliest infantile misconceptions, which are deeper than the phallic castration fear and shifted exhibitionism partially acknowledged by Flugel. In this emotional problem, we are dealing with the infant's undigested horror of the Giantess of the nursery, for which man later compensates with spurious superiority. Man has been unable to produce any better a defense than the tottering He-Man psychology. And this needs—clothes.

There are some pessimists who predict the ascendency of a gynocracy for the comparatively near future, an eventuality which would make prediction of the future of clothing even more difficult. What sartorial conclusions women would reach in a world dominated by women is anybody's guess.

Flugel's 1930 enumeration of the literary visionaries who see the world advancing towards a state of nakedness is already incomplete. *The Ape and the Essence,* Aldous Huxley's recent satire on the post-atomic world, in which America is rediscovered via Australia, mirrors a world dominated by demoniacal autocrats, where sex is forbidden except for two weeks out of the year. To deter sex, punishment is severe (violators of the taboo are buried alive), and women's clothes are inconspicuous, their only adornments being four red warning signs of NO placed on the breasts and buttocks. Amusingly enough, the genital proper is obviously not considered "sexual" by Huxley, hence fear is victorious even in the fantasy. Huxley's four NO signs are an argument against Flugel's deduction, provided that literary visions are arguments in the first place.

It is even less conclusive to use practicing nudists as argument. Those who have been analyzed proved to be neurotics.[9]

Moreover, Flugel completely disregards the influence of religion, in his occasional remarks about religion treating it as rather antiquated and inconsequential. But even those holding unorthodox opinions of religious dogmas cannot deny that religion, especially in our times, is a vital power affecting the great majority of people. Even those who are not devout believers in their own denominations, or who more or less opportunistically hold on merely to external religious vestiges, prefer not to come out into the open with their objections. Consequently, religion's objections against immodesty, and arguments pro clothes, are widely accepted.

Finally, the whole idea of "progress" as an arithmetical or geometrical progression forward and upwards, which is obviously assumed by Flugel, is a rather unrealistic one. Indeed, it is a contradiction of obvious facts. In the ideas of the last part of the nineteenth century, and the first decade of the twentieth, this *direct* development of the human genus to better and higher levels of culture and humanity was frequently foreseen. In the last four decades this "from better to better" philosophy has been rudely upset by successive waves of barbarism, enforced by successive waves of dictatorship from the right *and* the left. Goethe's words have proved sadly prophetic, "Progress has not followed a straight ascending line, but a spiral with rhythms of progress and retrogression, of evolution and dissolution." What consequences this will have in the atomic age it is difficult to foresee.

[9] See, e.g., an analysis of a secretary of a nudist society, in *Money and Emotional Conflicts*, l.c., Chapter "Dependee."

Index